The Tragedy and Triumph of an American Family

Higher Than Eagles

MARALYS WILLS
and Chris Wills

LONGSTREET PRESS
Atlanta, Georgia

Published by
LONGSTREET PRESS, INC.
2140 Newmarket Parkway
Suite 118
Marietta, Georgia 30067

Printed in the United States of America

1st printing, 1992

Library of Congress Catalog Number 91-77194

ISBN 1-56352-025-7

This book was printed by R. R. Donnelley & Sons, Harrisonburg, Virginia. The text was set in Bembo by Typo-Repro Service, Inc., Atlanta, Georgia.

Jacket and book design by Jill Dible.
Jacket photo by Stephen McCarroll © 1979

ACKNOWLEDGMENTS

This wasn't an easy book to write. Of course not, you say, thinking I must mean reliving the sad parts as I committed them to paper. But that isn't what I mean. Those scenes wrote themselves. I simply poured out what I felt, and through many drafts they stayed the same.

The hard part was everything else. Trying to decide which events would matter to others, how much detail to include, even where to start the story — all the while keeping it factual. Though the events all happened as portrayed, the dialogue was, of necessity, recreated from memory. If people didn't say *exactly* what is written, they very well could have.

The encouraging critiques by family, friends and professionals kept me going at times when my faith might have waned. Out front was Rob, my husband, who, while not perfectly patient with the need for so many revisions, always believed it a story worth telling — and supported the manuscript with enthusiastic listening and endless dinners out.

My children — Kirk, Kenny, Tracy, and especially Chris, gave unflagging help and encouragement. Chris was the other half of my memory, reliving the parts I never experienced.

My thanks to teacher Pat Kubis, who made me see what belonged in the book and what didn't—and for her staunch belief that I was publishable, and my friend, Pat Teal, for her help and enthusiasm. And to editors Robert Elman and Nick Lyons who gave that "reaching down" kind of help authors fear has disappeared forever from the publishing world. And to editors James O'Shea Wade and Noel Young, who offered so much encouragement.

My critique group—we call ourselves "The Literary Elite"—hung in from the beginning: Dorsey Adams, Win Smith, June O'Connell, Pat Walker, Barbara Benedict, Vicki Bashor and Stu Borden. After twenty-five published books among us, we hate to admit how much we still need each other.

Thanks also to supportive readers: Christy Wills, Greg MacGillivray, Gil Dodgen, Paul MacCready, Melissa Mather, Deborah Schneider, and Karen Boenish—and to Chelley Kitzmiller and Hillis Barnes for ideas that made a difference.

Most of all I am grateful for my agent, Susan Golomb, for her enthusiasm, ideas, and guidance, and my editor, Jane Hill, who made it all happen. How lucky I was to find an editor with her warmth and perception. When James O'Shea Wade said, "Don't give up. Make this dream come true," he knew it would be because of someone like Jane Hill.

PREFACE

I am the mother of six children — five boys and a girl. Three of the boys became hang glider pilots and two were champions. Together they drew us, their parents, into unpowered flight until we found ourselves unable to resist, swept away by its beauty, by the magic of multi-colored kites sliding silently into the wind, by the exhilaration of aerial dances performed above a mountain.

This is a story about our oldest son, Bobby, who became not only the American, British and Canadian hang gliding champion, but a legend in the sport — about whom *Sports Illustrated* wrote, "Like Paul Elvstrom, the great Danish sailor, he seems now to own a special part of the wind that not even he can see and no one else can find."

Yet none of it happened easily. If Bobby succeeded, as he'd vowed through childhood, in doing what had never been done before, it was because of traits that drove us crazy as he was growing up. When he became a pioneer of natural flight, it was only because he always did what he intended and because we could never stop him, especially when we tried.

In the end this is a story about a family. Though Bobby's life was equal parts travail, triumph and tragedy, he changed us more than we ever changed him.

1

MARALYS: I never thought I'd lose a son to hang gliding. It just never seemed possible that the sport we'd watched and applauded — the sport we'd taken on as a business and nurtured from infancy — could turn around and bite us. And Eric! How could it have been our third son, Eric, they called about, when all along it was Bobby who took the risks, Bobby who'd made a private pact with Luck?

Of all our six boisterous children, only Bobby lived on the edge of disaster. He drove his truck as though pursued by hit men. He rode his Bultaco motorcycle full bore down dirt roads at night, mindless of potholes, going airborne over whatever road junk he couldn't see. He flew his hang glider off unfamiliar mountains, playing the odds like an eagle — imagining he could make the flight work out and not worrying about the wind or the terrain or who would pick him up down below.

So why was it Eric — affable, non-daring Eric — they called about?

I remember that I was caught off guard . . . things had been going so right in our family, and Rob and I had come to expect it — as though we deserved our good luck after all the difficult years with Bobby, as though we'd paid our dues raising five rambunctious boys and now we couldn't be touched. Bobby was the one who lived dangerously, and he seemed destined to escape.

As a family we were flying high indeed, and nothing was going to bring us down.

I have only a vague impression of Eric leaving that Saturday, ambling long-legged through our kitchen, his wavy hair too long as always, his manner relaxed and pleasant. He was twenty. I suppose he was, as usual, loose and unhurried, whether he was in a hurry or not. Eric had always been one of those kids you enjoyed having around because he accepted life like a philosopher — with amusement and perspective.

"Where are you going?" I asked.

"Flying," he said, taking a banana from the fruit dish.

"Who are you going with?"

He shrugged, peeling down yellow strips. "Danny Wilson and some guys. You don't know the rest." His blue eyes turned in my direction, a dismissive look. "I've gotta go, Mom. They're waiting."

"Okay," I said.

An unremarkable conversation. I was busy making breakfast and didn't notice what he was wearing, didn't find out where they'd be flying. Later I asked myself, *Why didn't you look at him there in the kitchen, really look at him as he left, so you'd have something to remember?*

But why would I? I never imagined he wouldn't be coming back.

We were having company for dinner that evening. It was a March morning, and I was on my way to the grocery store, driving down Seventeenth Street, thinking absently that the sky had a strange pall for spring, that it looked oddly red and smoggy, even ominous. Suddenly I envisioned disaster, an earthquake or an atomic blast — something worldwide, nothing personal. Because I had once reacted badly to a family emergency, I vowed at that moment to be brave. I actually sat up a little straighter in the car and took a deep breath and set the pointer on my mental clock to BRAVE.

And then I forgot all about it.

Afternoon was smoggier still. Rob and I went to a swim meet and watched our fourth son, Kenny, then a broad-shouldered seventeen, set a county record in the butterfly. But we didn't stay for the whole meet.

While Rob went out for nuts and beer, I skimmed over the house: picked up tennis shoes, gave a cursory dusting to the trophies that crammed the mantle and the top of the television. They represented six different sports, and I was once again thinking how curious it was that our children had made us known as a sports family when Rob and I had been raised as eggheads. It was just one of those accidental turnings down a path you hadn't planned on — exactly like the hang gliding.

When the call came, I looked up from setting the table, impatient because I was running late as always.

A male voice asked, "Is Mr. Wills there?"

I said he wasn't but I would take a message.

There was no response, just a muted sound of breath drawn in.

Come on, I thought. Please say it.

The man took his time. "When will Mr. Wills be back?"

Something came to me, some overtone that made the voice vaguely familiar. I said, "Is this Danny Wilson?"

"Yes. I have to talk to your husband." He sounded different — hoarse and strained — and I was instantly curious. I thought, this is me, Maralys, you see me at the shop all the time, you know me lots better than you know Rob. I said, "You can talk to *me*, Danny."

Still he hesitated, and through the silence I felt his unwillingness to say more. The moment was short, only a few seconds, because suddenly I knew what it was about. I began to tremble. I said, "It's Eric, isn't it? Eric's had an accident."

3

"Yes," he said. His manner was calm, strangely matter-of-fact. "I'm afraid he's D.O.A."

I stood rooted to the spot. Uncomprehending. Refusing to understand. He'd used police jargon. A code. Mothers don't know police talk.

Yet I knew full well.

Holding the phone away, I screamed for my daughter, Tracy. She came running and stood in the doorway like a skitterish, long-legged colt, her hazel eyes wide with apprehension. She was fifteen. "Eric's dead," I blurted, too stung to be easy on her. I turned back to the phone. From a chasm, a hole so deep I could scarcely speak out of it, I heard myself asking, "Where?" heard the words, "San Bernardino," and realized I couldn't listen further.

"I can't talk," I said, breaking down. I hung up the phone and gathered Tracy in my arms. We clung to each other, sobbing.

After that I went on autopilot and a voice — mine — began making phone calls: cancelling our dinner guests, calling our second son, Chris, to come home from UCLA.

I found a dishrag and wiped the drainboard — chased every crumb and speck, loaded the dishwasher, packed food into containers, put dishes away — as if it mattered, as if a clean kitchen was important.

A neighbor appeared and put an arm across my shoulder. "Why don't you let us do that? Come on, Maralys, sit down."

I looked at her, dazed, and shook my head; it was impossible. I couldn't sit and I couldn't explain. Instead I wiped the stove and found the broom and swept the kitchen floor. The neighbor stood by and watched. Neither of us understood. But I understand now. I was clinging to what I knew, staving off hysteria with small, familiar acts so I'd feel anchored and the world would seem real.

Eric, I thought. *Eric, where are you?*

Gradually the house filled with friends; mysteriously,

they were simply *there*. One by one, with tears in their eyes, they drew me into their arms. But in the midst of their coming I drew back, stricken with fear. *Rob!* What would he *do?*

Suddenly I envisioned a second disaster — Rob hearing the news and going crazy, exploding in some terrible, unpredictable way. Rob had never accepted even the small setbacks in life. Though deep down I think he hopes for the best, his lawyer's mind conjures up the worst. Since the beginning he'd taken minor injuries to our children as an assault by fate, cursing the damage and the injustice, often blaming me in lieu of blaming a God he couldn't quite believe in. What would he do now? I simply couldn't predict.

And then Rob was there, standing puzzled in the door-way. All these people, I could see him thinking, not our dinner guests. What was going on?

Our neighbor, Ed — Big Ed, who knows what to say — went to him swiftly, laid a hand on Rob's shoulder. "Rob . . . I'm sorry," a deep, comforting voice, "Eric's had an accident."

Rob waited, his jaw tightening. "How bad?"

"It's bad. Very bad."

Still Rob waited.

Quietly. "It's as bad as it can get."

Rob sat down. He stared up at Ed. Then he put his hand over his face and cried.

I hurried across the room to gather Rob in my arms. We always return, I thought. In the beginning there was just us, and now, without Eric, there is just us again.

It wasn't true, but that's how it seemed.

For the next few days we stumbled through everything that had to be done when you're finalizing somebody's life.

After the funeral, we gathered in the living room to talk. The formalities were over, but our hang gliding business was still there, a broken down car momentarily abandoned. Sooner or later we had to walk back and decide what to do.

Nobody wanted to speak. The subject seemed almost obscene.

We spread out around the room, and I looked across at Rob. He sat heavily on the blue couch, an elbow propped on its upholstered arm, his chin in his hand. His eyes rested on Chris, twenty-two, who'd been the rock in our family forever. Who was born mature. A younger, shorter version of Rob — round cheeks, strong chin, hazel eyes that moved restlessly — Chris was unwilling to begin discussing the business he'd started.

Rob said, "You all know what we're here for — to make a decision about Wills Wing."

Chris shifted in his chair. "I wondered about it, coming down from school."

I felt his unspoken question: Am I going to have to give up flying?

Bobby, who'd been called home from a movie-making stint in Hawaii, said quietly, "I thought about it, too, coming home on the plane."

It was a flat statement, unemotional. He said it with his gaze fixed at some point on the rug. Sitting on the fireplace hearth, his unusually long legs seemed to stretch halfway across the room. They were heavy legs, filling every inch of his jeans, and his feet were consistent — he wore size thirteen shoes. With his head bowed, Bobby's chin nearly touched his chest.

I thought, It is for you, Bobby, that Rob is asking the question.

Then Rob spoke directly to Bobby. "This business isn't for Mom and me, and Chris doesn't need it. He's headed for medical school. We only started it in the first place for you and Eric." He paused, leaving words unsaid. "If we let it go, what will you do?"

Bobby shrugged but didn't answer.

I studied him as he sat there thinking his private thoughts, and I reflected on his hang gliding and the differences between him and Chris. For whatever extra Chris had outside the sport, Bobby had that much less, but in flying he had more — infinitely more. In the air Bobby was master, flying with so much grace he was always the pilot other pilots watched. As obsessive as Chris was about flying, Bobby seemed born to it. Chris had knowledge, but Bobby had instincts.

"Bobby," Rob said, "it's your decision."

No, no, I thought, that's wrong. I said, "Rob, we can't put this on Bobby's shoulders, it isn't fair. Either we keep the place open or we don't."

Under his breath Rob said, "We must be insane even considering it. We've already paid a horrible price for this business . . . horrible."

I nodded. Somewhere down deep I knew that what had happened once could happen again, and I thought, Why would we even *think* of going on?

Then I looked at Bobby again, and something about his face made me see things clearer. Twenty-three now, but with a look of resignation that took me back years. I thought of his childhood — the illness, the unhappiness, the monumental battles with his dad. Even more, I remembered the kind of boy he was — sadistic at times and funny at other times, but different, always different, forever searching for ways to express the offbeat ideas that floated through his head.

Offbeat ideas, yes. Also screwy. Funny. And useless. "His life is a joke," Rob said in those days. "He's headed nowhere."

So that's how it is, I thought. Bobby's past was the key. A difficult past and largely behind us, but important nevertheless. Because you couldn't decide what Bobby ought to do until you looked at where he'd been.

When I thought back to the beginnings, to the events that

would shape our decision, I realized the rest of us were merely *there*. The beginnings were all Bobby.

2

MARALYS: Even as a young boy, Bobby was strangely ambitious. He'd set himself a goal, sink his teeth into it and hold on, the grip of a willful puppy. He approached all his interests with that same doggedness, but I remember best the summer he turned eleven. One night at dinner he announced, "I'm going to build the world's biggest underground fort."

Across the table from me, Rob raised his eyebrows in a "What now?" expression.

"I've been thinking about it a lot," Bobby explained. "I know what I have to do."

Looking at Bobby sideways, I saw the long face, the hazel eyes that drooped slightly at the corners, the lank brown hair he never combed. But that was just the outer boy. He had an intensity about him, an earnestness that made you listen when he spoke. Like other mothers of driven children, I'd learned to take him seriously. "Where did you get that notion, Bobby?"

"I just got it," he said.

Rob and I exchanged glances—the universal signal of parents recognizing the onset of something familiar. My husband's expression, with its hint of amusement said, Well, here comes another of Bobby's Big Ideas.

"The fort sounds interesting," Rob said, careful to be noncomittal.

"I'll get Chris to help. Eric, too. We've got a bunch of extra shovels."

On my right, ten-year-old Chris looked up momentarily, then went on eating. He would wait and see. Eric, only eight, nodded and smiled — a little squirt, no doubt glad to be included.

Just then Bobby coughed briefly, the empty, dry cough of an asthmatic. I felt a familiar tightening inside and saw Rob's passing look of bitterness. Bobby's asthma was long-standing and intractable, and we each reacted in our own ways — me with discouragement, Rob with anger.

But Rob bit back any comment and asked instead, "Where do you plan to build the fort, Bobby?"

"Out there." Bobby pointed to a strip of dirt between the lawn and a bordering orange grove.

Rob nodded. "That should be far enough away."

I guessed he was thinking, as I was, that the project would confine itself to that empty area and the lawn between us would catch most of the excess dirt.

"And how will you know when it's the world's biggest?"

Bobby turned and fixed Rob with an expression so self-assured it bordered on scorn. "I'll just know," he said. "It'll be bigger than any fort you've ever seen."

Only after Bobby had gone to bed did Rob say with a laugh, "I'm glad they put a good foundation under this house, Babe. Bobby seems to have in mind something about the size of the Holland Tunnel."

Thus began the Year of the Underground Fort. And also the year that our relationship with Bobby deteriorated noticeably.

In those days Rob and I seemed to have a thousand children. Six was a large number even to us — one child too many to keep on my mental screen at all times. When someone was missing, I would know the numbers weren't right, but not always which child was absent.

With five boys and a girl, silence was an unknown commodity in our house. So was boredom. Everyone did everything—sports, music, pet projects, a minimum of schoolwork and a maximum of fighting with siblings—but it was Bobby who did more of everything than anyone else.

His electric trains were a case in point: Bobby crying, "More track, Granny, I need more track," and Rob's mother, Helen, rushing to supply him until his trains overflowed onto the patio, and the patio resembled a railroad switching yard . . . Bobby becoming an expert at ping-pong by pleading with anyone who'd play him, "one more game—*just one more game*" . . . Bobby practicing his piano pieces over and over until his teacher cried, "For heaven's sake, Bobby, it's *fine*! Let's move on to something else."

And so it was with the underground fort.

Then the predictable happened: *nobody* worked as hard as Bobby, and soon he grumbled to his brothers, "You're too slow," and left to prowl the neighborhood for recruits. Before long he'd filled our backyard with energetic boys, and the far edge of the lawn disappeared under a cloud of flying dirt. After a time I grew accustomed to the cacophony of backyard construction—Bobby's shrill voice rising above half a dozen others, shovels clanking and grinding.

But one day there was trouble. I came home from the grocery store to find the yard quiet and Chris sitting defiantly atop the pile of dirt, with Bobby, skinny as a shovel-handle, standing over him ordering him back to work. It was the first mutiny in a thousand boy-hours of digging.

Bobby was beside himself. "You're lazy, Chris!" he shrilled, arms flapping. "You're a quitter! You're a bum!"

Chris was not the kind of child you yell at. He took just so much, and then he stood up, very dignified, dusted off his pants, and trudged away toward the house.

Before he got far, Bobby did an end run and blocked his

brother's path. "Come back!" he ordered. And then a little desperately, *"Why* won't you dig? Huh?"

"I'm tired, Bobby."

Bobby stared at him. He didn't understand tired; tired was not in his vocabulary. "All right, then," he said with finality, *"it's not your fort anymore."* With that he broke down and began coughing, a paroxysm of effort that hunched his shoulders forward and turned his eyes dull. Watching through the window, I thought how everything was relative — that fighting was the worst thing that happened in our family — until you remembered the asthma.

Chris waited until Bobby finished. Then he said, "I don't *care* about the fort anymore."

Bobby couldn't believe his ears. Grabbing Chris's arm, he changed tactics, wheedling softly that he knew Chris cared about the fort, he must care, he *had* to care, wouldn't he *please* come dig, and finally, "I'll give you my marbles, all of them. Even the aggies."

Chris paused. "The aggies?"

Bobby said yes, the aggies, and there were fourteen in his collection.

Chris thought about it. "Don't shout at me any more, then. I don't like shouting."

"You'll *dig*?" said Bobby, smiling.

Chris said he would — for a while.

The two went back to the mounds of dirt and I stood a moment longer, watching. As Chris eased down into the hole, he looked back over his shoulder. "Bobby," he said matter-of-factly, "you don't have to give me your marbles."

Three years earlier we'd built the house on a half-acre of land adjacent to an orange grove in Southern California and moved there with our four boys. (Two more children, Tracy and Kirk, came along later.) Rob and I had designed the house as we wanted it, with beam ceilings in the family room, two fireplaces, and a kitchen window overlooking the backyard so I could work at the sink while I watched the boys playing and fighting.

But we couldn't have the house exactly as we wanted. Because of Bobby's asthma, which he'd had since he was five, we couldn't put carpets in the children's bedrooms. Instead we installed oak floors, which I tried to keep free of dust. A joke. There is no such thing as dustfree when you have six children. Dustfree is when they're all somewhere else and a cleaning crew is home mopping.

Lately there'd been more dirt around than usual, what with all the digging and some of the outside coming in, and Rob began making noises about Bobby's project being bad for his health.

I disagreed. "Rob, *everything* is bad for him! Why pick on the fort?"

When it came to Bobby's asthma, I thought, nothing was certain. In spite of his having had it for six years, the disease was a mystery to Rob and me: it was a slippery illness, springing up for no reason at times when he ought to be well, disappearing with equal unpredictability.

But Rob and I had never stopped searching for answers. Like itinerant peddlers, we trotted Bobby to doctors from Santa Ana to Beverly Hills. We bought air purifiers and breathing machines, sprayed all our wool fabrics, served unpopular alternative foods like rutabagas. But sometimes I thought we'd have done as well mumbling incantations and burning incense. The remedies of the twentieth century simply weren't working.

I was sure the fort was no worse than anything else, but Rob thought otherwise. He finally confronted Bobby one morning at breakfast. "Didn't sleep much last night, did you?"

Bobby shrugged. "I'm okay." He sat hunched over the table, the black circles under his eyes all too confirming of a night spent coughing.

"We think you're not okay. We think that fort's a problem."

Here it comes, I thought, like the trains . . . another of Bobby's projects about to be snuffed out.

Our son's expression changed. He sat up straighter, alert and defensive. "It's *not* a problem, Dad! The fort isn't hurting me a bit."

"I say it is."

"It's not!" Bobby got up to leave for school, moving quickly, talking as he went. "I'd *know* if it was the fort. Don't you think I'd know?" He disappeared before his father could say anything more.

Rob stared after him. "I'd as soon talk to a mule."

In the silent aftermath, I wondered why Rob couldn't show Bobby more sympathy, why he couldn't discuss instead of declare. I walked to the window and stood looking at the careless mounds of dirt, the lumber scattered about, the shovels lying at odd angles like hastily dropped pick-up-sticks. So many hours invested, so much enthusiasm. Before we called a halt, we ought to be sure.

So I kept still, hoping Rob's anger would blow over.

It did. Bobby kept out of Rob's sight for a while, which wasn't difficult, since in those days Rob worked erratic hours in a distant city, often arriving home at the children's bedtime. Bobby shoveled when Rob wasn't around and disappeared into his bedroom early at night.

One afternoon, though, Bobby couldn't dig. He left his brothers and friends outside and came into the house and dropped onto the couch. It was rare to see him sitting, rarer still when he couldn't summon enough energy for one of his obsessions. For the first time I began seeing the fort Rob's way.

"You know, Bobby," I said from the kitchen, "Dad may be right." He was sunk so low into the couch he was barely visible. "That project could be adding to your problems."

Bobby's energy came back. Quickly he stood up, threw me one of his defiant looks and left the room. It was as if I hadn't spoken. Though he didn't return to the fort that day, the next afternoon when I came home from an errand, Bobby was out there again.

I had just gone out to get him when Rob's mother drove up, pulling into the blacktop area behind the garage. As we exchanged greetings, she threw open the trunk of her aged Cadillac, revealing a virtual mineshaft of big wooden planks.

Making a quick decision, I shook my head. "I'm sorry, but we can't let Bobby have these, Helen."

She straightened abruptly. Helen was a pretty woman, with almost-black hair that highlighted her wide, dark eyes, and a generous, expressive mouth. She conveyed warmth and sympathy that drew strangers to her like magnets. Helen seemed to love everyone.

I gestured toward the planks. "Rob thinks the fort will have to go, and I'm beginning to agree with him. Close the trunk, please — we don't want Bobby to know these are here."

Helen stood quite still, dismayed. "My stars — why not?"

I tried to explain. But she made no move to do as I asked. Instead she looked shocked. "Surely you don't mean this, Maralys. He *loves* the fort!" Her blue-flowered smock rustled in the breeze, and she stared across the yard, her eyes possessively taking in the mounds of dirt.

I felt the rising of an old, familiar anger. *He loves the fort!* As if that were all that mattered! As if his sickness and my wishes were unimportant. Once more Helen was interfering, usurping control of our children. Once more I was quietly seething.

For eleven years, Helen and I had been locked in unspoken conflict over our boys. Our philosophies were nothing alike. She seemed to think children required instant gratification — that they should want for nothing, wait for nothing, work for nothing. Since I believed children's characters were strengthened by small doses of minor deprivation, I became, in Helen's eyes, something of an obstacle. But she worked around me and always pleasantly. "I know you're too busy to play with them, Maralys, so I've brought a few little toys . . .," meaning two or three shopping bags full.

I seldom faced her down. It was hard to pick a fight with someone brimming over with love.

"Oh, dear, dear," she cried now, her face crumpling in sympathy. "The fort is his whole life!" She gasped, a virtual gusher of emotion.

"It has to go," I said coldly. Her bathos had frozen me into an icicle.

She never brought anything more for the fort. Yet big wooden planks kept appearing, I didn't know from where.

That night Rob and I bore down on Bobby, and for a brief period, perhaps a week, he stopped digging, and the fort shut down like a union job on strike.

Bobby went on wheezing, and when he didn't improve, I felt Rob and I had merely added deprivation to illness. He was listless now as well as sick, wandering around the house bored and unhappy. When he finally sneaked back to the dirt mounds, I let him go.

Once more I listened at the kitchen window. "Come on, you guys!" Bobby cried. "Dig! Make it deeper — right here. You want some candy? I'll get you some!" The piles of dirt grew until Chris finally asked hopefully if it wasn't the world's biggest underground fort now.

"No," said Bobby. "It isn't. It needs one more room."

I'd never been down inside, but I began imagining their project as some kind of subterranean hotel to which the management constantly added new chambers.

One rare day when the project lay quiet, Chris suggested I come outside to look. Carrying an unlit light bulb on the end of an extension cord, he trotted ahead of me happily. "You're gonna be surprised, Mom."

I followed my sturdy son across the lawn. "How is that light going to reach a plug?"

"It isn't. We've got five more extension cords up there."

The fort had changed since I'd been out there last. Instead of a shallow mini-excavation, it was now a raised area covered over with soil — something on the order of a freshly dug grave. On one end was a tunnel-like opening.

At the tunnel's entrance, Chris plugged in his light and crawled away out of sight, dragging the extension cords behind him. "Come on down, Mom!" he called from the bowels of the earth.

I got down on my hands and knees. The tunnel was narrow but hard-packed, and I made my way down it gingerly, wondering if it was possible the thing might cave in — something that hadn't occurred to me before. Somehow I hadn't pictured my own sons digging anything deep enough to be cave-inable.

A few yards down the tunnel I stopped. I could see all I needed to see. In the middle of a small earthen room sat Chris, a rabbit sitting in his rabbit hole, holding his light bulb and grinning irrepressibly. Light from the naked bulb threw strange shadows across his face, creating a ghostlike apparition, all teeth.

Boards covered with tar paper sagged slightly a foot over Chris's head, high enough for a small child to stand. The little chamber seemed surprisingly tight and strong. Waving his hand expansively, Chris explained that there was space enough for two kids besides him. "If you can come down farther, Mom, I'll show you the other room."

Reluctantly, I inched deeper into the ground. It was cool in there. Musty. Beyond Chris the hollowed-out earth was damp and dark. The place smelled of ancient rains and rich decay.

"See?" Chris pointed toward a gloomy pocket. "That's our second room."

I strained to make it out, but the light didn't penetrate.

"We've got another room on the other side of that one. But the fort's not finished yet . . . that's what Bobby says."

Nor ever would be, I thought, because once it was complete, what would he do? As always, Bobby was geared to the creation, not the using. But it's a mother's job to go along with Pretend, so I said, "When will he consider it finished, Chris?"

"He says when we can get two guys in the third room, sitting down. Then it'll be the world's biggest underground fort." He raised the light a little higher. "Isn't it neat, Mom?"

"Yeah, it's neat. Just like the Hilton."

He laughed. Then I noticed Bobby had crawled in behind me. "You like it, Mom?" Bobby asked.

"Sure," I said. "You're quite an engineer." I could see he'd done a good job of packing the walls and shoring up the ceiling. Hard to imagine all this as the work of a child. "It's much better than I thought. And larger, too."

"We're going to make it even bigger. We're —"

"Bobby," I began sternly, automatically. I stopped. The lecture could wait. Why spoil a nice moment? "If you'll back out, Bobby, I think I'll leave now."

"But you do like it . . ." Bobby said, retreating toward the outside.

I made my way back out the tunnel and stood up. "It's a good fort, Bobby. It really is."

He nodded without comment, the solemnness of his long face hiding what he felt. But the pride and pleasure were there, right under the surface.

From that day I knew the fort was more to Bobby than child's play. It had taught him a few things about construction, given him confidence in what he could do with his hands. There it was, a child's vision made tangible, with importance of its own.

I could see Bobby's asthma wasn't the only thing that

mattered. His goals and achievements counted for something, too.

Bobby's wheezing continued. As the weeks went on, his symptoms were no longer intermittent. He walked around most days with his shoulders hunched forward and his chest curved inward. He struggled for breath. We began his allergy shots again, which were useless, as always. Other medications made him irritable and nervous without relieving his symptoms.

Helen had read that nebulizers helped, so on our next visit to the doctor I asked about them.

The doctor shook his head. "Sorry, no nebulizers. They can cause dangerous dependency. But I'll start you on cortisone, Bobby." He gave me careful instructions. I had the feeling we'd reached the drug of last resort.

Once again my attitude shifted. Bobby was really *sick*. Whatever the fort meant to him hardly mattered anymore, not if it was destroying him. I took a firmer stand, ordered Bobby to stop digging. But I'd reckoned without his terrible will. It was stronger than mine, stronger even than Rob's. I gave orders, but Bobby ignored them. It was as though he knew something we didn't, as though our opinions about the fort didn't count. He dug when I was at the grocery store, snuck out to the dirt when I wasn't looking. Better than anyone he knew my limitations: with six children I couldn't watch him every minute.

Late at night Rob shouted at me. "I want you to get him out of that damned fort!"

"I've *tried!*" I shouted in turn. "But he keeps sneaking back. Why don't *you* do it?"

"On principle I'm leaving this to you. Show some strength, why don't you? I can't hold down a job and run the household, too."

The next day after school I tried to approach Bobby rationally, forcing myself to stay calm. I said, "You didn't get much sleep again last night." When he shrugged and tried to keep walking, I said, "Stop a minute, listen to reason. The fort's a disaster. It's—"

He broke in, "I tried quitting—for a whole week I stopped. You saw it didn't help."

So that was it. He simply didn't buy our theories. I said, "Answer me one question, Bobby. Do you really believe you're doing okay?"

He hesitated. "I would if the medicine was any good. But it isn't. What I should have, if you wanna know, is a neb." He reached for the patio doorknob.

"The doctor said you can't have nebulizers, remember? He explained everything . . . about dependency . . ."

Poised to leave, he threw me a quick, defiant look. "Well, the pills aren't working, but the nebs Granny gives me are!"

I stood stock-still, shocked. "Helen's giving you nebs?"

"Sometimes." His voice dropped. He knew he'd said too much.

I stared at him. I could have marched on Granny with an army.

Eyes glittery, he went on. "Everything I want to do, you make me stop. That's all Dad does—makes me quit whatever I'm doing. That's what he's like. First the trains, now the fort!" His eyes blazed his anger.

"Because you do everything to excess!" I shouted. "You—"

"And you're just like Dad, you take his side every time." He was talking faster and faster. "You don't care about me any more than he does. *Granny's* the one who cares!"

Something hit me then. "Is she bringing you the lumber, too? Is that where you're getting it?"

No answer.

"I thought so." I could feel the blood rush to my face. "Well, Granny's love is going to kill you!" I tried to stare him down. "If you want to know who cares about you, it's Dad! Because Dad's making you do what's best!"

Bobby stared right back: his defiance showed in every muscle of his body. All five-six of him stiffened in anger. "Dad doesn't care about me," he said bitterly. "If he did, he'd try to show it!"

When he walked off, he left a rift in our family ten miles wide.

That night, I tried to explain Bobby to Rob. "Rob, listen, please . . . listen to Bobby's logic. He thinks we're all against him, and he remembers how he quit the fort and it didn't help. Can't you at least talk to him?"

Rob stopped me with a look. "Talk. Baloney. When did talk ever accomplish anything? Bobby makes a monkey out of you and he cons my mother royally. As for her . . .," he grunted in disgust, "she skulks around the place like a Russian spy. I caught her passing boards to Bobby three blocks away. Those two are sneakier than the KGB."

Unaccountably, we both laughed. I should have known it was hopeless trying to explain one family member to another.

We hadn't discussed Bobby when we woke up the next morning, but when we saw him sitting at the table, the same old asthma distorting his posture, Rob gave me one of his furious looks. Late for work, he stalked to the drainboard and grabbed an apple. Then he left the room, swearing through gritted teeth, cursing the fort. The front door slammed.

Bobby didn't look up.

I sat down across from him. "Bobby?"

He stared resolutely into his cereal bowl. It was full of Rice Krispies, now too soggy for any snap, crackle or pop. I guessed he hadn't eaten more than a couple of bites. Back in the bedrooms, I could hear the sounds of children noisily dressing for school.

I stood up to put my hand on his shoulder. "Bobby, please listen . . ."

He whirled on me, pulled out from under my hand. "If I stop now, I'll just go on wheezing, you'll see." Defiance straightened his shoulders, gave strength to his voice. "Some day I'm going to do something you and Dad can't take away from me." He stood up and reached for his lunchpail. "I'm not like your other kids. I'm not a quitter. *I* keep going!"

As he went out the back door, he flung one last observation over his shoulder. "You and Dad don't know *anything* about raising kids!"

Well, we didn't know much about raising *him*, I thought ruefully, and never had. He'd outwilled us all the way, even as a baby.

The back door slammed as the front had earlier.

I dropped down onto a kitchen chair. What had changed since he was a baby? Not much, I thought. How well I remembered trying to dress Bobby at eighteen months and his crying out, "Do it by self! Do it by self!" while he refused to let me put one more chubby arm into a sleeve, one more foot into a shoe. I tried to humor him, but there wasn't always time for a small, fumbling child to do it by self, so sometimes I picked him up bodily and finished the job. But he always got off the last shot. The instant my hands left his sturdy body, he pulled off his clothes again, exactly to the point at which I'd begun helping. And he always knew where that point was.

Now, ten years later, he still had the upper hand.

That afternoon Bobby's wheezing was worse. He'd come home from school and shoveled before I knew he was there, but it hadn't lasted long. I gave him a treatment on the Bennett machine, watching him inhale oxygen and a combination of medicines while I stood behind him, urging him to breathe deeper. It did no good.

I gave him his cortisone a day early. He was supposed to be three days on, four days off, but it always took a day and a half to take hold. I felt we couldn't wait.

Rob came home late to dinner. One look at Bobby and he spat out, "He's been digging again!"

Bobby glanced up without answering, tired eyes uncaring. With an effort he drew in a breath. When he exhaled, he whistled.

Rob pointed an angry finger at me. "And you let him do it!"

Like small animals running for cover before a storm, the other children began disappearing.

"I didn't *let him!*" A shrill response, the voice of a fishwife.

Quietly Bobby slipped away.

"He did it. That's what counts." Rob's eyes were dangerously black. "I say you let him. Who's the adult around here? Who's in charge?"

Staring down the hall after Bobby, I shouted right back. "*He* is! Haven't you figured that out yet?"

On our way to bed that night we heard Bobby wheezing more than usual, the sounds penetrating the hall like reminders from a distant prisoner rattling his chains. I tried to get past Bobby's door without hearing . . . as though what I didn't hear couldn't affect me. I tried not to dwell on the fact that somebody in there couldn't breathe. He made me feel I was choking.

And the sense of helplessness — that was the worst.

In silence Rob and I went to bed. After a while he got up. When he didn't return, I looked through the house for him. He wasn't anywhere.

Then, hearing sounds in the backyard, I went to the window. There was Rob out by the fort, a shovel in his hands, working in his undershorts. I thought, What's he doing out there? What is that crazy man doing shoveling in the middle of the night?

My eyes adjusted, and in the moonlight I could see him digging and throwing dirt, and I realized he was tearing down the fort. I thought, Oh God — poor Bobby. Bobby will never understand, he'll hate us for this.

Rob worked like a madman, shoveling and throwing, as if by fury alone he could still the wheezing in our house. He slammed and dug and tore down, raging against the earth, a man gone crazy in the light of the moon.

I knew I couldn't stop him. He'd taken the fort out of my hands. He was ending it, putting it to death. A resignation settled over me. Rob was doing what I could never do, in a way I could never do it: harshly, without compromise. But, sometimes, I thought sadly, death was for the best.

When Bobby went out the next morning, his underground fort was gone. The asthma wasn't gone — only the fort. And our problems with Bobby had just begun.

3

CHRIS: The hang gliding didn't start with Bobby, it started with me. In the beginning, Bobby didn't *care* about flying, so our conversations were mostly one-sided—me talking about planes and my various ideas for getting airborne and him listening with a far-off look on his face. He did his own kind of flying, but it was on the ground.

It makes you wonder why he ever started hang gliding. Hang gliding is *slow* and quiet. It's peaceful. You wait for the wind. Sometimes you can barely feel it happening. Nothing like motorcycles.

But that's how it was. In the early years only I dreamed of soaring, but the dream stuck in my head and wouldn't go away.

All through high school I read aviation magazines and sat around talking planes with Ramsey Price—who was Bobby's best friend and also mine. Price and I imagined ourselves in the air, trying to guess how it would feel to leave the ground and float over people and buildings. Pictures of experimental aircraft led us on. "Price," I'd say, "*that* one we can build!"

All this time Ramsey Price and I kept trying to drag Bobby along, but he was only *curious*, only half-interested, and he didn't pay much attention until after I built my first plane, the *Red Baron* biplane, and nearly crashed trying to tow it. I was a sophomore in high school then and Bobby was a junior, living with Granny because Dad had kicked him out. So he missed most of the construction, which he would have considered a laugh, because the *Red Baron*—a full-size copy of a model "line control" plane I'd built with Price—was made of broomsticks, brown wrapping paper, piano wire, and aircraft dope.

Even Mom and Dad hardly noticed what I was doing until one day I had to soften some large wooden strips by boiling them on the stove. To keep the strips inside the steam, I lashed them to the cupboard doors. When Mom came home from the store, a lot of cupboards were tied with string and the kitchen was full of steam. She stood there squinting through the mist. "Hey—what's all this?"

"My plane," I said.

She kind of laughed. "You're *cooking* your airplane?"

I explained about bending the wood to make an airfoil.

"Oh," she said. "Yes. Well, try to take the cupboards out of traction by five, will you? I have to cook dinner."

Other than that she didn't say much, except the day she was outside when one of the strings caught fire. She sniffed and asked, "Chris, what are you doing now, *barbecuing* it?"

Once the dope was on the wrapping paper, I added metal skids to the nose and under each wingtip, and a wheel behind the pilot, and then I painted the whole thing red, with black Maltese crosses on the top wing and tail. I thought it looked great, like an old German plane.

Bobby managed to be there the day Ramsey Price and I and a bunch of people and Mom and Dad went out to an unused street for the *Red Baron's* first official takeoff. A fairly big crowd was waiting for us when Price and I pulled up, and I could tell by the way Price jumped out of my truck he was as excited as I was.

He was almost seventeen then, six-two, with curly light brown hair and eyes that were brown like a cocker spaniel's. Crowds fired up his adrenalin. "Look at this mob, Chris, we oughta be doing something outrageous. Maybe you should try flying it upside down."

"I'll be happy enough if it works right side up."

Funny about our thinking, the way nobody worried or mentioned danger. It was like a big party, everyone standing around the street talking as we unloaded the plane and I tied it to my truck.

With the rope knotted tight, I put on a leather helmet and squeezed down inside the cockpit and Price climbed into my truck and started the engine, holding up when he saw Dad and Mom jumping into the back. Dad shouted for someone to hand him up our 8mm movie camera.

Ram began driving slowly, then faster and faster, and the plane rolled down the street and in seconds left the ground.

It went up smoothly, and I thought, I'm flying! but right away I overcontrolled and it dropped hard and smacked the pavement. Sparks flew out of the nose skid, and the metal flattened, so I had to put on a new skid. I told Ram to get the truck going faster next time, and we worked out thumbs up or thumbs down signals to control the speed.

The second time Ram revved the truck up to our agreed-on forty MPH, and the plane lifted off fast and veered to the left. It was still going up when I tried to control it by giving right aileron on the control stick. Nothing happened. I didn't know there'd be a delay, so I tried to bank more, and the next thing I knew it was banking hard the other way, and I was tipped up at a sharp angle and about to ground loop. I held my left thumb down as dramatically as I could while I gave full left stick.

Just as I thought, Well, I'm out of here, the plane straightened again and Price slowed and I came down and landed hard. It was only seconds, but everyone talked about what had happened like they'd seen a crash, and people kept using the words "lucky escape." There was no mention of a third flight. Price was giving me a technical critique of my flying errors as the crowd started leaving.

After that it was generally assumed the *Red Baron* was an obsolete craft — by everyone except Bobby, Price and me. We went out a few more times and I learned not to overcontrol, but gradually I lost interest in a plane that could fly only at the end of a rope.

Eventually I put an ad in the paper and tried to sell the *Red Baron* for twenty-five dollars. People came to look. Some laughed and others thought it "interesting," but nobody wanted to buy it. Bobby offered to pay money, except he wanted it only five dollars' worth, and I said I wouldn't sell it for five dollars, I'd burn it first. With all that paper and glue, the *Red Baron* made a spectacular fire.

My next plane was an experimental aircraft, built for my senior-class project in high school. Our neighbor Leo Pfankuch, an aeronautical engineer, came over to help, and with his advice I began building a conventional airplane with a chrome moly frame and wooden wings with a 1930s Clark-Y air foil. The biggest problem was that only Bobby knew how to weld, so I was always waiting for him to get around to it. The next biggest problem was the wings, which consisted of thousands of small pieces of spruce, fitted and glued together like an endless jigsaw puzzle.

By the time Dad said anything I was three-quarters finished. I'd bought a Volkswagen engine and was getting ready to cover the frame with cloth. Dad came out to the garage, and suddenly he was taking it seriously. "What are you going to do with this plane, Chris?"

I thought the answer was obvious. "Fly it," I said.

"Fly it?" He shook his head. "I think we'd better talk about this. You don't have a pilot's license. You've never flown anything except the *Red Baron*."

"It'll be all right. I'll take it out to the desert where nobody's around."

He did a double take. Then he laughed. "It's not the people on the ground I'm worried about."

It didn't occur to me he'd be *worried*. I'd always known I could fly, you can tell when you've got a feel for things. I stood there wondering how to prove it. Then I said, "Mr. Pfankuch can fly it first! *He's* got a license." It wouldn't be the same, but it was better than nothing. "I'll fly after he checks it out."

Dad said, "Leo Pfankuch might not want to offer his life for your plane. It's possible he'll want to live a while longer."

"I'll ask him."

He shook his head. "I'm sorry, Chris. I don't think it will work."

Dad was my excuse for giving up. But the real reasons were that summer came and Bobby wasn't helping and the project became overwhelming. Besides, I'd already gotten an *A*.

The search was over for a while. I hadn't given up on aviation for life, just for the moment, while money was a problem. In the back of my mind I still saw myself flying. I even worked weekends at a glider port, "running the wings" of gliders all day for a half-hour flight at the end.

Not expecting to be airborne soon, I hadn't thought Ramsey Price would keep looking—until the day he ran into our house with a *National Geographic* under his arm. By then it was 1972, and I was a sophomore at Cal State Fullerton. Ram stood at the foot of our stairs yelling for me to come down, he had something to show me. He'd never been more excited.

We spread his magazine out on the breakfast room table, and he threw it open carelessly. "So what do you think, Wills?"

I stared down at the page, dumbfounded. The picture showed a young guy flying! The plane wasn't much—a bamboo frame and a lot of black plastic and a man hanging by his armpits. But the big news was big enough—the guy's feet were off the ground!

I began reading the text: "I wrestle with the bamboo poles, and above me 256 square feet of plastic rustles and flutters. To its strength and to the aeronautical savvy of three high-school boys, I—a licensed pilot of 25 years' experience—am about to entrust my mortal body.

"The place is a hill above Newport Beach, California. We are celebrating, on this May 23rd, the birthday of German glider pioneer Otto Lilienthal by staging a hang glider meet."

Suddenly my heart was pounding. Right then I knew Price and I had found what we'd been looking for. My hands started to itch.

"We can make one, Price."

Price laughed. "Read on."

I turned the page and read aloud. "Like many hang glider fans,

Richard Miller combines meticulous engineering and trash technology."

"If we do it," Price interrupted, "it'll sure be trash. So what's the next move, Wills?"

I didn't have to think long. "We'll start today. Where does it say how to make one?"

His expression changed. "It doesn't. If you want the truth, it's just an article about a few crazy weirdos. Nobody figures anyone'll be nuts enough to try it."

Except us, I thought. As soon as we figured out how.

The answer came the way answers usually do. You think a while and suddenly you've got it. "Wait here, Price!" I tore upstairs to my room and came back with a ruler. Price was sitting where I'd left him with one of his half-amused, half-skeptical grins, never taking himself too seriously. You had to like Price, it was something people couldn't help.

I laid the ruler across the page. "An average man's about six feet tall, right? And this guy in the picture measures two inches. That's three feet to the inch, and the hang glider's . . ."

"Four inches," Ram finished, "which would make it about twelve feet wide."

I said, "That's close enough."

Ram was laughing. "Sure that's close enough. What else do we need to know?"

"Nothing, Price." I stood up, telling him we'd divide up the jobs, that I knew where to get bamboo and he could buy plastic for the sail. "And better get a good kind, as thick as you can find."

"Six mil, wouldn't you say?"

"Sure. Or thicker." I didn't know one mil from another, but six sounded about right. Only Price would know stuff like that.

"And duct tape," he said. "We'll need lots."

About three rolls, I figured.

Ram reminded me that it was already Wednesday and we'd have to hustle if we wanted to get it built on Thursday.

"We'll test it Friday," I said, "and be flying by Saturday." Why was I out of breath?

Price headed for our front door. "So get started, Wills. I don't want to be stuck looking at a bunch of plastic and thinking, Why aren't we building a hang glider?"

"You're telling *me* to get going?"

He was halfway down the driveway when he turned. "What about Bobby? You think we should get him in on this?" Bobby lived nearby in a rented apartment and saw Price all the time because they both delivered soft water for the same company.

"If he wants," I said. "Sure. If you can talk him into it. He'll have ideas. But I don't think he'll be interested. The thing will be quiet and slow — way too slow for Bobby."

"Maybe." Ram stopped where he was and scratched his head. "He may think it's boring. But he liked the *Red Baron*, so maybe he won't."

I shook my head. "The article said twenty miles an hour. When have you seen Bobby going twenty miles an hour anywhere, anytime?"

Without answering, Ram laughed and gave me a thumbs-up. In his usual careless way, he spun his VW bug around in the middle of the street, bounced off the neighbor's curb, and kept going.

The bamboo was deep in the back of the Tustin Lumberyard, like I'd thought. And I bought extra duct tape in case we ran out.

Ram showed up on Thursday with a roll of clear plastic that was so big, when you saw him coming it was like a roll of plastic with legs. "Weighs a ton," he said, "but they wouldn't let me buy half a roll. You sure we can afford this hobby of yours?"

I said a thousand dollars wouldn't be too much to fly.

He grunted. "That's you. I wouldn't pay a thousand dollars to do anything I can think of. I'm in this because I figure it'll be exciting and cheap." He put out his hand. "You owe me for half the plastic."

We did a quick accounting. Bamboo for ten dollars, five dollars for the duct tape, twenty-one for the plastic. I was scribbling figures on the garage wall when he waved me off. "Oh, forget it. Let's get going. What'll we do first?"

I wasn't sure. Grabbing lengths of bamboo, I began laying them around here and there, and as I did, ideas came. You could bind two pieces at right angles and form two sides of a square and then two more.

. . .

Images of how the pilot's cage — it was a kind of cage — would go together began coming faster and faster. "Here, Price, hold this!" I could feel the old excitement, the sense of great beginnings starting once more. Another plane taking shape under my hands, a plane I'd seen in a picture — airborne!

There was no question it would fly!

Price and I worked until dark Thursday, and then all morning Friday. After Price left, Bobby dropped by. I could hear him coming a mile away. Tires squealing, he spun up our driveway on his Bultaco motorcycle. His hands were in his jacket pockets, and he looked cold. The reasons were obvious: it was February and overcast, and he'd probably been going seventy around the curves.

"So that's it?" he asked, frowning at our machine. It was a big bamboo cage, lashed at the joints with Boy Scout knots that Price had learned before being kicked out of Boy Scouts (for serving another Scout a pan-fried turd). Gray duct tape covered the rope, and it was topped by a plastic sail. I thought it looked airworthy.

"You're going to take off on *that*?"

Not crazy about Bobby's attitude, I tried to ignore him. Even so, I had to admit it looked clumsy. The duct tape was thicker than bandages and the plastic sagged and in every way it was the opposite of stream-lined. I braced for further cracks.

"You really think it's going to fly, Chris?" There it was, dammit, he was laughing.

"Yes," I said. "What did you expect?"

"I expect you'll do a lot of hauling and no flying." He lifted the hang glider and made a face. "This weighs a ton."

"We've seen the pictures," I said. "We know what it'll do."

"Yeah?" For a moment he looked interested. Then he reconsidered. "Too bad you're not flying a picture." Walking long-legged and careless, the way he did, he crossed the blacktop and got back on his motorcycle.

Later that day Bobby came back. He knew Price and I were going to test the hang glider, and one thing you could depend on with Bobby — if something big was probably going to happen, he was going to be there.

4

MARALYS: The doctor gazed at us thoughtfully, drumming his ballpoint point pen on a leather-edged blotter. Across the desk from him, Rob, Bobby and I waited to begin a conversation nobody wanted. In the year and a half since the underground fort, Bobby's asthma had gotten worse, not better, and our trips to the doctor had become a useless pilgrimage. Bobby couldn't go on as he was, fighting for breath, nor could he continue to hang by a cortisone thread — a drug strong enough to thwart an attack, but also threatening to his immune system and his growth.

Eventually Dr. Simon said he could think of no alternative except to recommend Bobby for the Children's Asthma Research Institute and Hospital (as it was called then) in Denver. Informally, the place was known as CARIH, but to desperate parents the word connoted Court of Last Resort. We'd come now to talk it over.

The doctor started to speak, then reconsidered. Nodding at our son, he said, "Bobby, would you wait out in the reception room?"

Bobby stood up slowly and turned a face to us that was both scared and angry. The circles under his eyes accentuated the fear. He shuffled out of the room.

So it's going to be that bad, I thought.

"As much as you don't like this," Dr. Simon began, "it's time to make a decision. Bobby's thirteen now, almost too old to send away. If you wait much longer, Denver won't take him."

I turned to Rob, expecting him to say something, to put up a fight. He didn't.

"I've talked to the chief physician at the hospital. They've agreed to accept him in spite of his not meeting some of their criteria — long hospitalizations and so on. Usually they want proof he can't lead a normal life at home."

Rob's chin jerked up. "He can't! The fact that he sometimes appears normal is sheer willpower — Bobby's refusing to accept his illness. Nothing stops him. He'd have to be dying."

The doctor smiled. "In the long run that's good. Asthma can be emotionally crippling — sometimes more than physically. It's better he's a fighter."

"Oh, he's a fighter, all right." Rob's expression was ironic, and I knew what he was thinking. Bobby was a fighter in every sense of the word. But then, I thought, so was Rob. Sometimes it seemed fighting was the only way those two ever related.

"Well . . .," Dr. Simon searched our faces, "shall I make the final arrangements?"

Suddenly I felt an emptiness looming ahead — the prospect of years without Bobby. Worse still, I saw it the way he would, as banishment from the family.

I sat there remembering my own childhood. As a girl, I, too, had been sent away — shuffled off periodically by a confused and unhappy mother, sometimes to live in boarding schools, at other times fobbed off on relatives. Not all those substitute homes had hurt me. But some had — and I recall them still with surprising bitterness.

I wasn't ready to do this to Bobby. "Isn't it possible to send him for less than two years? To a child that can seem endless . . . almost forever."

Taking a deep breath, Dr. Simon explained patiently that two years were considered the minimum effective time.

"Any shorter and the patient relapses when he gets home. Then the hospital has to start over. I'm afraid, Mrs. Wills, if you're not prepared to let him stay, there's no point in his going."

I glanced at Rob. His face had hardened. "It's a drastic step. I don't like it. There must be some other place — something closer."

The doctor studied Bobby's chart. "Looks like you've exhausted Southern California."

"Albuquerque?" Rob persisted. "Isn't there research being done there — at the Lovelace Clinic?"

"There is, but I don't know much about it. If you'd like to give it a shot . . .," he shrugged, "I wouldn't put off a decision too long."

We took Bobby to Albuquerque. Alone with him, we all grew closer. The dry air did wonders for his asthma, and after a few nights' sleep the circles under his eyes faded. Between testing sessions we sat in restaurants and talked. Rob said, "You're feeling good, huh, Bobby?"

"Yeah. I didn't wheeze at all last night." Bobby stared out the restaurant window. His thin, boy's face was just beginning to stretch out. He pointed at the horizon, and I saw a starkness you wouldn't find in California. Dark mountains lay in one direction, in another the flat land stretched endlessly away: empty land, where shrubs struggled to grow a few feet, and the dull yellow grass gave up and clung tenaciously to the ground. "You could ride a motorcycle out there," Bobby observed. "You could go a long way."

"You sure could." Rob looked at his son with interest. "You'd like that?"

"I like anything where you're free." Bobby's eyes grew bright. "Anything where you can just keep going and nothing gets in your way. You could keep riding, and if you didn't need gas, you could go for days. Maybe you could take gas — so you wouldn't have to turn around until you felt like it." Chin in hand, he gazed into the distance. "I'm going to do it some day."

"Maybe you will," Rob said.

"I've got lots of ideas," Bobby offered. "I think about them all the time."

"What kind of ideas, Bobby?"

How rarely, amidst the confusion of six kids, we were able to talk like this.

"Oh, for inventing things. I dream up new stuff to make, things nobody's ever thought of. Different bikes . . . and other machines you can ride."

"Do you?" Rob asked.

The two of them looked at each other like old cronies discussing fishing.

"Yeah," said Bobby. "Only I never have time to make them, because of school and all that. I'm always practicing the piano or I have to eat. There aren't enough hours to do what I want."

Rob said, "You have to pick and choose, Bobby. Do what's most important to you. Adults don't have time to accomplish everything they want either."

Bobby sat up straighter. "I think *I will*." He looked at Rob earnestly. "When I'm older I'm going to figure it out, Dad, so I do *all* the things I want. You wait and see. I'll be different!"

Albuquerque had no answers. Their tests showed that Bobby had suffered a severe allergy-related hearing loss, whether permanent or not they couldn't tell. And his lungs were pre-emphysemic. Emphysema, they warned, was not reversible. But they offered no cure. Beyond bringing Bobby, Rob, and me closer, the trip had done little good. The Home for Asthmatic Children in Denver had become our last hope.

We saw Bobby only four times during his two years in Denver—four brief on-campus visits, none satisfactory. It was all the Institute would allow. Since children sometimes regressed after family contact, parents were considered part of an asthmatic's problem. No visits might have suited the school better, but what parent would agree to that?

The Home for Asthmatic Children was on the outskirts of the city, a small, neat campus with clipped lawns and a scattering of trees, white clapboard dormitories without rugs or curtains, a hospital, an austere dining room, and a recreation hall.

Bobby had been there six months when Rob and I and three of the boys drove to Denver to visit him. It was the week after Christmas, and we'd brought armloads of presents and a mix of the love and curiosity reserved for someone familiar who might have metamorphosed into a whole new person.

But something was wrong, we knew it right away. "I'm all right," Bobby said dully as we wrapped him in hugs. If he was glad we'd come, we couldn't tell. He smiled only grudgingly and at first had little to say. We didn't let that stop us. Full of plans, we swept him away to sledding in the mountains, to movies, restaurants, and a few nights at the home of friends. The boys, with their noisy normalness, soon captured Bobby's attention, and his reticence faded until he finally seemed part of the family again.

It was hard saying good-bye to him, even worse trying not to notice the tears he was trying not to let us see.

Six months later, in July, we made the trip again. Bobby had just turned fourteen. Though Rob and I had eagerly anticipated a second reunion, our first glimpse of Bobby was a shock. He had the look of someone who'd been sleeping under a bridge. Even from a distance we could see that his hair was long and shaggy, his posture stooped in an attitude of defeat. Across the trimmed grass he shuffled toward us, expressionless. He hardly looked like our son.

For a moment I stood rooted, staring. What had they done to him, what on earth had happened? Sucking in my breath, I covered my distress and hurried across the lawn. "Hi, Bobby!" I called, arms outstretched. I stopped short.

A flash of anger lit his eyes. His expression said, Don't touch me! I dropped my arms. He was like a cornered animal braced to defend itself.

Rob, too, pretended nothing was wrong. "Well, Bobby," he said, briefly touching his son's shoulder, "what would you like to do first?"

Bobby shrugged. "Does it matter?"

Above his head, Rob and I exchanged dismayed glances, then together we propelled him toward a car full of brothers. In the way of exuberant boys, Chris, Eric and Kenny galloped right past Bobby's depression, throwing out questions as they went. They didn't seem to notice how little he answered, how stiffly he sat.

"You going to stay with us tonight, Bobby?" Eric asked.

A moment's hesitation, then a sharp look, a dart of anger thrown in my direction. "No. I'm going to sleep in my dorm." Timing his exit dramatically, Bobby got out of the car and shuffled off toward the campus.

I felt as terrible—as rejected—as he wanted me to.

For a few awkward days we all tried to reach him, and finally he talked. "I hate this place. The boys in my dorm are rotten and the food isn't worth eating." Clearly, he ate as little of it as possible, which explained how he looked. I'd never seen him so thin.

He wheezed a bit, too. But when he did, he whipped a vial out of his pocket, looking me in the eye. "They give us nebulizers here," he said, daring me to challenge him.

Trying to do something about his thinness—even more about his morale—Rob bought him meal vouchers at a nearby restaurant. "Go there as often as you like, Bobby. If the vouchers run out, write me for more." Then we took him to the Rockies for an overnight campout, and there the rain poured down and seeped into our sleeping bags, and Rob and I lay awake all night pulling in our legs to avoid the water puddling at our feet. Next morning we climbed out of our soggy bags exhausted and stiff. But the campout wasn't all bad. Bobby had had a good time — and he finally smiled.

Leaving Bobby behind again was agony. I asked the school if we couldn't bring him home now, and they asked if I wanted to undo the medical progress he'd already made — which was apparent in his lungs, they said, if not on his frame.

I didn't, of course. But a small voice asked tormenting questions. Why wasn't he adjusting? Was there going to be some dark, unknown price for his physical health?

In Bobby's final months, the director of the home called me unexpectedly, the first such communication we'd had. With an edge of impatience he said, "You'll have to do something about the presents. The situation has gotten extreme."

"The presents?" I was baffled. "What are you talking about?"

"You know. The things Bobby's grandmother sends in the mail. The gifts."

I stiffened. "She's never said a word to me about gifts."

An intake of breath from the other end. Disbelief, perhaps. Then a brisk scolding. "I'm surprised you don't know. They come almost every day. Toys, games, equipment — sometimes in bunches. They're doing more harm than good, of course, damaging Bobby's relationships with the other boys. The last straw was the television. We — "

"A *television*?"

"That's right, Mrs. Wills, it arrived this morning. We'll have to send it back."

I was trembling with anger. "I can't believe she'd do this! A *television*!"

Instantly I saw the whole scenario: Bobby singled out with daily offerings as though he were royalty — showered

with gifts that bespoke rank, special privilege, excess—
opening his packages before the jealous eyes of his cottage
mates. No wonder they hated him!

"I'll talk to her," I said. "But it may do no good. She does
as she pleases."

Rob was furious and phoned his mother and shouted at
her.

Helen sulked. Then she defended herself. "I was only
trying to help. The poor boy, he's miserable there. You don't
know, Rob. He doesn't tell you. But he tells me. Denver is
the worst thing that ever happened to him."

No it isn't, I thought. You are. Then I chided myself for
being uncharitable, though it didn't diminish my anger.
Love without the tempering of good sense was probably
worse than no love at all.

Bobby was fifteen when he came home. Rob and I went
to the airport to meet him, excited and full of that tentative
hope one brings to a new day or a new relationship. Whatever had been wrong back at Denver we could fix. A few
hours in his own home and he'd be good as new.

Medically, the home had been encouraging. In the last
few months Bobby's lungs had shown a remarkable return
to function. The asthma wasn't cured, but his lungs could
now cope with it. If his lungs were better, I supposed he'd
look better, too—taller, happier, sturdier.

He didn't. Not any of those things. When I spotted him
coming down the airport ramp, he seemed exactly as I'd last
seen him—no taller, thin and spiritless. Once more Rob
and I did all the hugging and exclaiming and Bobby merely
looked at us.

Something inside me twisted. He was home now; why
was he so *sad*?

As we started down the escalator, I stole little looks at
him. He was carrying a box under one arm. His brown hair
was neatly combed, his clothes institutional-clean. I

remembered that plaid shirt — now somewhat faded — from years ago. With a pang I realized it hung as loose now as it had then.

We waited in the baggage area. I kept thinking, It's all right, Bobby, you're back, your life will be normal now, just wait. "All the kids are dying to see you," I said.

"Are they?" The hazel eyes raised to mine. The look in them was pure accusation. Of what, I didn't know.

Bobby didn't speak to us in the car. Instead he opened his box and played a solitary game on a toy called Labyrinth, which required the manual dexterity of a neurosurgeon, except that Bobby made it look easy. He'd obviously spent hours practicing.

We took him to the airport tower for lunch, thinking he'd enjoy watching the incoming planes. If he did, he didn't say so. Actually, he didn't say much of anything. Rob and I could think of no way to make conversation except with questions, which Bobby answered stiffly and in monosyllables. He wasn't enjoying it, obviously, and neither were we. After a while we gave up and finished lunch staring out the window.

It wasn't the kind of homecoming I'd had in mind. I didn't know it then, but our years of peace were over.

5

CHRIS: Bobby shook his head, looking at the hang glider I was about to test. "I don't know, Chris. It doesn't look anything like a plane. It looks like a beach umbrella."

That was his opinion. I was going to test it anyway. I figured we'd be flying soon, it was just a matter of working out the mechanics.

At the top of Lerner Lane, a mostly empty street behind our house, I lifted the frame over my body, grabbed the bamboo crosspiece and ran, ran like crazy considering the weight, with Price pushing from behind.

We didn't expect a lot, but we thought there'd be more than nothing. Afterwards, Price stood in the street, scowling. "This is a joke. If we want a *real* test, we'll have to try it in the back of Bobby's truck." So we heaved it up, and Bobby got in the cab and Price and I knelt in back to hold the glider down just in case.

Figuring the best test was a fast test, Bobby gunned the truck all the way to the cul-de-sac. Right away the sail billowed out and the plastic crackled like a flag in a hurricane and the kite strained and lifted. Price and I held on hard and barely kept it in the truck. If the thing got away, we were in deep trouble.

When Bobby finally stopped, Price and I went crazy, laughing and banging each other on the back. "It tried to fly!" we yelled. "It tried to take off!" At the moment I wasn't remembering that Mr. Pfankuch had said even a kitchen table would fly if you gave it enough horsepower.

"Now that we know what it'll do," said Price, "there's got to be a better test on the ground," and that's when I thought of the terraced half-acre lots up the street.

We hauled the kite up Skyline, and at the top of the highest lot, which was covered in thick weeds, we tied a rope to the frame, and I got up inside. This time Bobby pulled and I ran and Price pushed, and we all stumbled and tripped in the weeds until we came to the first dropoff and jumped down. That was when Bobby landed wrong and sprained his ankle.

For the rest of the day, Bobby leaned against a palm tree near the street, watching.

With Price on the rope, we took a few more runs, and I could swear at times I felt the kite lifting, so just to get the feel of flight I jumped into the air. And I saw Bobby laughing, a quiet laugh, half to himself.

"Did you see it flying—some?" I asked him.

He gave me a strange look. "Chris, your feet were on the ground the whole time. Flying is when you're not on the ground."

"Shoot," I said.

Price asked if I wanted to try again, and I said no, the lots were too small and we needed more slope. We'd have to go somewhere else.

One more day, I thought as we left. Twenty-four hours and we'd be flying for sure.

Bobby's truck blew up before we could go out testing somewhere else. We needed a bigger hill, which wouldn't be anywhere close to the house, and I don't remember how this happened, only that we must have said something to our neighbor, Mrs. Underwood, because she said she'd drive us.

Mrs. Underwood didn't have a truck, she had a station wagon. It took a lot of maneuvering to get the hang glider into her car, with half of it sticking outside on the tailgate, and three of her kids, and Price and me and my girlfriend, Betty-Jo, and Mrs. Underwood all inside. Bobby's ankle was a swollen mess, so he didn't go.

Mrs. Underwood said, "Where to?" and Price and I talked it over and decided the reason the kite wasn't flying was because we needed a sea breeze like they had at the Lilienthal meet. Price said, "Mrs. Underwood, if you don't mind, take us to Newport Beach."

It turned out the Lilienthal field was full of unfinished high-rises, so we drove around until we found some gigantic terraced lots—about fifteen feet between terraces, with a gradual slope facing the ocean. While Mrs. Underwood and her kids sat at the bottom, Price and I and Betty-Jo hauled the hang glider from one level to the next.

Then, gripping the kite, I ran down across the terraces—run, jump into space, run, jump—without anything happening. Feeling like I might have been flying without knowing it, I yelled up the hill, "You see anything, Price?"

"Yeah," he yelled back. "I saw you jumping."

"I mean do you think it was flying?"

"Are you asking is jumping flying? No, it's just jumping!"

"Shoot," I said when I got back.

Betty-Jo smiled. "The kite was good for *something*, Chris. When you went off the edge, it kept you from breaking your leg." Which is how she looks at things.

That was when Ram stood up and started swearing, the way he does. "There's got to be a trick to this." Talking nonstop, he got his shoulders inside the cage and took off galloping across the terrace.

Above his head the hang glider bounced and swayed, but the speed wasn't there. Even with Ram's tent-pole legs it was just a slow-motion run. When he reached the edge, I figured he'd draw up short like a horse at a hedge, but he didn't, he kept going. On the third jump his knees collapsed and he went down hard.

After he recovered, he turned around. "How'd it look, Wills?" he shouted back to us.

As Ram said, jumping and flying are not the same.

We walked back to Mrs. Underwood, who asked, "Well? What now?" and Price and I explained we had to go scouting for a bigger hill. "We'll find one by next weekend, if that's okay with you."

"Sure it's okay." Laughing, she gestured toward her children, who were staring at us with their mouths open. "I'll take you anywhere you want to go. You can't beat this for entertainment."

The hill we found on La Paz Road was 250 feet tall and fairly steep and came with a good sea breeze. It had everything except a landing area. In case we ever went that far, we could be in trouble because the hill ended against a highway, and on the other side of the highway was a lake. Which wouldn't be too good if you happened to be flying and couldn't stop. But nothing like that had been a problem so far. Not stopping was something we'd worry about later, after we cured the problem of not starting.

We pried the glider out of Mrs. Underwood's station wagon, and I hefted it to my shoulders and Price and I and Bobby—who was still limping—and Betty-Jo started up the hill, thinking we'd go all the way to the top.

I couldn't. A third of the way up was my limit.

Price said, "What's the matter, why are you stopping?" and Bobby said, "Look back, Chris, this wouldn't be any flight at all!" and Price said, "Bobby's right."

I said, "*You* carry it, Price."

"Hell," said Price, "it's not that heavy. We carried it all over the place last week. I know what it weighs."

"Yeah," I said, "across a few empty lots we carried it. This is a mountain."

Ram lifted the glider. "It's a hill."

"It *was* a hill," I said. "Now it's a mountain."

It wasn't long before Ram decided we'd gone far enough. "Who wants to fly more than halfway down anyhow?"

We sat down to rest. I looked around at all the empty hills, mostly brown, and I knew the empty wouldn't last, that someday there'd be houses on every one, and I wished we'd get airborne soon and be flying while the hills were still bare.

I stood up. "Come on, you guys. Let's fly."

Betty-Jo grabbed my dad's movie camera and rushed down the hill.

With Price helping, I settled the glider over my shoulders, holding the bamboo in a death grip. Pointing down the hill, I yelled, "You ready, B-Jo?"

She held up the camera.

Ram shouted, "Don't take him if he doesn't get off the ground!"

She called back, "You don't want the beginning?" and Bobby said, "Yes we do! Don't miss *any* of it!"

Ram shrugged. "Well, quit if nothing happens."

Inside the bamboo, I took a deep breath. Fidgeted. Thought about it some. Squared my shoulders. There was a tippy feeling about being up inside a cage with a steep hill dropping away at your feet. If you gave it much thought, you'd forget the whole idea.

I started to run. But the hang glider was dead weight and I couldn't get up much speed, and besides I kept having the sensation it was top-heavy and the kite would bail out and there I'd be, splatted all over the hill. After a short run I stopped.

Bobby said, "You need more horsepower, Chris," so he tied the rope to the front of the frame, and towed me down the hill at a fast limping run. Price pushed from behind and I ran and jumped (to see if I was flying) and ran and jumped some more.

And nothing.

It wasn't happening and none of us knew why. We all plopped down and Betty-Jo came up and handed me the camera, saying it didn't work, that it ran a few seconds and for no reason stopped.

"It has a problem," I said. "Sometimes you have to slap it."

She gave me a funny look. "I don't think I can do this."

Then Price was talking a mile a minute, spouting his theories about why everything was going wrong.

Nobody answered. Down the hill, the hang glider sat on its side, defying us. I knew Bobby was thinking we might as well forget trying to make a dead-weight hang glider fly.

About then Price said, "I'm thirsty as hell. You got any drinks, Betty-Jo?"

She was reading a book. She looked up and shook her head. "We finished the Cokes. But Mrs. Underwood might have something, she—"

Price didn't wait. Taking off at a gallop, he shouted back, "Maybe you'll get lucky and I'll bring you some."

Bobby stood up and limped slowly down the hill and Betty-Jo closed her book. "You won't be too disappointed, Chris, if . . . the hang glider never flies?" She seemed anxious. "You can get a pilot's license some day."

I smiled grimly. "Before or after I get my M.D.? I won't have enough money for a license until I'm . . .," I stopped to calculate, "past thirty. That's too long. This will work, B-Jo. One way or another we'll make it work."

Soon Price came back with an unopened can of beer and handed it over. "This was all she had, and Bobby said we could have it. I'm giving you first swig." He watched me swallow. "I've been thinking, Wills. Speed has got to be the answer. We have to run all out."

The kitchen-table theory a la Price. "Sure," I said.

"But we haven't done it."

"Right," I said. "Who wants to go falling on his face? Nobody." I took another big swallow, and after awhile I felt the alcohol begin its slow climb up my body. I said, "Let's analyze it, Price. What's the worst that can happen? Broken bones—right? You fall wrong and there goes an arm or a leg. But it's not the end of the world. It breaks—you let it heal." I suddenly felt braver.

"Give it back, Wills." Price weighed the can and scowled. "You could have left me a decent amount!"

I wasn't thinking about beer. "We've been holding back—this whole time we've never let go!" I walked to the hang glider feeling new power, new energy. We'd been a couple of chickens, Price and I, afraid of getting hurt. But sometimes you had to commit to something, go all-out if you cared enough. You had to take a few chances.

I could feel the beer talking in every limb.

In a crazy cocksure mood, I picked up the hang glider. This was going to be a different try, a committed try. I no longer cared whether I wiped out, no longer worried the craft wouldn't fly. This time I would go like hell.

Under the hang glider I straightened my shoulders and started to run. It wasn't easy at first. But I dug in, pushing forward. I knew I was going to fall, I could feel falling on its way — an out-of-control sensation that I was about to topple forward in a spectacular high-speed crash. But I didn't care. I ran faster, forcing myself, pushing with all the power in my legs.

Faster, down the steep slope, still faster. Always about to fall but somehow not going down.

And then something happened. The weight lightened just a fraction. Began to lighten more. Then gradually became a featherweight, as if someone had lifted the glider from above. As if the machine had lost pounds. My steps grew farther apart.

I picked up more speed. Without the burden, I ran easily over rocks and grass — fast, then faster. Then faster still because I felt so much lighter.

The hang glider vanished completely.

Odder still, *I* was lighter. I ran down the rough terrain, weighing nothing, running, running, light as an atom . . .

I was doing a moonwalk, half on, half off the ground. And then even the ground disappeared.

I was running over nothing!

My legs churned, my feet ran, but I ran on air.

Below, the ground moved past without me. For seconds . . . or minutes . . . or an hour . . . I floated above the ground, not part of it.

I could hardly breathe.

My head felt light and empty.

My body was empty. But suddenly my brain was full of shouting, shouting to the whole world, screaming news at the top of my lungs. Look, everyone! Look!

I'm flying! I'm flying!

I, Chris Wills, am flying!

6

MARALYS: Bobby wasn't normal. Even for him he rocketed beyond the limits of expected behavior, and I began taking notes — why, I wasn't sure. *If I don't write this down*, I thought, *I'm not going to believe it later.*

Only days after he came home, a wild black rabbit blundered into our backyard, inspiring Bobby to organize a three-brother-posse bent on its capture. At first Eric and Kenny were willing enough to dash around for the sake of a new pet, and the three soon had the quaking bunny cornered against our fence — until Helen arrived with her ancient Cadillac and her implied promise of toys unlimited.

The chase ended abruptly. As the younger children sprinted for the Cadillac, Bobby stood a moment, horrified. Then he began shouting, "Come back! The rabbit's getting away!" When they didn't, he ran after them, yelling and waving his arms. "Come back! Come back!"

No response. Outside the car, Bobby clutched at his brothers' clothes and arms, pulled and yanked, ordered them back to the fray. Finally he turned on Helen. "Leave!" he demanded. "Drive away! NOW!"

"Oh my stars!" cried Helen. "What's wrong with you?" Rolling up her windows, she started the engine.

By then, of course, the rabbit was gone. But in some ways Bobby was gone, too. The child who staggered into our family room, moaning and livid, was like nothing I'd ever seen before. "I'm going to *teach* those boys!" he wailed, "they never finish what they start! They're a bunch of brats! I'm gettin' sick of it! Sick of it!"

"Bobby—"

He whirled on me, his expression tormented. "Why don't you teach them? They're quitters! I should beat them up!"

A part of me seemed to split off, observing in amazement that my son was crazy. The other part tried to deal with him. "They don't *have* to chase your rabbit, Bobby. I'm glad you haven't hurt them. You showed a lot of self-control." Was I doing it right? "Get your racket. You have a tennis lesson."

Chris appeared. Thirteen now and taller than Bobby by half a head, he seemed years older. Stepping between the boys, he helped maneuver Bobby into the car. But once we got to the tennis club Bobby wouldn't get out, and it took words and words before he shuffled off with his head down, tennis racket hanging in a limp hand. *Wonderful,* I thought, *a mentally disturbed kid in the hands of a gung-ho tennis pro!*

But craziness is unpredictable. As I walked to the courts later, Bobby ran by with a light step. "Sure he had a good lesson," the pro said. "Why? Did you think he wouldn't?"

"Uh . . . no. Of course not."

He decided to walk with me. "He tried hard as a matter of fact."

I just looked at him.

"Actually," he said, "I've never seen a more competitive kid."

The bittersweet days of his return from Denver continued, with Bobby blowing hot and cold; generous and selfish; kind and cruel; pleasant and petulant. One day I looked at him hard and thought, *He's not wheezing—this is a miracle*, but then he hurled a well-aimed tennis ball and caught Eric in the neck, and as Eric lit out after him, I forgot all about miracles.

School wasn't going well, either. At our blue-ribbon high school, Bobby seemed to be in a daze. He was never on time in the morning, no matter how much I pushed and cajoled, and I soon found out he was late *between* classes as well, drifting in ten to twenty minutes behind everyone else. More than once I asked, "Bobby, what do you *do* with your time?"

It wasn't a question he could answer.

Though his latest aptitude tests marked him for accelerated English and math, performance suggested he drop out of school immediately and go to work. When I sometimes doubted his capacity, I reminded myself that back at the home for asthmatic children he'd won the school's chess championship (ping-pong too) and they'd told me his I.Q. was 147.

His problems ranged in every direction, it seemed. But the fighting was the worst.

One night Bobby came into the house late for dinner, and passing behind Eric's chair, he suddenly yanked it backward, halfway to the floor.

Predictably, Eric jerked around bawling, "Cut it out, Bobby!" but he only succeeded in launching the chair out of Bobby's grasp, so that he and his seat crashed to the floor with a sound of splintering wood.

Caught by surprise — as I usually was — I shrieked, "Bobby!" and flew out of the kitchen. By then Eric was scrambling to his feet.

Seeing the two of us in pursuit, Bobby danced, laughing, just out of reach. He was of course infuriating. His jeering laughter made me want to throw something, to fell him on the spot, but some remnant of good sense reminded me that my aim is questionable. The two disappeared among the bedrooms, their progress punctuated by slamming doors.

Seething, I picked up the broken chair, hoping I could forestall an additional scene by hiding it from Rob — at least until after he'd had dinner. Around the family room table Chris, Kenny, Tracy and Kirk waited apprehensively.

Eric returned first, anger showing on his adolescent jaw, his mild blue eyes uncommonly bright. Frustrated that Bobby had been too quick for him, he picked up his fork like a weapon. "One of these days," he growled into his plate, "I'm gonna get him!"

Until Bobby was sure Eric had cooled down, he lurked near the doorway with only a portion of his very large feet visible just beyond the doorjamb. Eventually he returned, but even then his appearance wasn't that of a chastened child. He slunk back, wary and cunning.

I said, "Sit down!" and thought for a moment he might actually do it. Instead he paused behind Kenny's chair, apparently up to no harm until he clapped his hands thunderously just behind Kenny's ears.

Kenny went off like a rocket. Out of his chair and up, screeching as only "Cobra Ken" could screech, "MOM! DO SOMETHING!" in the four-alarm voice developed by a younger child to scare off predators.

Once more I raced into the family room. On the way, spotting an open window, I slammed it shut, not wanting the neighbors to know I'd turned into a shrew. With murder in my heart, I lunged for Bobby, wanting to get my hands on him with an ache that was nearly physical. He'd made our dinner a shambles and turned me into someone I didn't like. He deserved a licking.

I tried to grab him, but he eluded me. Grinning, he dashed outside and let the door bang behind him. I burst through and stopped. He'd already crossed the yard and further pursuit was useless. I'd done that a few weeks earlier, sprinted across our half-acre trying to run him down, yelling at him to stop, knowing what I meant was, Come back so I can wallop you! He never stopped, of course, and I never generated enough speed to catch him. I felt like a fool. Nobody with a shred of dignity would do that more than once.

That night I was torn between telling Rob how awful our family life had become (in Rob's presence Bobby never behaved this way) and hiding my own inadequacies as a disciplinarian. I had pride after all. I was supposed to be intelligent, the one in charge. I'd once been a school teacher, and not a bad one at that. Why was I such a flop as a mother?

Finding no answers in myself, I began blaming Rob for not being home most evenings until dinner was long over. Why was I taking the brunt alone?

For the moment, I said nothing. I wanted Rob to love his oldest son.

One particularly bad night after the house had finally quieted (Rob was still at work and Bobby was tinkering in the garage) I went upstairs to talk to Chris. Steady, calm Chris. I found him sitting at his desk. He looked up from his books, and I launched into the injustice of having to cope with Bobby. "He's driving me crazy, Chris. You saw what he did tonight—turned Kenny into a raving maniac. I can't stand it, I don't know what to do." I waited hopefully for Chris to agree with me that yes, Bobby was a rotten kid. I didn't care what he said, actually, I just needed comfort. A few commiserating words.

When Chris didn't answer, I finally stopped and looked at him curiously. "It's funny, Chris, I've come up here to blow off steam, but it's a one-way conversation. You aren't saying anything. Why?"

Chris shifted uncomfortably in his chair . "You know, Mom," he was having a hard time saying it, "all the best times I've ever had in my life, I've had with Bobby."

I sagged against the doorframe and felt shame creeping along my skin. What had I been *doing*? What ghastly mission had I been on, trying to undermine brothers for the sake of a little solace? Dear God, it had taken a child to remind me! Hand on the doorknob, I said, "I'm glad you feel that way. Forget everything I just said."

I never complained to Chris again.

Still it became impossible, finally, not to spill over onto Rob. Soon, because of Bobby's antics, all the adults were fighting, each pitted against the others. Helen undermined our authority with money and gifts. Conversely, I demanded that Rob stop shouting, not be so harsh.

He turned on me irritably. "Babe, if your sweetness-and-light approach is so damned effective, why is it I come home every night to your complaints?"

I thought he'd missed the point. "Can't you see, it's *your* understanding he needs, Rob, yours more than anyone's. He needs patience from a father."

"Baloney."

As usual, we were getting no sleep, arguing about our oldest son. Rob rolled away from me in bed. "He needs *discipline*. He gets plenty of understanding—far too much of it—from you and my mother."

On Helen's infrequent visits she usually had tears in her eyes, pleading with me, "Bobby needs love. Oh my stars, can't Rob see it?"

Actually, whatever it was Bobby needed, none of us knew.

Eventually we took Bobby to a psychiatrist, whose approach, we discovered, was nondirective. For a few sessions he and Bobby played chess. Then the doctor discontinued the chess and they sat. He was waiting, I suppose, for Bobby to open up, but Bobby felt no need to bare his soul to this stranger. *He* wasn't unhappy, anyway. We were.

Week after week for a whole hour, Bobby and his psychiatrist sat, saying nothing, while we paid thirty-five dollars an hour. Even Bobby saw through that.

"What do you do in there?" I asked one day.

"Nothing."

"Nothing?"

"Nothing."

"I mean, doesn't he say anything, Bobby? Anything at all?"

Bobby shrugged. "He doesn't say anything. He just sits. And I sit. It's boring. We don't look at each other or talk or anything. Look, Mom," Bobby turned to me, a hint of a smile in his eyes, "why don't you just pay *me* the thirty-five dollars and I'll be good?"

I laughed and he smiled good-naturedly.

It was an idea, at that.

So much for psychiatry.

Things came to a head just after Christmas. On an evening when Bobby and Eric had been fighting more than usual, Rob and I decided to go to a show.

Rob stuck his head into Eric's bedroom. "Keep the lid on tonight, Eric, okay? You stay out of Bobby's room and I'll tell him to stay out of yours."

Eric looked up from his practicing, trumpet in hand. "You can tell Bobby, but it won't do any good. He just busts in here whenever he feels like it."

"Well, he won't tonight," Rob said grimly, "if you don't bother him."

"Yeah," said Eric with a shrug. The look in his eyes said he knew better.

Rob gave a similar warning to Bobby. Then for some reason he told Chris to write down the name of the theatre. He'd never done that before.

We'd been in the movie only a half-hour when we saw the usher with his flashlight. Stopping at row after row, he finally reached us. "Mr. Wills?" he whispered, and Rob gave him a surprised nod. I stared across at him. Squatting there in the aisle, the usher embodied everything ominous—the shrilling phone at two A.M., the black-and-white police car pulling to the curb. My breath came faster.

"Phone call," the man whispered. "An emergency."

Rob stiffened. The news seemed to paralyze him, so he

got up with maddening slowness. He walked toward the lobby heavily, each step slow and deliberate. I wanted to scream, Rob, hurry!

In that same ponderous manner he took the dangling phone. "What is it, Chris?" A moment of listening, followed by soft swearing. Then he said, "Hang on. We'll be right home."

Before I could ask questions, he was walking swiftly toward the door.

"Rob, what is it?" I ran after him. "Rob!" Anger has never sat well on my husband. More than anyone I know, it makes him different, unrecognizable.

He marched away, shutting me out.

"Answer me!" Hurrying behind him like an inferior, I shot out urgent questions, but they were like buckshot hitting a haybale, absorbed with no effect. I was frightened and angry all at the same time.

He threw open our car door and had the engine going before I was quite in. Cursing again, he finally said, "It's Bobby! The bastard has injured Eric."

"How? In what way?" It was pointless to ask. If he knew, he wasn't going to explain.

The house was strangely quiet when we arrived. Rob exploded through the front door and into the bedroom wing, but all we saw was Chris on hands and knees, scrubbing the hall carpet. At our approach he jumped up quickly, almost guiltily.

"What are you doing, Chris?" I pointed to the rug.

"Just cleaning up a couple of spots is all." Later I would know the spots had been blood and I would find a wastebasket full of broken glass and wood chips and realize Chris had been dispatching evidence to shield Bobby.

"Where is he?" Rob demanded. "Where's Eric?"

Chris put a finger over his lips. "He's in his room. Probably asleep."

"Asleep?" Rob was incredulous. "If he's asleep, what are

we doing home?" He started for Eric's room. "Where's the injury? I have to see it."

"Dad, maybe I shouldn't have called you. It might not be as bad I thought. I bandaged it. Maybe you should just let him sleep."

Rob snorted and flung open Eric's door. "If it's bad enough so we had to come home, by God it's bad enough to see." With no attempt to modulate his voice, he snapped on the light.

In the sudden glare, Eric rose off his pillow, blue eyes blinking and confused. One look and I could breathe again. He seemed all right. I noticed how handsome he'd grown in the last year—his hair thick, light brown and wavy, his face lengthening to a future manliness.

And then I saw it—the middle finger of his left hand encased in a thick white bandage, laid on the blanket as though for safekeeping. The professional-looking bandage extended down over Eric's hand and wound around his wrist.

Rob spotted it the same moment I did. He stared down, disbelieving.

Behind us Chris said, "You see, it's covered and—"

Rob spoke right through him. "What happened, Eric? I want to know exactly what went on here tonight." Deadly calm, but it wouldn't have deceived anyone: he was a simmering volcano, ready to blow.

Eric rose to one elbow, keeping his injured hand out of the way. "Bobby came in here and socked me and I chased him and he slammed the patio door just as I got there. My hand went through the glass."

Reaching down, Rob took Eric's hand. "Take the bandage off, Chris."

Chris brought scissors and began cutting. In spite of my apprehension I noticed the way he worked: unhurried, confident, each snip taking a measured amount of cloth as though clipping bandages were his everyday work. In a few minutes he was down to the last layer of gauze. With slow, careful fingers he peeled it back.

I stared down, horrified.

Part of Eric's finger was gone. Sliced clean. A canoe-shaped hollow left only scant flesh covering the bone. As we looked, blood seeped up and oozed across his finger.

Rob cursed softly.

I felt sick. How could Chris have doubted whether he should call us? The finger had to be seen by a doctor, and quickly—only what could a doctor do? The flesh simply wasn't there.

Eric said, "Cover it up. I don't wanna see it."

Chris began rewrapping the wound, layer by careful layer. He'd been talking, lately, of becoming a doctor. At that moment I thought, *Look how he uses those hands.* For the first time I couldn't imagine him doing anything else.

Suddenly Rob erupted, cursing violently. It was as if he'd been generating energy as he stood there, his frustration simmering until it overheated and burst. There was a different look on his face, dangerous and frightening. He started for the door and I knew where he was going.

I lunged for him. "Rob, it was an accident!"

He shrugged me off. In several furious strides he disappeared.

I stayed with Eric, frightened for him, even more frightened of what was coming to Bobby.

"What will they do to my finger?" Eric asked, watching Chris as though the finger belonged to someone else. "How will the doctor fix it?"

Chris shrugged. "I'm not sure—" and stopped, hearing sounds from Bobby's room. Rob's voice, bellowing. Then the sickening thud of flesh on flesh.

I rushed out, hurtling toward Bobby's door.

The scene was horrible. Rob stood just inside the doorway hitting his son, cursing and shouting, while Bobby cowered on the floor. Hands over his head, he tried to deflect blows.

"Bastard!" Rob shouted. "You've done it now!"

"Stop it, Rob!" I screamed. "Stop!" I threw myself between them, so that some of Rob's blows struck me. I grabbed his arms. "For God's sake, he's your son! Rob! Stop!"

But it was as though he couldn't stop, as though all the anger and frustration of the last six months poured out of him in a raging, uncontrollable torrent. His face was awful. He was a crazy man. Demented.

But so was I. Wild with fear and anguish, I grabbed for his hands, his shirt. I held on to him, shouted at him. I even hit him.

Panting, Rob finally pulled back. He stopped the pounding and loomed over Bobby as if holding him at bay. For a few moments he glared down at the boy on the floor. Then he straightened and walked out.

I waited while Bobby got up off the floor, every part of him in a shambles: his clothes, his hair, his expression. Defiance blazed out of his eyes — no, more than defiance, sullen hatred. He hated Rob, hated me. He snarled, "Get out!" He'd become a vicious animal.

Still I stood there, feeling terrible. "Bobby . . ." I wished I could say something that mattered.

He wouldn't have me. "Get out!" he shouted again, so I left him.

At the moment I no longer worried about Eric's finger. I feared for Bobby's soul.

7

MARALYS: We rushed around in the middle of the night preparing to take Eric to St. Joseph Hospital — everyone except Bobby, who was still in his room. I couldn't have felt worse about him. Whether he'd been entirely at fault I'd never know, but at this moment his alienation from the family seemed complete. I was the mother, yet I had no way to help him. Bobby wouldn't speak to me and Rob was adamant in his anger.

Sick at heart over what had happened and feeling like a traitor to one child while I tended to another, I left Bobby in his own unhappy company and went to the emergency room. There our family doctor carved a piece of flesh from Eric's forearm and grafted the slice to his finger. The scar on Eric's arm would fade in time, he said, and the finger would fill in around the graft.

But Rob was unmollified. "Injuries are permanent," he growled on the way home. "Scars are forever. His finger will never be the same."

Nor will Bobby's psyche, I thought.

Chris spoke up. "The finger will be okay, Dad; you'll see."

Once again we sent Bobby away. This time we shipped him off to the San Fernando Valley, to Helen and her husband, Neal, "for the sake of our other children," Rob said.

In my heart I disagreed. I felt we'd done it for ourselves, to end all the disruption. Bobby went silently, stoically. Yet I don't think he minded, really. It was I who minded, I who cried, I who felt guilty and angry. He was our son. For good or for bad, we owed it to him to keep him.

I cried to Rob. He told me to be still, that I had no choice in the matter.

For a while I could think of nothing but Bobby, and I drifted through my chores absent-minded and depressed. One day I drove off our side street and straight into the path of an oncoming car. Screech! Swerve! A flash of metal skimming my flank. I stamped on the brake and spun sideways just as the other car flashed by. Shaken, I forced myself to keep going. But when it happened again a few days later, I realized my emotions were going to get me killed. From that day on I kept reminding myself: Helen and Neal loved Bobby every bit as much as we did.

The pain eased. Gradually I fought down my conscience — or I just rationalized — but in any event I came to believe Bobby was happier with Helen and Neal. In time my guilt centered on the knowledge that life at home was easier without him. This was a different kind of pain: knowing I'd given up, literally failed at being a mother to this one boy and turned the job over to someone else. And, worse, to someone whose philosophy I didn't agree with.

Private soliloquies snuck up on me: *I love you, Bobby, it's just that you're so much easier to love at a distance.* I yearned to tell him about the trip Rob and I took when he was a baby, about our jumping out of a motel bed at three in the morning and driving straight through because we couldn't stand being away from him one minute longer . . . about the almost physical ache of wanting him back in my arms.

I still feel that way about you — when you let me. But he hadn't allowed us to be loving the last few years. He didn't want us near him, didn't wish to confide in us. At a distance, somehow, we all found it easier.

Is it part of the Grand Plan, I wondered, that parents be weaned from their children in a series of bruising steps?

When he was eighteen, Bobby came home to stay.

We're a family again, I thought in relief, as though I'd been holding my breath the whole time he'd been gone.

After all our reunions with a son who seemed destined to remain spindly, I now had a surprise of another kind: the boy who wheeled an arc welder into the garage was an entirely different person! I stood there staring at him.

Though we'd seen him sporadically over the eighteen months he lived with his grandparents, I'd somehow failed to notice how much he'd grown. Nothing of the child remained. The thinness, the suggestion of frailty had disappeared, and a new, tougher aspect had come to his frame. His face seemed bigger—longer in the nose and jaw, and I could see that his big hands and feet were larger than ever. When he glanced my way, I was looking into the face of a near-stranger—a stranger who must be over six feet tall!

"It wasn't easy," said Neal, as we watched Bobby carry clothes into the house. "It almost killed us. But if he turns out all right, it was worth it."

"You deserve a medal," I said, and meant it. Then for no good reason my optimism was in full flower, blooming away once more. Bobby was home, and we were going to turn him into a normal person, at last. He'd go to college, choose a profession, make a mark in the world . . .

Instead Bobby moved into the garage and became an inventor. From that day on, the garage was his because nobody else could get in it. "*Where* is my socket wrench?" Rob demanded one Saturday. He searched the workbenches, the tool box, then the garage floor. "Look at this!"

retrieving the greasy wrench from the cement. "Son of a bitch!" Curses. Shouting.

The next Saturday . . . same scene, different tool. I came to dread Saturdays because they were invariably ugly.

In the fall of 1969 Bobby enrolled in local Saddleback College. I never learned what he did there, only that he went each morning, faithfully carrying his books, and came back in the afternoon to set his texts on his bedroom desk and leave them undisturbed until the next day. The hours between school and school he spent in the garage. Even late at night the place was alive with the clatter of his working, the sparking of his arc welder.

"Bobby," I said, casually at first, "shouldn't you be doing some homework?"

"Don't worry about it, Mom. It's my sweat, not yours."

"I do worry."

His answer was a quick, unconcerned look in my direction, then dismissal.

As the semester wore on, my anxiety grew. Talking to Bobby in the garage was impossible; half the time he didn't even hear me. I resorted to flicking the light off and on.

Bobby simply waited me out, patient and calm.

He was now too big to punish or threaten, so after a while I gave up. He was right; it *was* his sweat. Meanwhile, night after night he sat on the cement surrounded by half-finished work—and also by grease and dust and disorder. He didn't mind the confusion, but he was slowly driving Rob crazy.

Fall became winter and then spring, and I knew the passing months had added little to Bobby's book-knowledge. Instead, he motorized our old wooden trash cart and called all the kids, "If you want a different ride, come on out!" With all his brothers and Tracy aboard, he chugged in bumpy, light-hearted triumph down our cul-de-sac.

"Hold it right there!" Rob ordered the first time he saw the thing in motion. Moments later he dashed outside to take pictures as the trash cart rounded the curve with children hanging all over it, an octopus of flailing arms and legs dotted with grinning faces.

Next Bobby built a souped-up hot rod which screamed like a 747 on takeoff and brought all our neighbors to their doors.

From a rusty rototiller he found abandoned in a ditch, he created a bizarre cliff-climber. "Watch this!" he said, grinning, and we stood by as the spiky machine clawed its way up a steep hillside with Bobby riding on its back.

He even mounted a Briggs and Stratton lawn mower engine to an ordinary ten-speed bicycle and putt-putted through the neighborhood, straight-faced and somber, but confiding to us privately, "You should see people laugh."

But the extravagant bicycles — those were his triumph. Young boys gathered from miles around to ride the high-bike, which towered twelve feet in the air on two triangular metal stems . . . and his two double-deckers, which were marvels of cockeyed engineering. On the latter, the top-story man was eight feet off the ground and had his own handlebars, seat, and synchronized pedals.

Bobby was the only person I ever saw who could mount those elevated bicycle seats unaided; he made it look easy. Giving his bike a light push to get it rolling, he simply climbed up the assorted welded tubes until he reached the top. Even as he ascended, the machine continued to roll smoothly as though guided by an invisible hand. Though Chris assured me others could do it too, I saw only the failures, those who fell sideways buried under a contraption the size of an oil rig — or the rest who resorted to propping the bike against the garage roof and crawling onto the seat under the eaves.

As Bobby and his friends pedaled around the neighborhood, they inspired so many double-takes — suddenly stopping cars, honking horns, waving people — that even a short trip became an adventure. Years later *Sports Illustrated* would call Bobby "the neighborhood's most attractive nuisance."

One afternoon Bobby came home grinning. "Chris and I thought we were in trouble today. We were riding the double decker and came to this intersection, and there was a cop on his motorcycle, watching. He motions us to pull over, and right away I think, Oh oh, here comes a ticket, I don't know what for, and I shout down to Chris, 'We better do what he says.' We get the bike over to the curb and I jump down from the top. But the cop isn't writing, he's just looking. He gets off his cycle and says, 'How do you get up on that thing?'"

Bobby laughed. "He really wanted to know, too, so we showed him. He said, 'I'll be darned,' and got back on his motorcycle and drove away."

Eventually Bobby did get a ticket — for breaking some obscure city ordinance forbidding "any bicycle with pedals more than six feet off the ground." Hard to imagine for whom, other than Bobby, the law had been designed since few bicycles would be even remotely capable of breaking it.

Knowing he was licked, Bobby stood resignedly in the courtroom as the D.A. handed over the the complaint. To Bobby's surprise, the judge read it once, did a double take, read it again, and gave Bobby a long look. "Am I reading this right? Mr. Wills, have I got this straight? . . . You have a bike with pedals more than six feet off the ground?"

"Yes," said Bobby.

"And that's what you're here for?"

"Yes, sir."

The judge shook his head. Turning to the D.A., he said in annoyance, "Case dismissed." As Bobby walked off trying not to smile, he heard the judge add, "Don't bring me any more cases like this!"

On Earth Day 1970 Bobby made his first and only mark

on campus. Riding his high-bike seventeen miles to school, he managed to arrive just as Nobel Prize winner Dr. Willard Frank Libby was making an outdoor speech. "I could see him as I rode behind the audience," Bobby said. "He looked up and did a double take, and I guess he lost his place in the speech because he stopped talking. People turned around and started laughing. Then the college president sent a guy running after me, saying, 'Get that thing out of here.'"

Bobby smiled. "I tried to leave, but a photographer rushed up to take my picture."

The next day Bobby was front-page news: "Towering Cyclist Rides into Nobel Prize-Winner's Speech." Rob bought extra copies of the newspaper to save for Bobby's children. "At least they'll remember you for *something* down at Saddleback."

Except for this brief moment, Bobby left college that spring without causing a ripple.

Once Bobby wasn't in school, Rob looked at his son and saw only greasy hands and feet, uncombed hair, and a flagrant unconcern about his future. "When are you going to put this aside and *do* something, Bobby?"

Deep in tools and half-finished projects, Bobby said, "I *am* doing something."

"That's playing. You know what I mean — something that has a future."

"Maybe this does have a future, Dad. How can you say it doesn't?"

Rob stared down at the garage floor in disgust. "These are *toys*. You're spending your days amusing yourself, headed nowhere."

Up went the barrier. Bobby tuned him out.

Rob's frustration spilled over onto me. I was the softhearted mother. I didn't see a problem when it was right under my nose. I wasn't concerned enough to do anything.

Unlike Rob, I knew an immovable object when I saw one.

Actually, I was grateful for progress, however limited. "Do you realize, Rob, he's not fighting with the other kids anymore? And he seldom wheezes. If we give him time, he may invent something useful." Of course, Bobby's bedroom looked like the dwelling place of a hobo and the garage was worse, but what did a few rumpled areas really matter?

"He still wheezes," Rob growled.

"Not much. And he knows what to do about it." What he did was carry a nebulizer in his pocket at all times, an ever-present bulge that we came to accept as the natural outline of his hips. Occasionally he turned and took a quick whiff, as a man might turn away to sneeze. Bobby's asthma had finally become his problem.

"You think it's enough?" Rob went on bitterly. "Wheezing less and fighting less? And inventing worthless gadgets? How much time do you want him to have?"

One Sunday, hearing Rob's angry voice, I went to the garage to find him thrashing about looking for a tool. He was swearing. Slamming cupboard doors. Kicking tools aside. "You got my crescent wrench?" he demanded.

"No. I've got mine." Bobby sat on the cement floor, bare feet extended out in front of him, between his knees a large wheel gripped in a human vise. Frowning, he tightened a nut over a bolt.

Rob glared at him. "It's a funny damned thing, isn't it, that my crescent wrench would get up and walk off."

Bobby didn't answer.

Rob took a deep breath, and I saw he was trying to control his anger. "Look, Bobby, it's time you went back to school. Or if you're not interested in school, get a job, put some of your mechanical abilities to work making money. You're nineteen, almost twenty. You've played long enough."

Bobby looked up indignantly. "This isn't playing, just because I like what I'm doing. You never said Chris was wasting his time working on planes."

"Chris was on his way to college."

Bobby laid down his tool. "I'll never be Chris. I'm not *like* everyone else, I'm different!" He gathered new energy. "I'm never going to do what other people are doing, you might as well know — what's the point of it? There's no use living if all you ever do with your life is stuff other people have already done!"

Standing in the doorway, I felt like cheering him on, applauding his individuality. The trouble was, there seemed little left in life that someone hadn't already done. Where would he find frontiers? Only the highly educated seemed to have access to the new and untried.

Rob said, "The point is, Bobby, I'm supporting you and I'm tired of it. *I* have to make a living, *I* have to think about money." He waved an arm over the garage. "Who do you think's paying for all this? Well, I'll tell you who . . . me!" He looked down at the floor disdainfully. "Nothing will come of any of it."

"Some day it will," Bobby said mysteriously. "You'll see."

8

CHRIS: Flying!

I looked down and saw the ground spinning by under my shoes and felt the wind coming into my face, and gravity wasn't there. My body was light and free and weightless. I was floating, skimming, not connected to anything—sailing away in a new dimension, where the horizon went on forever. I swung my legs. Air was everywhere—above my head and under my feet.

I wondered how long I'd be up and whether I was going to land on the road or keep floating until I hit the lake. I tightened my grip. And suddenly it was over.

I came down hard, hitting with my feet. The hang glider flew out of my grip and spun over my head and stopped in a patch of weeds.

I stood there staring after it, not knowing how I stopped or why. I hadn't meant to quit.

A commotion spun me around. High up the hill Betty-Jo held up the camera, cheering, and Price boomed down the slope yelling like an Apache. Bobby came running up from below.

They got there in seconds. Price was laughing, shouting, pounding me on the back. "We did it, Wills! We did it! Son of a bitch, that sucker finally flew!"

"That was great!" said Bobby, grinning. "Way to go!"

Betty-Jo ran up and threw her arms around me and said she couldn't believe it.

I said, "Did you see how flying sneaks up on you? First you're running and then you think you're running but you're not." The sensations swept over me again. "I mean, it's not a matter of jumping at the kite, the kite decides for itself when to start flying." I started pacing back and forth. "Could you see how high I was?"

Betty-Jo said she could.

"I saw it all," Price said, ready to start analyzing the details. "You were up about six inches."

"*Six inches!* The heck, it was more like six feet."

"Inches, Wills. I'll give you ten inches."

"Feet," I said. "I was the one in the air. You saw it, Bobby. How high?"

Bobby shrugged and said it didn't matter. "Nobody was measuring, so probably you're both wrong. A foot—maybe two feet. That's not important, it's how far you went that counts."

Price lightened up and said with a grin, "I was looking under your feet, Wills. They're big enough so nobody could miss where they were." He laughed. "Feet or inches, who cares . . . I'm out of here." He was off, running toward the hang glider.

At a slower pace, Bobby hopped after Price to help bring back the kite.

Betty-Jo smiled. "It must have been neat."

"It was," I said.

Without thinking, I reached for her and kissed her, caught her by surprise. I couldn't stop grinning. "It was the most exciting thing I've ever done, it was—"

She broke in with a smile. "*The* most exciting?"

Ram and Bobby speeded by, carrying the hang glider carelessly like a balsa wood toy, proving even heaviness is partly attitude.

"Second best," I conceded, "but I wish I could tell you how it feels to lift off . . . the way you go weightless . . ." I was suddenly out of words.

"I saw your face, Chris. I could tell."

We heard a yell from the bottom of the hill, a lady yodeling, and I looked down and remembered the Underwoods. Mrs. Underwood was waving. She pointed and laughed, and I could tell she was congratulating us, so I returned the wave and mouthed a thanks and watched her go off with her kids and sit down.

Ram flew next, running down the hill all out, shouting his head off. He ran hard, but it took so long I thought he might not lift off. When he finally did, his feet churned empty, pedaling through space. He was up for a couple of seconds—then down. He hit like a rock and rolled over and over, but then he got up grinning and shaking his fist like he'd won a contest.

Afterwards Bobby said, "Neither of you guys stayed up very long," and I agreed we hadn't and I didn't know why—unless, subconsciously, we were bailing out.

He said, "I'll see what I can do," and minutes later he was under the kite, barefoot, pushing off with massive force, like an engine pulling a train.

But instead of flying, Bobby stumbled and went down. I could see he'd taken a wrong step and turned his ankle — and this time turned it good. For once Bobby didn't act like it was nothing. He could hardly walk.

We stopped long enough to examine his ankle, which was a swollen mess, with little red veins around the puffy area. Waving us off, he said, "Forget it, go fly." He sat down to watch.

Price and I took two more flights apiece, neither very long measured in seconds, but a lifetime in sensation. Off to one side Betty-Jo kept her camera on the action, and I began noticing the pattern — how we'd fly a few yards, twenty or thirty, and come back to earth, and I realized it was all we wanted to do . . . that neither of us felt like going high or staying up long. Somehow, mysteriously, we signaled the glider and it came down.

Though the sensations were incredible — freedom, and lightness, and endless space, everything I'd imagined — we weren't sure we wanted to be away from gravity long. It was too scary, too unknown. What if we couldn't come down at will? What if we went higher and higher — and then fell?

We were crazy, Price and I, but not completely crazy.

For hours that night Ram and Bobby and I told the story. The excitement hit us all over again and we had to say it fast or it wouldn't keep. Mom and Dad were laughing and Dad kept saying, "Is that so? Truly?" wanting to know where we flew, who was there, the time of day, all the conditions. He kept asking us to repeat the details and he didn't seem to mind that we were loud enough to be heard all over the neighborhood.

Part of me stood back and watched, thinking about the way my parents got involved — and how Dad looked like one of us that night. For a lawyer, I thought, he was more like a kid.

A few weeks later Bobby's truck was fixed, so we told Mrs. Underwood she didn't have to drive us anymore but come anyway, and we called Mr. Pfankuch to tell him we'd be at a new hill in San Clemente, and four of us squeezed into Bobby's beat-up truck with Betty-Jo sitting in my lap.

Right away Bobby made us wish we'd gone with Mrs. Underwood. We'd barely left home before he was squealing around the curves on Skyline, and once on the freeway he rammed through traffic like A. J. Foyt. For him driving was competition. Bobby would accelerate up to somebody's rear end, check the adjoining lanes, and if there was a space between cars, he'd scoot into it like a crab between two rocks. His reflexes were world-class. But any one of those drivers could have messed us up, and it made me mad that Bobby figured he could never fail.

On my lap Betty-Jo faced straight ahead, stiff and tense. Halfway there she whispered in my ear, "I'm never riding with him again!"

I said, "Dammit, Bobby, slow down!"

He glanced at the speedometer. "What's the matter, Chris? I'm doing seventy-nine, barely moving." Across the cab he shot me a fiendish grin. "You're not scared, are you? Be glad I'm not doing ninety."

I said, "Betty-Jo gets car sick, *okay*?"

No answer. But the needle dropped back to seventy and Ram remarked pleasantly, "What they say about you, Bobby, is probably true. You'll drive like an idiot all your life and then die from an infected splinter."

The idea amused Bobby. Anyway, he had no plans for dying—ever.

Bobby parked the truck with a squeal at the foot of our new hill near Camino de Estrella. It was 450 feet tall, almost twice the size of the hill on La Paz, and it faced the ocean.

People were waiting for us. A dozen cars sat near the landing area, and when we pulled up, spectators drifted over to join us. It was only our fourth weekend in San Clemente, but people could see us from the freeway and the word had spread. From the first day they asked if we'd be coming back.

Our friends gathered around, and a man in glasses came up and said, "I'm a Boy Scout leader. Where did you get your plans?"

Price and Bobby laughed, and I said, "Out of our heads," and he looked disappointed.

Then Mr. Pfankuch—thin, with pants a little baggy— strolled over and said, "The crowd seems to be getting bigger. You've really started something here." He grinned. "If I was younger, I'd do it myself."

"Go ahead, Mr. Pfankuch," I said, but he shook his head and said the line was long enough already. And he was right. About half the crowd was friends, and all wanted to fly.

After Price carried the kite up the hill, he was puffing so hard he could barely speak, and that's when he came up with the Price Rule for using the hang glider. "For every ride down," he announced, "you guys have to carry it up the hill twice—once for yourself and once for us."

To my surprise, nobody objected. I said, "Good thinking, Price."

Because his ankle wasn't healed, Bobby sat down to watch. I wondered why he was willing to come each time and just *sit there*, but after a while he said, "Do you guys know you always shift your bodies back just before you land?" I said I didn't, and he said, "You flare the kite like one of those seagulls landing on the beach," and I knew then what he was doing—figuring out the principles of flight.

But Price had his own theories: "I've noticed whenever we kick our legs, we have a soft landing." After that the two of us kicked our legs every time, and sure enough our landings got better. By the fourth week it wasn't *us* crashing, it was our friends.

I'd always known hang gliding would be exciting, but when others got into it, flying took on a whole new dimension. Our friends, who hadn't been around for the learning part, saw only the go-for-it part, so they threw themselves down the hill without worrying. Their crashes were spectacular. Sometimes they dove into the ground at full speed like kamikaze pilots, or they flipped and landed with the hang glider on top of them. They dug furrows, plowed through cactus, sent up explosions of dust. The crashes got to be the best part of flying, the part we tried to get on film and later carried around to show at Kiwanis and Lions Club—or to any group who wanted laughs.

Naturally our friends kept breaking the kite, but they usually honored the contract and carried what was left of it back up the hill. We used so much duct tape we began buying it a dozen rolls at a time. Bamboo splints and tape over the plastic rips kept the kite going all day, and eventually we learned how much damage it could take before it needed major repairs. Every week we practically remade the hang glider. But it was worth it.

In the beginning, Betty-Jo alternately took movies and timed our flights with the stopwatch, but we soon said, "Forget the stopwatch, Betty-Jo, and stick to the movies. We can't afford to miss a single flight." So she was filming that fourth Sunday when everything broke loose. By mistake I flew right into the camera and knocked her all over the hill, and later Price sailed over one of his friends and into somebody's motorcyle, and the cyclist got so mad he rode his cycle into the side of Bobby's truck.

And then a friend from my college chemistry class, Jim McCaffery, cartwheeled on his first flight and lost his glasses, and everyone stopped and spent about an hour poking through the two-foot-tall grass and never found them. After a while McCaffery took another flight, and when he got near the ground he decided he didn't want to crash again, so he just let go and the glider flew off by itself.

Near the end of the day it was Betty-Jo who found McCaffrey's glasses—not that she was looking for them any more. You might say it was an accident. She sat on them.

Each week we got our developed movies back from Rochester, New York, and spent hours studying them frame by frame to learn more about flying—except for the first week, when we got a big surprise. I remember how excited we were as we tore upstairs to my bedroom for the Big Showing. It was going to be great, seeing ourselves for the first time. I threaded the film on Dad's projector and somebody turned out the lights and the image began—but we had a massive shock. All the footage was upside down!

After a lot of discussion and Ram swearing and saying What the hell is this? and coming up with various theories, I got Betty-Jo to show us how she held the camera—and, sure enough, she'd been holding it upside down. "I'm sorry," she said. "It looked the same both ways."

So now all the best footage was lost. But then Bobby said, "You could hold the projector upside down," and I did, but that got to be old. So I tried playing with the film editor and after a while I figured out you could run it backward, and sure enough, the images came out right side up. But there was still one minor problem: all the action ran in reverse. A scene opens with dust and flying objects and confusion, and then out of the mess a hang glider rises up and miraculously flies backward up the hill. It was very funny, but not funny the way we'd planned.

About then Dad bought a new 8mm camera, and things got simpler. But there was still something strange and unsatisfying about the crash scenes. Every crash ended with the kite ramming the hill and giving a big convulsive jerk just as the film cut out. When we thought about it later, the jerky endings were Price's fault. He'd made such a big deal about wasting film that Betty-Jo never waited to see the victim crawl out from under. Anyone watching our movies just had to asssume the flyer survived.

We had feelings of destiny about those films. Gradually they were wearing out, and some instinct told us to preserve them. Our instincts were right: a few months later our flying had changed so much the bamboo-and-plastic kites seemed like holdovers from the days of Otto Lilienthal.

9

MARALYS: Rob's patience was running out. "Bobby's twenty," he growled one day, "how much longer is he going to vegetate in that damned garage?" He couldn't go near the place now without railing at the greasy inventor sitting on the floor.

Innured, Bobby no longer defended himself, he simply waited out the storm. Clearly, Rob was just one of the obstacles implicit in an inventor's life — a second being that the days were only twenty-four hours long and, as anyone could see, he needed more time.

At last Rob issued an ultimatum: "Bobby, you either find a job or move out!"

Relucantly, Bobby went to work as a mechanic in an auto agency and for the first time in his life had his own money — though he never seemed to buy anything. Instead he complained, "They cheat the customers, Dad. They tell us to charge twenty-five dollars for a two-dollar part, and they say if we don't see anything wrong with the car to find something. I got in a big argument with my boss today. He didn't fire me, but I thought he was going to. I can't work there anymore."

"I understand perfectly," Rob said. "But there must be an honest agency in town. Try somewhere else."

Bobby did, and was hired as a menial in the largest Oldsmobile agency in Santa Ana — a job with attractions he hadn't expected, namely the delivery of repaired cars to their owners. Suddenly Bobby had an unexcelled opportunity to discover—and report back to Chris and Ram—the performance limits built into every model and engine. Using the freeways as a testing ground and keeping out of the clutches of the law God knows how, he kept top-speed tallies of every Oldsmobile then produced.

Rob and I were blissfully ignorant of all this, and also that Bobby sent messages along the high school grapevine: "Come out to the test curve today, I'll show you the spin-out speed of model X." Apparently the agency never caught on because Bobby drove so fast he always delivered the car before it was expected anyhow.

With his full-time job and "entertainment" sideline, Bobby's inventing narrowed to weekends and Rob and I seldom saw him. Our Saturdays and Sundays were devoted to watching our other children perform—in swim meets, tennis matches, and water polo games. One weekend we had children competing in four different counties.

Only Eric was missing from our whirl of activities. For a long time, now, he'd been the son I hardly knew. "Where's Eric?" Rob would ask, and I'd look around and realize he'd slipped away. His comings and goings were silent, unobtrusive, almost mysterious. Gradually we realized he wasn't peforming well in class, and fearing he might not graduate from high school, Rob enrolled him in a military academy, whose sole purpose, as far as Eric could tell, was to make sure his hair was kept permanently, obnoxiously short. On home leave Eric's conversation centered on the desirability of getting out of military school and coming home to grow hair.

Now that Bobby had a job, there seemed to be a temporary truce operating in the garage. For a few months Rob left him alone to tinker amidst his grease and metal. But one night Rob came home late and walked into the family room with an expression I knew right away meant trouble. Without preamble he marched to the table where Bobby sat alone, eating, and said, "Tonight is the night you clean up the garage." Even as he issued his ultimatum he spotted the ratchet that Bobby had set by his plate, and for an instant he glared at the tool with profound distaste.

Startled, Bobby put down his fork. "Why did you come in all mad? Can't I even eat?"

"Finish dinner and then get out there." Rob looked at his watch. "I want that job done by bedtime." As though it would just magically happen, he turned his back on Bobby to drape his suit coat over a chair.

Silence. Bobby's eyes went from his plate to Rob's back before he said peevishly, "How come you're always picking on me?"

Rob whirled around. "Because I own this place, dammit, and I want it habitable! Now get moving! You have an hour and a half." He started for the back of the house.

I thought, Bobby's never cleaned up anything in his life, why on earth does Rob think it's going to happen tonight? He'll have to *show* the boy, go out there and work with him. But the chances of that were almost nil.

Suddenly Bobby pushed his chair back. His face held a different expression, not the sullen stubbornness usually reserved for his father, but something else, a new undercurrent of strength. "I'm tired of your yelling, Dad," he said quietly, "the way you shout at me for no reason when I haven't done anything. That's all you know how to do."

Rob hadn't quite left the room and now he stopped. "Oh, is that so!"

I held my breath, fearing Rob's reaction. And indeed, he suddenly looked fearsome: shoulders squared, eyes dark with anger, jaw tight. "You don't like it here?"

"You yell at me every single day and — "

"Be quiet, Bobby!" I hissed.

"You don't have any right to bully me," Bobby went on.

"You're always on my back."

"Tell me about it!" Rob advanced on him, jabbing his finger at the air. "I have no rights, eh, is that what you think? While you're sitting there eating the food I pay for, the dinners for which you've never contributed one single dime! You're telling me I have no rights . . ." He moved closer.

Bobby watched him come without flinching. "All you think about is money," he said. "That's all you care about! Well, you can *keep* your dinners!" He shoved his plate away and, pushed too hard, it skidded off the table and fell to the floor. Spaghetti curled on the linoleum, peas rolled like spilled marbles. The plate lay in two pieces. For one silent moment Bobby stared at it, aghast, his face revealing he hadn't intended what happened.

Rob lunged at him.

"No, Rob!" I shouted and started forward.

My words were useless.

As Rob came on, Bobby scrambled out of his chair and ducked sideways, but not in time to avoid Rob's fist. With fury in his eyes, Rob landed a clumsy blow on Bobby's chest.

Bobby pushed him away. Taller than his father by half a head, Bobby either didn't try or didn't dare strike back. There was no fear on his face and no confidence either, only wary waiting. He dodged as Rob swung again and somehow avoided his father's fists — but only momentarily. Rob had the momentum, the anger. I was frightened and screamed at him to stop, but he ignored me. I searched wildly for the right words, cast about for a weapon. Why, why was I so ineffectual?

Shoulders hunched into a thick mass of aggression, Rob swung again and again.

At last Bobby fought back. He pushed his father, grabbed Rob's clothes, and finally struck the arms that pummeled him.

Rob drew back for a great swing and Bobby swerved and Rob hit nothing, and then the two moved in close, grunting and pummeling and shoving. It wasn't a movie fight, nothing neat or well-aimed; everything Rob and Bobby did was awkward, deflected, and went where it wasn't intended. Yet it was the most horrifying spectacle I'd ever witnessed and worse than any movie. No cimematic portrayal could have prepared me for the sight of two grown men fighting in a "civilized" family room.

I danced around uselessly, groped for their arms. Infuriated, I tried to hit them myself. My anger mixed with bewilderment that Rob had never found a better way to deal with his oldest son, that it was always this same child with whom he lost control. Why, when he'd never administered so much as a spanking to Chris, did he allow himself to stoop so low with Bobby? With all my other emotions came a heavy, gut-sick feeling of revulsion. Rob looked terrible, like a monster. I hated him.

Kenny appeared in the doorway, then Chris, their eyes round O's.

For terrible minutes the fight surged across the family room. The two punched and grunted and pushed. Finally Bobby fell to his knees. Struggling to regain his feet, he butted against Rob, and one of them, I never knew which, backed into our huge plate-glass picture window. With a resounding crash, the entire wall came down.

Instantly they stopped fighting.

For mini-seconds glass tinkled and settled into grotesque shards, large and small, with parts of the window still in place like shark's teeth. The hole was so large it seemed as if the whole north side of the house were gone.

Rob and Bobby stared.

You deserve it, you fools, I thought.

Even before the sounds had quite died away, Tracy and Kirk rushed into the family room, and seeing the two men still squared off and glowering and the window scattered sharp and ugly on the floor, Tracy, eleven, burst into hysterical sobs and ran away again.

"Get out!" Rob bellowed at Bobby.

"I'm GOING!" Bobby shouted back. He turned on his heel.

"And take this with you!" Rob seized the ratchet Bobby had left on the table and hurled it through the opening.

Bobby didn't look back. Striding like Gulliver across the room, he went out, letting the back door slam behind him.

Sick inside, I gave Rob a look containing all the loathing I felt and walked out to go comfort Tracy. I found her leaning against her bed, sobbing. Taking her shoulders I said, "It's all right, it's over now, honey. They won't fight any more." I was telling lies. What assurance did I have that anything was over? "Everything will be all right, Tracy." I held her and rocked her in my arms, seeking solace as much for myself as her, soaking up the sweet wonder of a gentle girl. Sitting on her bed, I held her until she quieted. "Lie down now, baby. Get under your covers."

"Why did they do that?" she asked, her face still distraught.

"Oh, Tracy, I don't know. They were angry."

"They scared me."

"They scared me too. But it's over now."

"Are they going to fight again?"

"No."

She let me ease her into bed. "Tell them not to. I don't want to hear it."

I assured her there'd be nothing to hear.

She squirmed down deep. Then she pulled out again and tried to sit up. "Mom, who's going to clean up the glass?"

I paused before I answered, feeling my anger return. But I couldn't inflict it on her, not on Tracy. Taking a deep breath I said, "I'm not sure who's going to clean it up." I swallowed hard and held back my words. *I'm not going to touch it!*

She sighed as I turned out the light.

Though I had no way of knowing I'd told Tracy the truth, I had. Rob never touched Bobby again.

A few minutes later I went to bed, but I didn't sleep. The awful scene came back, so unlike any brawl on the silver screen. How many moviemakers, I wondered, had ever *seen* the fight of two inexperienced men, who grappled and grunted and fought in close and never once landed a blow that had much effect . . . normal men who fought as if they couldn't fight?

I kept seeing the window coming down, a harsh symbol that the tenuous thread between father and son had finally broken.

I saw nothing ahead for our family but grief. Again, it seemed, we had lost our oldest son.

An hour went by and Rob didn't come near our bedroom. Instead I kept hearing noises, something happening out in the garage, scraping sounds, then Rob's footsteps on the patio, where all the floodlights were on. Slamming sounds issued from Bobby's bedroom.

Eventually I got out of bed and drew back the curtain. For a long moment I stared in disbelief. Outside on the ping-pong table, illuminated harshly in the light from a naked 150-watt floodlight, lay stacks of Bobby's clothes.

Horrified, I threw on a robe and went to the back door. All Bobby's possessions were strewn across the blacktop and the garage was empty. His bicycles, hot rods, tools, and machinery filled the area and overflowed around the side of the garage. I followed the trail of gadgets, and there I found Bobby, out of view on the narrow driveway at the far side of the garage. He was sitting on one of his hot rods—not doing anything, just sitting, staring straight ahead. His bare feet lay flat on the cement, his hands gripped the machine's steering wheel.

"Why don't you come to bed?" I said.

He didn't look at me. "I figure I have no bed."

"Sure you do. He'll get over it in the morning."

He shook his head. "This time he won't."

Tears rose in my throat, choking me so I could hardly breathe. "Of course you can sleep in your own bed. Bobby . . .?"

"I can't. I'm leaving. I just don't have anywhere to go tonight."

"Oh, Bobby."

Small sounds reached us: the incongruous chirping of crickets, somewhere a dog barking. For a minute or two we shared the narrow space, looking past each other without words. Then he said bitterly, "Go back in the house. You belong to *him*."

Did I? I wasn't sure any more.

I just looked at my son, trying to communicate my love and regret, knowing he would never let me touch him. I watched him, my heart breaking, and when it finally seemed I wasn't helping, I left. I had never felt more devastated in my life.

10

MARALYS: The next morning Bobby was gone. How or where, I had no idea, but I couldn't think about anything else. For days I was too angry to be civil to Rob. I walked by the gaping hole in the wall, glad it was there, wishing it were even larger, for it symbolized punishment, a kind of revenge I myself was helpless to inflict. The hole spoke for me. Take that, Rob, you idiot. You deserve it.

I'd move out before I'd lift a finger to fix the glass.

Word came to us from Ramsey Price that Bobby had found an apartment with a friend and also a better job working at the same place Ram worked, delivering soft water. One night Ram told me conspiratorially how he and Bobby arrived early each morning to be sure of commandeering the fastest trucks, and how they spent hours plotting their routes, the idea being to deliver the greatest number of water-softening tanks in the least amount of time while collecting the smallest number of speeding tickets. Soon he reported back that they were making more money and working half as many hours as everyone else. I knew then Bobby was going to survive.

It was perhaps three weeks after the fight when Bobby appeared unexpectedly. He simply walked in the backdoor as though nothing had happened. For a split second I stared at him in disbelief, as though he'd materialized out of the empty garage. *Bobby. You're home!* Did I dare hug him?

Would he let me? Did it matter? He'd come back, that was the important thing, he'd put aside his pride and stepped across the invisible line. I smiled at him, and he said casually, "Hi, Mom." It felt wonderful.

Rob was there. He said, "Hello, Bobby. Want some dinner?" as though he'd never been away.

A momentary look of surprise. "I guess so." Tentatively, Bobby sat down at the table.

Ignoring him affably, the other children went on eating and afterwards jumped up to go about their usual activities. Only I seemed to think it a dramatic moment.

Toward the end of dinner Rob said, "What are we going to do with all your stuff, Bobby?" Rob had stacked Bobby's machinery along one side of the blacktop, where it sat in organized disarray.

Bobby shrugged. "I don't know."

"Look," Rob said with sudden energy, "find a garage some place and I'll pay the rent on it. Make sure they'll let you plug in your welder and power tools — and won't object to your working late at night."

"You'll do that, Dad?"

"Sure." Rob laughed. "I have to get it out of here some time, and I wouldn't want to sell anything without your okay. If you find a garage, you can do what you want."

Bobby murmured, "Thanks, Dad." He looked around the room as though seeing it with new eyes, as though our place were finally comfortable again.

In our bedroom later, overflowing with relief and good feelings, I said to Rob, "I'm glad you and Bobby could talk. You both acted as if nothing had happened. I hadn't expected that. I worried that you wouldn't speak to him if he showed up. But then I thought he might never come home again."

Matter-of-factly Rob said, "He's decided to join us on our vacation. He wants to drive that old Mercury Commuter of his. I told him the car would never last the distance, but of course he thinks it will. We'll see."

"Let him drive it, Rob."

He sat on the edge of our bed ready to write in his journal. Pen in hand, he said abruptly, "*Of course* I'd talk to him — why wouldn't I? Whatever happens doesn't alter the fact . . . we're still a family."

A few weeks later we left on our trip, Rob driving the station wagon and Bobby his ancient white Mercury, which Rob assured him "probably won't get out of the state of California."

"Sure it will, Dad," Bobby said cheerfully, and insisted on carrying not only the extra luggage and two of his brothers, but also a couple of bicycles on the roof, whose handlebars spiked toward the sky like the four-point antlers of a bagged elk.

In the end it wasn't the car Rob objected to so much as the bicycles. "When you break down, Bobby, there won't be room for the bicycles to come in with us. We'll just have to ditch them somewhere. You're not being realistic."

"I told you, Dad . . . the car will make it," and to everyone's surprise it did. Three thousand miles without so much as a flat tire, and Bobby crowing that the bikes had been the best idea of all. Mountain bikes hadn't been invented, so it seemed madness that on our four-mile hike up a steep, rocky trail to Sequoia Park's Heather Lake, Bobby chose alternately to push and ride his three-speed, with all of us telling him he was crazy.

He wasn't, of course, not by his lights, because coming back he managed to ride lickety-split down the trail — between pines and over rocks and across water breaks with the aplomb of a deer running through the forest. Our fellow hikers on the path viewed him as something between a phenomenon and a spectacle, but we were all used to that.

With Bobby only the extraordinary was ordinary.

That spring Eric graduated from the military academy, finally escaping any further encounters with barbers. "I'm never gonna cut my hair again," he threatened, and I looked at him hard, the clean-cut boy with the wavy hair and deep blue eyes, and started to argue, then decided I might as well hold my arguments until the need arose. He was so handsome the way he was (some said the best-looking of our five boys) I couldn't imagine he'd want to appear any other way.

Yet he did: I would never see him look quite that good again.

In the fall Eric declared, "I don't want to live in this crummy, crowded area," and when I asked where he *did* want to live, he said the northern California town of Mount Shasta. He'd been there once and remembered catching fish. "And Shelley wants to live there, too."

"How will you earn a living?"

He gave me one of those patient, son-to-naive-mother looks. "I'll get a job."

I was ready to ask, How? With what skills?

He read my mind. "They have jobs up there, just like any town. I'll find something, Mom, don't worry."

But I did worry, and I tried to imagine the lovely Shelley disappearing into a minuscule town on the edge of nowhere. Where would they live, what would they do with Shelley's little girl? (After we met his new girlfriend, Rob's comment had been, "Sure she's beautiful, but did he *have* to choose a beautiful girl with a baby?")

Now Eric was ready to become an instant parent — at eighteen!

Within a week the two were loading all their possessions into Eric's new-used station wagon — a graduation gift from Rob — while the family gathered on the blacktop to see them off. Even Bobby was there.

"What're you going to do in Mount Shasta?" Bobby asked, watching Eric carry a box to the car.

"Get a job. And fish." Eric pushed the box into a niche in

back. "I like it there."

"But there's nothing *in* Mount Shasta."

"It's better than here." Eric slammed the tailgate closed. "I know I'll like it. And Shelley's gonna love it." Behind him the girl nodded, her great, dark eyes full of mystery, her long, rich brown hair falling over her shoulders. By anybody's standards Shelley was gorgeous.

"Well, you'll be back," Bobby said.

"No," said Eric, "I don't think so. That's where I'm going to live. I know what kind of place I like."

Rob looked sympathetic. "I wanted to get away, too, Eric, when I was your age. I know exactly how you feel. Perhaps you *will* stay. Well . . . keep in touch." Through the driver's window he and Eric shook hands.

I thrust a bag of sandwiches through the opening. "Eric . . ." There was so much I wanted to say to him, my young, vulnerable son who didn't seem old enough to do what he was doing. But my words would do no good. He'd been set on this move for months. Under Eric's sweet, calm exterior was a surprisingly determined core. I smiled at him. "When you get there, call us, okay?"

He said he would.

They backed out of our driveway, a brave pair, I thought. Brave and a little foolish. So good-bye, third son.

As the wagon started down the street, Eric waved.

He's gone, I thought, the boy who'd never communicated much, who'd rarely shared his inner thoughts — in a large noisy family, the quiet one who went unnoticed. Yet in his leaving I saw confidence and strength. There he was, moving to a strange town of his own choosing miles and miles away. And of all of us, only he wasn't worried.

The wagon turned right at the end of our street and disappeared. First Bobby gone, now Eric. Neither with much in the way of prospects, but gone just the same. Somehow I'd always thought when birds left the nest they'd know how to fly.

11

MARALYS: Hang gliding. Did it burst into our lives without warning, a flame ignited spontaneously, as I said to all my friends, or was the truth something more subtle, that the sport had been sneaking up on us for years in little doses?

I don't know. Chris did seem destined to fly, somehow, somewhere. He'd built so many non-flying or semi-flying planes, spent so many hours cutting, shaping and gluing, conspired so exuberantly with Ramsey Price, that I should have foreseen the possibility that *one* of those craft, even the oddest of the lot, might make him airborne.

But the rest of us . . . how could I have guessed we'd all become involved?

How clearly I remember our first look at the sport — Rob and I persuaded by Chris to go down with him to San Clemente one Saturday. His enthusiasm was contagious, irresistible. He'd been grinning nonstop for days. "Mom and Dad, you *will* come tomorrow?"

So we went, climbed part way up the hill and stood off to one side while yards above us Chris got himself under his plastic wing, ran a few steps, left the ground and hurtled by with his legs swinging and the sail rattling like a hundred fresh-washed bedsheets flapping in the wind.

The sound literally washed over us as he rocketed past, and I sensed what he was feeling, his triumph, his freedom.

Seconds later he landed farther down the hill, running hard to keep his balance. I asked, "Did you see his face, Rob?"

"Sure I saw his face. What you could see of it under the grin." Rob stood quietly shaking his fingertips, a gesture of inner excitement that comes without conscious thought. He watched Chris hoist the glider to his shoulders and begin the uphill climb, still grinning infectiously. "I can see why they like this, Babe. It's incredible!"

We watched flight after flight that day, caught up in the spell of Chris's and Ram's enthusiasm, sharing vicariously the sensations of speed, sound, lightness of body, a breeze in the face. They never flew by without laughing, never came near us without talking in exclamation points. By the end of the day we were as full of excitement as Chris.

Rob and I went to San Clemente often after that. When Bobby's ankle healed — and, with his penchant for bigger-and-better, he built a second, larger version of the original hang glider — our family life became richer and more exhilarating than I would have believed possible.

To our amazement, the new hang glider attracted swarms of spectators. It seemed two kites were more than twice as eye-catching as one, so more people saw them from the freeway and pulled off for a closer look. The hill became a carnival — cars everywhere, people milling near the landing area, up on the slope little knots of spectators with picnic lunches. A few camp followers appeared faithfully every Saturday and Sunday and waited for the boys if they were late. Ramsey Price remarked, "Seems like we can't stay home anymore. We've become their weekend entertainment."

Then, subtly at first, Rob and I sensed all was not well. Carrying sixty pounds — awkward pounds at that — up a steep hill isn't something you get used to. Though Ram thought he'd found a solution by shifting the task to friends, one day Chris observed in all seriousness, "We're running out of friends." And Bobby explained as though it were news, "The trouble is they get tired too."

There came a Saturday when they didn't go down to the hill at all—and a day soon after when Bobby boomed into the house shouting, "Chris! I've got it!" and declared from now on he'd take his motorcycle and *ride* the kites up the hill.

Chris was skeptical. "That hill's pretty steep, Bobby."

But steepness wasn't the problem. When Bobby tried to ride with the kite on his shoulders he: a) couldn't *see*, with the plastic falling over his eyes; and b) couldn't carry the hang glider without someone running behind holding the trailing plastic like a bridal veil. His friend Curt Kiefer, a good-natured and uncomplicated lad, stoutly tried to oblige but lasted only part way up the hill, falling to his knees gasping for air and dragging the kite, the motorcycle, and Bobby to the ground in quick succession.

As Bobby righted himself, he shouted back at Kiefer, "Why didn't you let go?" and Ram, who'd just gotten there, said acidly, "What do you think he is—some native runner from Kenya?" and Chris said, "You'll have to think of something else, Bobby."

Just as it seemed hang gliding would succumb to something as pedestrian as tired muscles, Bobby happened to be prowling around our yard and came upon the contraption he'd welded out of second-hand pipe for the chariot races in high school—an unwieldy vehicle that the boys claimed had enjoyed long-term residence under a backyard bush.

Bobby's chariot was all big wheels and thin rusty pipe, dotted with a few new welds applied in his rented garage. It was skeletal and crude, but the way Ram and Chris hovered as Bobby lifted it out of the truck one Saturday down in San Clemente, the moment was like the unveiling of a Bugati. I gathered it wasn't just a chariot Bobby was offloading—it was their whole flying future.

We were all there. Bobby attached the chariot to the back of his motorcycle, bungeed a kite onto the chariot, climbed on the cycle, and set off up the hill.

He appeared to be dragging an insect — a very large insect with a huge diaphanous wing that glistened in the sunlight. Suddenly we were all laughing. The motorcycle growled and the insect darted one way and then another and seemed to be flying, and at last there it was — on top!

From the bottom, Chris and Ram cheered and waved, and then Ram took off running for the top while beside us Chris danced around exclaiming, "It worked! It worked!"

"Amazing!" I said, and Rob said, "I didn't know it was going to look so funny," and Chris said, "Bobby likes being funny." And then he was sprinting up the hill after Ram.

For the rest of the day, the boys took flight after flight, excitement over Bobby's chariot running equal to their enthusiasm for being airborne. As for Bobby, he was seldom off his motorcycle. Between taxi runs up the hill, he rode down again pell-mell, leaving a boiling contrail of dust. As the day wore on, the spectators multiplied until crowds surrounded our boys after every flight.

Finally Bobby sought us out. "Hey, Dad . . . we're in business again. We're gonna go on flying!"

"With that chariot," Rob remarked, "uphill is almost as entertaining as downhill."

Bobby grinned. "Did you see all the people taking pictures?" and Ram came up and said, "He's gonna get a big head."

For no reason Bobby turned sober. "I thought maybe it *wouldn't* work — I don't know why." His expression became distant. "I thought maybe the center of gravity would be off, or the cycle wouldn't have enough power or something. Things always go wrong."

It was an odd change of mood, but I understood: Bobby's luck wasn't always good.

Ramsey Price turned him around. "Things might go wrong yet," he said cheerfully. "You could always break an axle."

By the end of spring 1972, Rob and I expected hang gliding for the Wills family had reached its zenith. What more could the boys do? They flew competently short distances. They were hillside heroes — certainly they'd conquered San Clemente. The newspapers had sent photographers, written stories. Fame (but no fortune) had come to them. It was all they could expect.

When we discussed Bobby's future, it was always with disappointment that at twenty-two he was a sometime pilot, would never be a student, and was destined to work at only the most mediocre jobs. Even Bobby had looked reality in the eye, I realized when I found some rolled, spindled, and mutilated papers discarded on the back porch. To my surprise, the sheets contained a sketchy contract and a line drawing of his double-decker bicycle.

Rob and I asked Bobby about the "contract" the next time he dropped by, but it was clearly a painful topic. He was sullen and closemouthed and revealed only after considerable prodding that he'd paid a promoter three hundred dollars to market his bike.

"Three hundred dollars!" Rob exploded. "And all up front, I assume. What has he done so far?"

Bobby shifted from one foot to the other. "It takes time, Dad. Nothing happens right away. But he really likes my bike, I can tell. I'm supposed to pay him a total of five hundred. Maybe he won't do anything until I give him the rest."

Rob was trying not to yell. "You've been taken, Bobby. It's a con game, I can tell by the contract. Don't give him more money. You'll just lose it. If the man hasn't done anything yet, he never will."

Bobby's eyes dropped. "I *can't* give him any more . . . I don't have it."

He made me feel terrible — made me want to loan him the money, foolish or not. Mentally I toted up my small private bank account; if something came of the project, I'd be ready.

In a kinder tone Rob said, "It may be a cheap lesson, at that, Bobby . . . for three hundred dollars."

As Rob guessed, Bobby's double-decker bicycle was never marketed. Rob never brought the subject up again and neither did Bobby. The contract drifted from spot to spot in our house and then disappeared.

12

MARALYS: Rob has always hated motorcycles. From the first day Bobby showed up with one, his father had a look of distaste, as though a bad odor had drifted up the driveway. "They're noisy, dangerous, and the recreational pastime of morons," he told me from time to time, and he warned Bobby, "You're flirting with death riding that damn machine!"

Bobby rode them anyway. One day I noticed that his stride was halting and stiff, and he confided offhandedly that he'd hit an open trench the day before while riding down a dirt road.

"A *trench*, Bobby? You're telling me casually you hit a trench, as though it's nothing, just an everyday event?"

He shrugged. "Mom, you can see I'm okay. I just didn't happen to notice it, that's all." He was already pulling away from what he guessed would be a tirade.

"Wait a minute. I wouldn't be pressing if you weren't walking funny. What *really* happened?"

He stopped and gave me a searching look. How much did he want to tell? Then his sense of humor got the better of him, and, laughing, he admitted that he'd hit the thing rather fast and he and the motorcycle went airborne, except that Bobby traveled a somewhat different route than his machine and came down separately.

"When you say fast, how fast do you mean?"

He hesitated. "About sixty."

"And you couldn't see the hole, I suppose."

"It was night."

I shook my head. "In the dark you're going sixty down a dirt road, driving completely blind. . . . Damn it, Bobby, you could have been killed!"

"I told you, all I got were a few bruised ribs."

"Luck," I said. "You had a charmed night."

He gave me a disgusted look and walked off quickly, but he could have stayed. I was finished. The difference between us wasn't brains; it was outlook. Philosophy. For him, traveling fast was so thrilling it outranked danger, and I supposed he'd have to grow old before it ever occurred to him he wasn't immortal.

Strangely, it was Ram who came close to dying at the handlebars of a motorcycle. Stranger still, by the time it happened, Rob had expressed grudging admiration for Bobby's "moronic pastime."

About the time that Chris began sweeping the family into hang gliding, Bobby was quietly entering motorcycle contests. Without fanfare, because it was Bobby's style to triumph offhandedly, he started bringing home trophies, which he placed on the dining room table with a casualness that bordered on indifference.

Thus we discovered accidentally in the spring of '72 that Bobby was about to enter the Elsinore Grand Prix, a one-of-a-kind race of two thousand participants over both city streets and the roughest possible terrain. I happened to overhear Ram quizzing Bobby—goading him would be more accurate. "You're going to race *both days*, Bobby? You'll never finish, one of your motorcycles will break down—or your lungs won't hold up in all that dust." I could feel Ram smiling. "A hundred miles each day? No way!"

"Well, I'm going to," Bobby said. "I signed up for it, so that's what I'm going to do."

After that, Rob suddenly wanted to see Bobby race.

About midday on a Saturday, Rob and I showed up in the backwater town of Elsinore and found a bridge that spanned a portion of the course. From there we watched Bobby come around four or five times on the ten-mile lap. To our surprise, it hardly seemed a "race" at all. The motorcycles down below labored up the rocky arroyo at laughable non-speeds — bucking, coughing, skidding, slewing sideways. Men fell off and knocked down others like tenpins.

But not Bobby.

He stood upright on his pedals, his arms bulging with effort as he muscled his motorcycle up the streambed. He dodged boulders, wrenched his front tire out of ruts, gunned his engine to keep it alive. And slowly, slowly, he passed other riders — always with no room to get by, so he had to detour into even worse terrain, or partially climb the bank. We stared down, fascinated. Perhaps it was a race after all.

Though we shouted down at him, Bobby's only response was a slight nod. He couldn't waste the effort looking up. Lap after lap, his intense frown never varied. I said, "I never dreamed this would be so . . . physical," and Rob said, "Nor I. It's nothing like I imagined."

We went back the second day. As we watched from the bridge, Rob's attitude changed. You could see the blossoming of respect, though I wondered if Bobby would ever know. "I'll tell anyone who asks," Rob said after we got home, "I went to scoff and came away to pray."

Late Sunday night Bobby stopped by, dull-eyed and spent. He staggered to the family room couch. "I almost quit today," he said, trying to catch his breath. "I didn't get much sleep last night. My asthma flared up, and I kept telling myself, I did this yesterday, nobody expects me to race two days in a row. But after a while I felt better, so I finished."

Weeks later Bobby strolled into the house with two mammoth trophies, nonchalant as always. That's when I knew it must pay to ride half-unconscious. On Saturday, out of a thousand riders, Bobby came in third. But Sunday, the day he literally willed himself to finish, he placed second.

A month later Bobby and Ram quit their jobs and persuaded Curt Kiefer to join them on a motorcycle trek deep into Mexico and down to the tip of Baja California, an adventure that would end in disaster for Ram.

Gentler in his objections than he might have been earlier, Rob nevertheless grumbled that the three boys were taking foolish, unnecessary chances in a land of dirt roads, sparse civilization, and occasional bandits. "What happens, Bobby, if someone gets hurt?"

Bobby said, "We've thought of that," and explained that because of the dust they'd travel separately and leave at intervals, with the first man waiting on a hill until he saw rising dust, then the second waiting for the third. Since Ram's was the motorcycle voted "most reliable," he would go last. Bobby leaned forward earnestly. "We spent time working this out. We figure the longest anyone would have to wait for help is one hour. If somebody doesn't show up, we go back."

Rob said, "It's too far. You'll never make it," and Bobby grinned and said, "You wanna bet?" They shook on fifty dollars.

They'd been gone less than a week when I learned that Ram was home again—in the hospital. It seems on the second day out, Ram was cresting a hill when an old Ford started up from the other side, and offering no warning dust, it was suddenly *right there*, and car and bike collided head-on, crushing Ram's leg between them. A Mexican family piled out to find Ram in terrible pain with a torn-up knee and a broken femur.

Nobody knew what to do, but miraculously a van appeared just then with two American ambulance drivers, and Ram said to the Mexican father, shooing him away with his hand, "Go on! Go!" lest the police come and throw the family in jail.

"It took nine hours to reach a town," Ram said later, "because the dirt road was crappy and the van kept bogging down in sand. The tires peeled off their rims and Bobby and Curt had to muscle them back on. Luckily, the medics had some codeine. One of them pulled on my leg, trying to keep it in traction, which helped the pain. So I'd fall asleep and the leg would bleed all over the van, and he'd tighten the tourniquet, and I'd wake up again and yank it off because my leg was hurting like hell."

Eventually the group crawled into the coastal town of Guerrero Negros. There a not-so-good doctor filled Ram full of painkillers and casted the leg without cleaning it. Later that day a local pilot took one look at Ram's bloody cast and glassy eyes and shook his head. "I no fly him — too sick." He thought Ram was dying.

Bobby and Curt, meanwhile, hovered at the clinic a day and a half until Ram waved them off impatiently. "The doctor'll get me out of here soon. You might as well go — there's nothing you can do." Bobby and Curt wouldn't hear of it, but Ram said, "Look, you're just cluttering up the place, and *somebody* has to make it to Baja."

Reluctantly they left.

The next day the doctor tried to give his patient a better image. He slapped a new cast over the old, took Ram off medication so he'd look alert, hauled him to the airport in the back of a pickup truck, and bribed a small airline into accepting him — *sitting up!*

On the final stretch, Ram's father, driven crazy by the delays, picked him up in Tijuana and began driving home ninety miles an hour. Ram said, "Why so fast, Dad? It's already been three days. Why kill both of us now?"

Back in Santa Ana, several doctors refused what looked like a certain amputation, but another, G. William Hawkins, one of the best in the area, agreed to do what he could. Ram was apparently not quite out when Dr. Hawkins began the surgery because he heard Hawkins say, "Oh shit! There's dirt in this knee!"

Price said, "Really?" and after that he remembered nothing.

Dr. Hawkins put a steel rod in Ram's femur. While he was healing, Ram wanted company, so Chris went to the hospital often. On one such visit, Ram said, "I wish you'd adjust this traction some — it hurts," and in a whisper, "I don't like the therapist — he's weird."

Chris bent over the apparatus to take a look. "It seems pretty straightforward to me. This part here controls this cable and . . . let's try this," he said, as though he knew what he was doing. "How does that feel?"

"Better," said Ram, and after that Chris adjusted Ram's traction every time he came, which was nearly every day. It wasn't long before Dr. Hawkins said, "So, Ram — I hear you're getting outside help with the traction."

Ram said he was and implied that Chris was a doctor.

Dr. Hawkins said, "I see," and coming closer, he examined the cables and pulleys with a practiced eye. "Well, it looks like your friend knows what he's doing!"

It was all Ram could do not to give himself away, laughing. The minute he could reach him, Ram was on the phone chortling to Chris.

By the time Bobby and Curt arrived home a week later, Ram was healing miraculously with no sign of infection. As for the two adventurers, they'd made it all the way to the tip of Baja and back, seven days of hard riding with no further mishaps until the last ten miles, when Bobby's cycle broke down and Kiefer had to tow him.

Rob and I listened to Bobby's story, incredulous. "And you never got sick . . . or sore?" I asked, and Bobby laughed and said, "We made it fine, Mom, no sweat. Do I get the fifty bucks, Dad?"

"You didn't make it," said Rob. "You had to be towed."

Bobby sat up straighter. "That's not true! I was sitting on my motorcycle the whole way and the wheels were moving even if the engine wasn't. So what do you call that?"

"I'd call it a Mexican stand-off," Rob said with a smile. But he paid Bobby the fifty dollars.

Bobby got a new job as a plumber's helper. He and Chris flew every weekend in the hours when they weren't at the hospital, reporting back that they'd learned to control the kites in ways they hadn't thought possible. "All we do is shift our weight to the left," said Chris, "and the kite turns left. We fly anywhere we want—and land where we want, too." They'd become so blase Rob and I assumed the hang gliding was on the wane and would soon fade to memory. Which shows how little we understood about aviation and its power to seduce those who love it.

A month or so later Ram persuaded Dr. Hawkins to let Chris into the operating room to watch the removal of the steel pin. "I'll be gowned and scrubbed like everyone else," Chris confided to me, his face alight with energy. "It should be interesting." He seemed barely able to contain his excitement. "I have to be there real early, Dr. Hawkins said about six."

I listened, pretending to be casual and not as pleased as I really was.

A few days later Chris saw surgery for the first time in all its retractors-and-hammer reality, and he reacted appropriately—he fainted. Quick to deny he'd lost consciousness, he admitted only that he "felt awful" and had to go sit down with his head between his knees. The whatever-it-was didn't last long. "I was back at the table in time for the important part," he said. "You should see the rod they took out of Ram's leg! It was two feet long and Dr. Hawkins *hammered* it out!"

"Do you still want to be a doctor?" I asked, trying to keep the anxiety out of my voice.

"It wasn't that bad, Mom."

Which I took to mean yes.

13

MARALYS: Keeping five boys under control in an urban setting — in any setting at all — isn't hard, it's impossible . . . and I'd like to see the woman who's alert enough to know where they all are, what they're doing and what they're thinking even a minimum part of the time. Since on weekdays Rob seldom appeared before the sun set and the tumult died down, I was grateful that our sonless neighbor Leo Pfankuch found their activities fascinating enough to spend time hunkered down with them nose-to-nose on the blacktop, and that his enthusiasm carried with it a salting of adult wisdom.

It was out of one such session that the next-generation hang glider sprang to life. "You're flying too high now for bamboo and plastic," he advised them in early summer. "We've got to find stronger materials." He offered to lend his aviation expertise and a touch of credit.

As usual, I was the last to know. I simply came out one morning to find Chris sitting at our dining room table pedaling my old Singer sewing machine like the tailor in *Fiddler on the Roof*.

Surrounded by bolts of material in red, white, and blue, Chris was so nonchalant he seemed above such motherly questions as, "What on earth are you doing with my sewing machine?" and "Whoever taught you to sew?" so I merely asked, "What are you making anyway?"

To which he answered calmly, "I'm making a sail for a *real* hang glider."

Since so far the only real hang gliders I'd seen were bamboo and plastic, I naturally didn't know how much more real a hang glider ought to be. I looked at him suspiciously. "And this sewing business. When did you learn that?"

"There isn't that much to it, Mom. I use your machine every once in a while."

"You do?" Well, that was news. Then I thought back. This was the boy who had — by himself and without fuss — replaced the engine in his first car, even put it all back together so it ran! By comparison, a sewing machine probably wouldn't seem the world's greatest challenge.

With the purchasing power of Leo Pfankuch, I learned later, Ram and Bobby were building an aluminum frame. Apparently the new kite would be similar to the old — the same triangular-shaped sail — except the supporting frame would now be aluminum tubing, held taut by steel cable.

For a week or so, familiar sounds issued from our black-top as Bobby, Ram and Chris argued about the design. In spite of having just left the hospital, Ram was over every day, propelling himself along on crutches as though they were his normal transportation.

Soon Betty-Jo took over the sewing. Chris must have bribed her. At any rate, cheerful as always, Betty-Jo guided miles of heavy Dacron under a zig-zagging needle, and when I stopped to commiserate, she said, "It's not so bad. I only have a few more panels to go." Gathering an armload of material, she carried it away and dumped it on top of other armloads. Our dining room looked like a yardage shop where somebody had gone on a rampage and unraveled every bolt in the place.

"Are you sure Chris measured right?" I asked. They seemed to have enough cloth for a three-masted schooner.

She shrugged. "He says it's right. I'm just sewing."

Out on the blacktop, things weren't going well. Bobby, Chris and Ram couldn't agree on the smallest details of construction. Bobby wanted to do everything "right" while the other two were in favor of less perfection and more speed. I could hear them caviling and bickering. Bobby was always the first to raise his voice, then Ram turned waspish, and Chris, initially conciliatory, eventually shouted at the other two to shut up and listen to *him*.

I went out there one day and found Bobby sitting on a motorcycle tire staring into space.

"What are you doing?" I asked.

"Thinking."

"Where are the others?"

His attention drifted off. Eventually he said, "Chris went to buy bolts, and I told Ram to leave."

"You told him to leave?"

"He's a jerk. He wants to throw it together all wrong. I told him to get out. I'm going to think it through before we go any further."

The next day I heard Chris saying, "I'm not going to sit around thinking, I'm going to build it. If it's not how you like it, Bobby, then start making it right."

The end result, I gathered, was a frame that fell somewhat short of Bobby's standards but exceeded those of Ram and Chris. Only much later would I learn how marginal the new kite really was. At the time Rob and I thought their new machine quite wonderful.

The bright "professional" hang glider actually flew. The pilot no longer had to hang by his armpits but rode like a king on a swing seat, using a triangular control bar for weight-shift control. With their new look, the boys attracted more attention than ever down at San Clemente.

Less than a week after the new glider was completed, Bobby walked into the house and announced calmly that the following weekend, on the Fourth of July, they were going to take their new hang glider to Saddleback Mountain.

Rob stopped paying bills and stared, for once taken entirely aback. When he found speech, he thundered, "Saddleback Mountain! That's over five thousand feet high!"

I could see Bobby retreating behind a wall of stoicism.

Rob said darkly, "That's a ridiculous idea, too idiotic to discuss. Leave me alone now, I'm busy."

"Will you at least listen, Dad?"

"Not to that nonsense."

From upstairs Chris had heard Rob's outburst and come rushing down to help. "We've *tested* the glider, Dad," he began. "We're already flying off a two-hundred-foot hill. What's the difference?"

"You don't see a difference, Chris?" Rob's tone was dangerously acerbic.

"No," said Chris. "If you fall, high or low doesn't matter, either way you could get . . ." he hesitated . . . the word *killed* hung in the air . . . "you could get hurt," he finished, "and besides, higher is better. You have more time to correct your mistakes. And set up your landings. Mistakes close to the ground — those are the dangerous ones."

"You don't have to explain about altitude giving you time," Rob said, "but what if the kite breaks?"

Bobby said earnestly, "We've been *flying* the kite all week, Dad, and I can tell by now — it's plenty strong. It held me, and I'm the heaviest."

"Why do you want to fly off Saddleback anyway?"

"Because it's different," said Bobby. "Because nobody's ever flown off a mountain before. Everyone we've heard of is still flying off sand dunes."

"I'm against it," Rob said. But he wasn't *as* against it as he'd been earlier.

I looked at the two boys hovering around Rob's chair, anxious, compelling, and I thought, Rob is smart, he'll stop them if it's not all right. For my part, I was fascinated, wondering what they'd do next.

Looking back, I realize my attitude was born of monumental naivete. Knowing almost nothing about aviation, I understood only what I'd seen, and so far what I'd seen appeared safe enough. Saddleback seemed merely an extension—higher and more exciting.

Chris was saying, ". . . and air is air. So what do you think, Dad?"

Rob laid down his pen and the room grew silent. Then a new objection occurred to him. "Forget the whole idea, boys. Saddleback Mountain is closed for the fire season. There's a chain across the road." With an air of finality, he turned back to his work.

A sly grin crossed Bobby's face. "Dad, I have bolt-cutters mounted under my truck and lots of master links—"

"Don't tell me." Rob groaned. "Don't say any more. I don't want to know." Lips tight, he began writing.

The two exchanged unhappy glances. I thought they'd give up. In a kind of last-ditch plea, Chris said to the back of Rob's head, "Bobby rides his motorcycle up there all the time and nobody bothers him. We've got it all figured out, Dad, don't worry." A pause, then a deep breath. "Are you and Mom coming?"

Rob took his time answering. "I suppose we'll watch," he said grudgingly, "from the bottom."

The boys turned to each other, grinned, and slipped away. They'd grown up, I thought. They knew when to quit pressing and hang tight on a gained advantage.

So they would fly off Saddleback . . . I was amazed, amused, and interested. If I'd known anything at all, I would have been afraid.

The Fourth of July arrived in a light haze. Standing outside with friends as the boys packed up their hang glider, I saw Rob look up at distant Saddleback Mountain and frown. The mountain was pale purple and far away, almost unattainable, it seemed.

"They must be nuts," he murmured.

Indeed, the mountain did look formidable, and for the first time I felt a kind of nervous thrill and wondered briefly if we were behaving reasonably. What were we *doing* cheerfully setting off to watch, even making a picnic out of it? This wasn't make-believe. It was real: our two sons were about to leap into five thousand feet of space.

I shivered.

Then the Underwoods arrived with their new motor home, and Rob and I handed them baskets of food, and with our four youngest children in our station wagon, we followed the motor home, which followed Mr. Pfankuch's sedan, which followed Betty-Jo's bug, which followed Bobby's truck toward a spot ridiculously far from the base of the mountain.

Along a paved, winding road, the caravan proceeded with funereal solemnity until Bobby led us off onto a dirt road that didn't go anywhere, we learned, except to an old, dry streambed. Wallowing in each other's dust, we parked in a long line, half on and half off the road.

Bobby jumped out of the truck and ran back to our wagon. Standing just outside Rob's window, he declared, "I think this is where I'll land."

I marveled at his matter-of fact approach to what was surely one of the big moments of his life. But when had he ever shared his inner excitement? He squinted toward the mountain, hand shading his eyes. "Yup, I think I can just make it here."

Rob didn't ask why Bobby would necessarily go first. Nobody had said he would, yet we all knew that's the way it would be. He did ask, "How can you be sure where you'll land?"

I was staring up at the mountain, some four miles away. Between that peak and us were ridges, outcroppings, canyons, every kind of terrain. I said, "Bobby, how can you possibly know?"

He smiled. "I've figured it out, Mom."

"And what if you *can't* make it?" Rob asked.

Bobby laughed. "Somebody'll have to come get me, I guess."

Suddenly Rob was angry. "We didn't come out here on the Fourth of July to go traipsing off in some canyon looking for you. And we're not going to get the Forest Service involved. I want you to know that ahead of time."

Bobby's grin faded. "I know what I'm doing, okay?" He sniffed and rubbed his nose with the back of his hand. "*You* won't have to do it anyway. Chris and Ram will see where I go down if it's anywhere but here."

Silence.

"You worry too much, Dad."

I waited for Rob to say, Somebody has to, but for once he let it pass. As Bobby began to walk away, Rob called after him, "Bobby . . . don't take any unnecessary chances!"

Bobby turned and waited, face solemn, hands hanging.

"Don't put yourself in jeopardy. Well . . . we'll be watching through binoculars."

For the merest second Bobby gazed past his father, then he touched his finger to his forehead—his salute and good-bye. "See ya back here."

Moments later the truck, with Chris driving and Betty-Jo and Ram in front and Bobby in back with the hang glider next to him rippling like a red-white-and-blue flag, roared past us along the dirt road. We turned to watch it pass. There go my kids, I thought excitedly, into the unknown.

With the rest of the family I settled down to wait, periodically glancing toward the mountain. The peak was high, with an infinite number of places for a speck like Bobby to launch. In my mind it became a contest, one boy against all that space: the boy would lose.

I shook my head to clear it. No, no. That wasn't true, he wouldn't fail—not Bobby. Not when he meant to succeed. It was something we'd learned about him, pit him against anything—a game, a parent, an opponent—and you could take bets the other side would lose.

In a sudden, euphoric rush I thought, You're an incredible kid, Bobby. You really are.

14

MARALYS: All up and down the road we stood with our necks craned in the direction of the mountain, those who had binoculars training them on an empty sky, the rest tilting back staring at nothing. Rob had of course pre-empted our family's powerful airplane-spotter glasses (which *he* brought home from Japan after *his* occupation).

But it was Leo Pfankuch, trained in all things aeronautical, who eventually said, "I believe I see him."

Rob swung his binoculars higher.

Itching to grab them away, I said, "Where? Where? Show me. Do you see him, Rob, do you see him?" and Rob said he saw nothing.

Leo Pfankuch held a finger near Rob's nose and pointed.

Rob said, "Oh . . . oh yes . . . ah-ha . . ."

When I finally got my turn, the sky was empty. Rob said, "Don't look at the mountain, Babe. He's not on the mountain. He's over on the far right horizon."

At last I found him—just a dot above a ridge, a wisp of something dark, and high—very high! My heart began to pound. That speck was . . . *Bobby!*

Immediately Rob took the glasses back.

And that was when a Forest Service truck pulled up and a brown-uniformed man got out and asked what we were looking at. One or two people might have escaped notice, but a crowd like ours was guaranteed up to no good.

Rob, with his fast mind accustomed to fielding curves in a courtroom, answered quickly, "Birds."

"Birds?" asked the man.

"We thought we saw an eagle." Rob was nonchalant.

The man in the brown uniform studied Rob thoughtfully, and a long, tense moment followed. Casting a suspicious look at Rob and then the mountain, the man got in his truck and drove away.

Rob muttered darkly, "They'll be looking for 'em now."

Slowly our eagle came closer. Passing the binoculars back and forth, we saw him floating peacefully, his speed imperceptible, his form motionless. Nothing could have seemed more serene. His progress toward us was the drifting of a feather without a trace of wind.

Gradually, he became larger, then visible to the naked eye. A murmur ran over the crowd, excitement buzzing heavenward as though something extraterrestrial were about to visit earth. Eyes strained upward, fingers pointed, faces waited tensely. The suspense grew.

As it came closer, Bobby's sail took on color. The red, white, and blue glinted in the sun, and below, an amorphous form gradually turned human.

My son! I was bursting with pride.

His flight seemed to last forever and seemed over in an instant. At the end he grew large quickly. With a staccato rush of flapping Dacron the hang glider swooped by overhead, pouring sound over us as though from a bucket, and swooshed to a stop only yards away.

As Bobby's bare feet touched ground, he ran a few steps and stopped. For an instant he stood alone under his kite, quiet and solemn.

Then we surrounded him. We banged his shoulders and pumped his hand. Rob kept saying, "Amazing! Incredible!" Father and son exchanged glances and an understanding passed between them, a long-overdue acceptance without words.

The moment passed and the questions started. What was it like? Was he afraid? How did it feel? Would he do it again?

I can't remember how Bobby answered, for I was immersed in feelings, not facts. Enough that Bobby had done this incredible thing, that Rob and I had been there to see him float down from his mountain and land at our feet. I tucked the memory away like a flower pressed in some fold of my mind, remembering those details I considered important: Bobby had dared fly from a peak nobody had tried before, a mountain twenty-eight times higher than any used by a hang glider previously, and he'd made the flight without knowing positively it would work, having only himself to trust. I couldn't read his face — except for a pleasant expression he was calm as usual — but he must have *known* he'd done something wholly, wonderfully different.

I couldn't stop smiling.

Later I would know we were right to think the occasion momentous: it was Bobby's first step in his quest to do with his life what had never been done before.

CHRIS: Ram and Betty-Jo and I found Bobby surrounded by people bombarding him with questions and laughing, so I knew he'd had a good flight. But he wasn't excited at all. He was cool and calm.

Ram asked, "So which way did you go?" and Bobby pointed and said, "Down the ridge. I was following a hawk."

"You liked that way best?"

Bobby just looked at him and smiled. "What other way have I tried?"

I said, "What was *really different* — from what we've done before?"

Bobby waited so long to answer I wondered if he'd heard. But then I saw his mind was way off, re-living the flight, and he said, "Well, it didn't seem as high as I expected because I could see everywhere. And I didn't get any feeling that just because the space was big I was extra small." He thought some more. Then he looked at me and said, "I had room, Chris, more space than we've ever had before, and I was high enough so I could pick where I wanted to go. I guess that's the best part. What I felt was free."

Right away everyone started talking about having a picnic, but I said, "If we eat now, it'll be too late for another flight."

Mom said, "Then we'll wait," and Bobby began loading up the kite.

Betty-Jo took me aside and said she didn't think she'd go — not if she had to drive down with Bobby. Price overheard and said, "So fly down with Chris."

She just looked at him.

As we were pulling out, Dad held up his hand. "You should know, Chris . . . the Forest Service has been nosing around. They'll be looking for you."

Bobby smiled. "We'll sneak him off. Once Chris is gone, what can they do?"

Ram offered, "They could shoot him out of the sky!"

"Be careful," Dad said.

As Bobby left the paved road and started up the Saddleback grade, I was thinking about all the illegal things we were doing — how Bobby used his bolt cutters to cut the chain across the road and then connected the two parts with his own padlock. Which explained why the Forest Service got into the act. They must have found his padlock on their chain.

Suddenly the back end of the truck whipped around and I looked across the cab at Bobby. The dirt road was bumpy and so narrow there wasn't room for two cars to pass. Yet here we were, with a cliff on one side and a bank on the other, safe speed about twenty-five, max, but Bobby was doing fifty — turning the wheel hard on the curves and letting centrifugal force spin the rear end around.

I said, "Slow down, Bobby." Swirls of dust billowed up behind us.

He eased off on the gas. But gradually he picked up speed again until we were fishtailing worse than before.

Ram kept falling into me until finally he got mad and shouted, "Look, Bobby, I wanna know if you're planning to kill us, because if you are, tell me now and I'll hike back!"

After that he didn't go much over forty.

When we stopped, I knew I'd survived the worst part—flying down had to be safer than driving up.

Up top the wind was blowing through a few scraggly pines. Not much there, just dry chaparral, in some places twenty feet thick, and scattered rocks. In the distance a hawk circled, and Bobby shaded his eyes, watching. "If we ever get good enough, we'll know what he's doing."

"If we live that long," said Price.

Bobby laughed. "Did I scare you?"

A careless shrug. "You were always at least two inches from the edge."

I walked over to the spot where Bobby had launched. A bluish haze prevented our seeing the ocean, but to the west were the Santa Monica Mountains, to the north, Mt. Baldy. The land dropped off sharply, and down below somewhere was Escape Country, a private park for motorcycles and fishing, and nearby, the road where I intended to land. It was cool up there—nearly a mile high, so the air had a sharp edge.

I set the kite up quickly, slid my fingers over the cables, and checked the nico stops, small clamps that pinched the cable where it folded back on itself. For the first time I thought about how we'd pounded the nicos with a hammer instead of using a nico-press tool. The idea didn't sit too well. The cable was the strength of the kite; without it, even the metal tubing would fail. I wished now we'd stopped to find a nico-press.

After I'd hung the swing seat from the top of the control bar, I asked Bobby if there was anything I needed to know.

"Nothing important," he said.

"But there *is* something . . ."

He hesitated. "It's not that much, Chris. But when I got down, my arms were killing me."

"Is that all?"

"When your arms ache and you're still a couple of thousand feet up, it can seem long." He stared out over the valley. "Another thing. I thought I'd stay higher than I did."

I nodded. Bobby had wasted a lot of altitude detouring over to the ridge.

As I lifted the kite, Price said he wished this was him. He was leaning against a tree with his crutches on the ground, and for the first time I felt sorry for him.

"It'll be you," I said, "one of these days."

For a minute we stood there, not talking. It was a long silence, each of us thinking different thoughts but nothing particular we needed to say out loud. Then I felt the wind coming up the mountain. "Well . . . here goes." I gripped the control bar, steadied the kite, ran a few steps — and stalled off the edge.

The kite sank. My feet scraped through chaparral.

A chill went through my hands. Gradually I pulled the bar in, balancing increased speed with avoiding brush, and slowly my speed increased and my descent slowed, like someone had grabbed the kite from above. I let out a long breath. The kite moved forward like normal. Flying.

Below my feet, dark green ridges flowed downward like a river. The sail rustled steadily, a reassuring voice whispering that the wind was there, supporting the kite.

All at once I was filled with the most intense feelings. The magnitude of the space around me came rushing in like a flood, and I had the sensation I was almost God-like, that I owned all that was below me and the air around me, too. I could do anything — see forever, fly forever, live forever, as though up here I was more than mortal, with incredible power which could never change. With all my awareness of immense space, I felt detached from the world. Time slowed. And speed seemed to decrease at this higher altitude, so at times it was difficult to tell if I was really moving; perhaps I was stuck in space. But no — the wind was still in my face, so I must be flying forward.

Testing my power, I pushed the control bar left, shifting my weight so the kite turned right. Yes, it worked. Even that high it worked the way it was supposed to, and I told myself, Air is air . . . yet up there the air was in such crazy abundance and nothing seemed the same. When I made a turn, it wasn't me turning, but the world turning around me. When I pulled back on the control bar to speed up, I didn't seem to move. The air just came at my face faster.

That was when I made a decision. The ridge Bobby followed had taken him out of the way, so he came in lower than he meant to. Detours were a luxury; you couldn't spend your altitude on luxuries. I would fly straight down the valley — the most direct route to the landing area.

Fixing my eye on the far horizon, I thought, If he came out too low with his long, curving flight, by going straight I'll get there with altitude to spare.

I would soon discover the flaw in my logic.

God, I was high! Tipping back, I studied the sail over my head, and doubts crept into my mind. Price and I, we'd been so careless — throwing the frame together in two days, more interested in speed than quality work, hammering the nicos in a hurry, maybe not tightening the nuts enough.

We'd been stupid, no other word for it, and here I was, still a couple thousand feet off the ground and hoping that what we did was good enough. If I crashed, they'd find the diaper pins securing the wingnuts.

And then I noticed something new — my arms were beginning to ache. I took one hand off the control bar and started to rub my forearm, but the nose went up fast and in one more second I'd be in a stall — which meant the kite would stop flying and the nose would fall through into a dive. I'd done it once, accidentally. I was horrified at the thought of doing it here.

I grabbed the control bar again. On other flights I hadn't noticed the force needed to maintain flying speed. Why hadn't any of us observed this before? Then I guessed the reason: we'd never before flown for longer than a minute.

To relieve the pain in my arms, I looped my right arm over the control bar and hooked my thumb under my belt, locking the bar in place. The pressure was now on my belt and thumb, letting my arms rest. I was thankful I happened to wear a belt; usually I didn't, but these Levis were new and not fully shrunk.

Bobby was right; with the pain in my arms I wished the kite would come down quicker.

And then it did.

Suddenly I was losing altitude fast, and the ridges, no longer below me, rose up on either side.

As I sank into the canyon, the sides got steeper and the ravine narrower. I looked ahead. At the far end it was *really* narrow, only twice as wide as my kite, but there was something worse: the narrow end was plugged by a gigantic pine tree!

I was still much higher than the tree and several minutes away, but there was no escaping the inevitable. There was no way to land in the ravine with its wooded, narrow bottom and near vertical walls. And my current glide path would probably not clear the tree. For what seemed like hours, but was probably only two or three minutes, I had no option but to hold on, hope, and stare at the ever-closer top of the tree. I no longer noticed my aching arms.

The kite picked up speed and panic rose in my guts. I looked around for an escape, a way to avoid crashing into the tree.

There was nothing. No room to maneuver, nowhere to land. The tree came closer.

My mind raced wildly . . . swerve to one side and try to pass . . . land on top . . . purposefully crash into the softest part of the cliffs on either side.

Desperation shot through me. I thought of one last thing, my only good option — I would stall over the top. I jerked my thumb out of the belt. The upper branches were coming at me, even with my face. I saw pine needles. Suddenly I pushed out on the control bar — hard but not too hard.

The nose flared and the kite lifted a few feet and for a split second I seemed to hang suspended above the tree, my shoes just touching the soft top branches.

Then the kite flew again and I flicked over the pine needles and came down on the other side.

Relief spread like warm, soothing water through my veins.

I was still flying!

At 150 feet above the ground, I was over a nice flat wash. In seconds I cleared some power lines and settled into a soft, gentle landing.

I'd made it! I was alive!

MARALYS: We found Chris about a mile down the wash, trudging along with the kite on his shoulder. Behind him was a deep, high-walled canyon blocked by an enormous tree.

Chris grinned sheepishly and eased the kite off his shoulders. "I came down a little short," he said. "I figured I'd be high enough to fly on past you, but . . . here I am."

Rob said, "You came down in one piece. Short doesn't matter as far as I'm concerned."

That went for me too, I said. I stood there looking at Chris, who was both embarrassed and excited, a pleasant mix like a sweet-and-sour sauce. And Bobby next to him peppering him with questions.

My two incredible sons. Lord, I was proud.

Chris was too stimulated to eat any picnic lunch. He couldn't stop talking about his sudden descent into the ravine and his miraculous escape from the tree. He wondered if there was some advantage, after all, to flying near a ridge.

In time Bobby and Ram managed to get in a few words. Laughing, they described their final trip down the mountain when a Forest Service truck coming up flagged them to a stop. The boys knew they were in deep trouble. But the Forest Service wasn't looking for them. Armed with the ultimate in misinformation, the man glanced at Bobby's white truck and said he'd heard there was a red truck on the mountain carrying a white glider, and he asked if Bobby had seen it.

Bobby and Ram nearly choked trying not to laugh but managed to answer coherently that they'd seen no such thing.

"The man told us to get the hell out of there," Bobby said. "After he'd gone Price and I broke up because we'd stalled him long enough so Chris had time to disappear."

Rob said, "You're luckier than you deserve."

"Well, we didn't get away completely," Bobby said, pulling a paper out of his pocket. "He gave us a ticket—for being on the road in the fire season." He looked at it fondly. "Ten dollars. Boy, it was worth it!"

It was Chris who brought me the clipping a few days later. Someone writing an aviation article had found an early statement by Leonardo da Vinci, a quote Chris must have found appropriate, because he dropped it on the dining room table as he left for his lifeguarding job. I found it during breakfast. "Once you have tasted flight," wrote Leonardo, "you will walk the earth with your eyes turned skyward."

He was right. From then on, Chris and Bobby indeed walked the earth with their eyes turned skyward.

And, because of them, so did the rest of us.

15

MARALYS: After Saddleback Bobby disappeared. He became an airborne zealot, a connoisseur bent on sampling every hill in Southern California. We rarely saw him anymore.

When he finally came striding into the house one night, it was only to get Rob's opinion on a legal document, which he handed over in the tentative manner of a child offering his last cookie. "I was going to sign this contract, Dad, and I thought . . . well, maybe you ought to see it first."

As Bobby waited by Rob's chair I sensed in him a deep current of contentment, though he'd never have Chris's effervescence. With Bobby you had to look for the subtle clues — the set of his shoulders or the way he walked.

In minutes Rob had read through the papers and was flicking them with his fingers. "If you sign this, Bobby, you're crazy. Sometimes I wonder about your judgment. This contract isn't worth considering."

Well, I thought, you ask Rob's opinion, you're going to get it, plain and unvarnished.

Bobby's expression changed. "I *knew* you'd find something wrong, I knew it. You don't *want* me to get ahead!" For a moment he seemed uncertain whether to stay or grab his contract and leave. He stood there with his long arms hanging awkwardly.

Rob asked, "Who is this Bill Bennett, anyway, and why

does he want you to sign your life away?" Perhaps sensing he'd come on too strong, he continued more reasonably, "Tell me about him, Bobby. Why have I never heard of him?"

Curious, I came in from the kitchen. Bill Bennett was a new name to me, too.

Bobby wasn't sure he wanted to tell us anything. He began without enthusiasm, "He's from Australia. He builds hang gliders and travels around to all the flying sites trying to sell them. He wants me to fly for him, demonstrating kites and selling them on commission." Seeing Rob's genuine interest, Bobby dropped into a chair and said with more spirit, "You'd like him, Dad, he's funny. He likes the way I fly. He saw me a few times out at Palmdale."

"Palmdale?"

"Yeah. That's where I've been going. It's a taller hill and right into the winds so you can soar."

"Palmdale," said Rob, clearly surprised Bobby was traveling so far. He picked up the contract again. "Have you studied this? It says, in effect, that all the flying you do over the next five years will be for Bill Bennett—that he owns you. You can't possibly agree to this, Bobby. I don't care how funny he is."

"But the commissions are *big*—three hundred dollars. I could make a living selling kites. He gave me one as a demo. It's really well-made." He sat there rubbing his bare toes against the carpet. "He said I can't work for him without this contract."

Rob sighed. "Okay, sign it, but know what you're doing. In five years you may have entirely different ideas. That's a long time, and it's not likely you'll be thinking the same then as you are now." He reached for his TV control. "You do have alternatives, you know. I say work for the man—fly for him and sell his kites—just don't sign anything. If you're good, he'll give you commissions, with or without a contract."

Bobby took his papers and left. Later we found the unsigned contract where such things were left to die — on the back porch.

Bill Bennett soon became a household word. Chris and Ram had found him, too, and in the weeks before the two started classes at UCLA, all three demonstrated kites for the funny Australian. Ram's injured leg, though stiff and somewhat weaker than the other, had finally healed well enough so he could fly.

In mid-September Chris and Ram found an apartment together in Westwood. On weekends they came home to their kites, and the tenor of the noisy conferences held in our family room was that soon they'd be selling hang gliders in great numbers and in no time they'd all be rich.

Rob and I listened on the periphery, noting after a few weeks that the day when they'd be rich seemed to have an ephemeral quality that vanished if you looked too closely. Certainly none of them had sold a hang glider this weekend or last, and the leads they developed always mysteriously evaporated.

Clearly something was wrong.

Not long after Bennett came into our lives, I had to rush Rob to Los Angeles's Good Samaritan hospital with a kidney stone. He was in agony, writhing in the car all the way. I still recall with a sense of exquisite relief the moment they gave Rob a hefty pain shot and he quietly slipped off to sleep.

The surgeon took out not one stone but three, reluctantly entering Rob's kidney to extract stones that lurked in various calyces waiting to become trouble.

When Rob was out of recovery and I called home to tell the children he was all right, Chris said, "Bobby set a world record today."

"What kind of record, Chris?" It was a Saturday, and I wasn't sure whether he meant motorcycles or hang gliding.

"He flew two hours and sixteen minutes at Palmdale

without coming down, and he beat the old record by more than an hour. Everyone's talking about it."

"Really?" I glanced over at Rob's bed, where he was snoring heavily, the drugged sleep of the still-anaesthetized. "I wish Dad was conscious so you could tell him the details."

"Tell him when he wakes up."

The drapes were drawn in Rob's room and the atmosphere was hushed. A little later he woke up, groaned, and opened his eyes groggily. "Hurts — Babe." Consciousness increased and so did the pain. He thrashed and gripped my hand. I rang for the nurse.

Twenty minutes later, as the painkiller took effect, he smiled at me and patted my arm. I stroked his forehead. "Rob," — I leaned close to his face — "Bobby set a world record today. He flew an hour longer than anyone's ever flown before."

The response was a drunken, "Ish that so, Babe?" and a smile, eyes regarding me languidly under half-closed lids. "That kid . . . wouldn't you know he'd do somethin' like that . . . just like him . . ." Still smiling, he drifted off to sleep.

The next day I had to say it all again. Rob wanted to know where it happened, whose record Bobby had beaten and by how much. In those days of daily pain and night sweats the news about Bobby helped sustain him. Eight days later he left the hospital, weak, walking poorly, leaning on my arm. He'd lost fifteen pounds, and he was pale and unable to stand straight, hobbling from wheelchair to car bent over like an aged arthritic.

Driving gingerly with my frail passenger, I maneuvered our station wagon into traffic. We'd gone only a few blocks when Rob said, "Take the Hollywood Freeway. We're heading north."

"Why?" I asked.

"I want to make a little detour — to Palmdale."

"Palmdale!" I turned to stare at him. "Rob, we have to get you home." He sat slumped on the small of his back, too weak to sit up. "You don't want to do that, not today."

"That's where he'll be flying, isn't it? It's a weekend. I want to see him. There," he pointed, "there's the on-ramp."

I was torn. It was an idiotic idea, but he was too weak to engage in argument and so insistent it seemed wise to humor him.

Our route led eventually to high desert hills where ferocious winds gusted up the slopes. Only three other vehicles were at the site, one of them Bobby's truck. Rob directed me to park the station wagon with the tailgate backed toward the hill, whereupon he crawled out of the front seat and onto its extended rear, stretching out on the hard metal in his hospital bathrobe. Lying on his back, he scanned the sky.

I tilted my head and squinted. Bobby was three hundred feet up, the only pilot aloft, and so high we couldn't clearly make him out, yet somehow we recognized his posture.

He flew an unfamiliar kite, red-and-yellow sail canopied against the sky, so he was more butterfly than hang glider. Slowly, languorously, Bobby soared back and forth, criss-crossing the sky on some unseen current of upward-moving air.

"Look at that, Babe." Rob rose to his elbow. "Just look at him."

The figure overhead moved into clear view, retreated a little, made a lazy turn and came back. The sun glinted off the sail, giving it a luminous quality. On the ground a tiny, kite-shaped shadow danced over the dirt.

Rob shook his head in disbelief. "Amazing."

For half an hour he lay on the tailgate, entranced. Then he admitted he was too tired to stay any longer. "We can go now."

I'm not sure Bobby ever knew we were there.

It was October when Bobby stopped by to tell us about the fledgling Southern California Hang Gliding Association and to suggest that Rob and I come to a meeting.

Rob said he'd never heard of the group and saw no reason why he should attend.

"Because they're putting me on the program this time. And Chris will be there, too."

"Oh?" Rob had suddenly become interested.

"On the program for what?" I asked, and Bobby turned to me with a "Where did you come from?" expression. Sometimes I was like a spectator in my own house. Whenever the boys rushed in with news, it was always Rob they addressed, Rob whose approval they sought, no doubt because he was so intense. Somehow there seemed to be *more* of him than me—more approval, more disapproval. When I entered the conversation, it was like the wallpaper speaking: they often seemed vaguely surprised I was even there.

Bobby said mysteriously, "It's something I did last week . . . you'll see."

That night, caught in heavy traffic on the freeway to Los Angeles, Rob grew surly. "I never should have agreed to this! I've got half a mind to turn around at the next exit." Yet for some reason he kept going.

The Southern California Gas Company's conference room was large and austere, its folding wooden chairs unpadded. When we arrived, a considerable crowd was milling in confusion near the speaker's platform, and Rob looked around irritably.

Searching for the boys and Betty-Jo, I could see this was a mixed bag of people whose common interest would be hard to discern. Besides the fact that few were geriatric, the sixty or seventy people came in all modes of dress, all ages, both sexes. I don't know what I expected. What did hang gliding types look like anyway?

Bobby rushed up. "I hope you didn't hurry, Dad. These

meetings never start on time."

"I did hurry," Rob growled, and I was thinking, Oh for heaven's sake, Rob, let up!

"Well . . . you're usually late. I figured you'd get here just about right."

"I'm sorry I wasn't later."

Bobby looked uncomfortable. "The problem is everyone has something he wants to talk about, so they spend the first hour arguing about who's going to speak. After a while they get going and show movies." He looked around anxiously. "I'll introduce you to Bill Bennett, okay?"

Rob shrugged.

Bobby led off into the crowd until he found a short man whose back was to us. The man was gesturing with both hands as he talked to a knot of four eager male listeners. Bobby tapped him on the shoulder. He turned around and was nothing like I'd imagined. Fiftyish, a little paunchy. Square face, very dark hair, bright, bird-like eyes. "Bobby!" he exclaimed with a grin, only it sounded more like "Bowby."

"These are my folks." Bobby introduced us, and I could see Rob sizing him up . . . so this was the famous Bill Bennett.

"Your son's quite a pilot," the man offered.

Rob said, "That doesn't surprise me." The tense lines in his face relaxed a little. "You two met at Palmdale?"

Bennett shook his head. "Not the first time. I wandered down to your little hill in San Clemente and saw him there. He was flying a dreadful machine with exceptional ability."

"Their kite was that bad?"

"Not bad, mate . . . terrible. Had a rear end like a Mack truck. It was so tail-heavy it's a wonder it didn't dig furrows in the ground. They coulda used it for a plow. I saw him flying this monster machine, and I said, 'Mate, you want to fly something good?' and Bobby said he did, so I got one of the kites off my van. Well, he straightaway took the damn thing and almost made it talk." Bennett grinned. "The rest is history. He's been flying my gliders ever since. And a damn good job of it, too."

Bobby seemed to expand and glow under all that praise. I glanced at Rob, now smiling. Bill Bennett had sprinkled fairy dust on him, too.

Bennett went on, "I like Bobby's style. He's bold. But he's not reckless. You can't be, in this sport. Too many blokes 'av paid dearly for their recklessness — me included. I've been around to see it."

"You've been in hang gliding a long time, I take it," Rob said.

"You might say so. Been involved one way or another since the early sixties. I was flying kites when most of these kids were in diapers." Seeing my look of surprise, he added, "Free flight isn't that old, you understand, a couple years maybe. What we did in the early days was tow above a boat, and they were all flat kites then — an invention of the devil. This kind of hang gliding, the Rogallo sails, is newer, and it's only just gotten respectable." Bennett grinned infectiously. "Meetings makes it respectable, you see. You put it inside a building, give it a president, and suddenly people accept it."

I nodded, fascinated.

Waving an arm at the crowd, he went on, "Half these blokes have never flown. They just come here with their theories — their mathematical formulas and equations and a bunch of fancy aeronautical talk that doesn't apply to hang gliding — and then they sit on their duffs until the next meeting. I like your boys. They're the kind of fellows who are gonna make people sit up and take notice. They're all action, your two — *and* they know how to fly."

Bennett had said all the right things. The contract was forgotten and Rob and I were his.

Chris called us to the speaker's platform for more introductions. Gesturing around Betty-Jo, he said, "Dad, Mom, this is Lloyd Licher, the president. My mom and dad."

I couldn't have been more surprised. The slight, diffident man shaking hands with Rob—he seemed almost shy—appeared neither presidential nor athletic, and in no way fit my idea of a leader of gung-ho pilots. With the mien of a scholar, Mr. Licher smiled apologetically. "We're getting a late start, I'm afraid. The committee is still working on the agenda. One of these days we'll get organized."

A few minutes later, with Bobby seated on the platform behind him, Lloyd Licher called the meeting to order.

Bennett was right about the theoretical groupies. The first speaker was a youth in glasses who must have been from Cal Tech because he drew formulas and equations on a blackboard, mumbling abstractly and mostly inaudibly until everyone began stirring. It was all Licher could do to make him stop.

Hurrying things along, the president announced a movie, another of Volmer Jensen's flying adventures, he said dryly, which brought titters from the crowd. Ramsey Price, sitting beside Rob, leaned toward us and whispered, "You'll see why they laughed. His movies are classics."

The lights went out and an 8mm image of fair quality flickered on a movie screen. Uninitiated in all this, I expected to see someone flying, but no . . . the scene opened with a group of determined men pushing an enormous glider—a wide, rigid wing with inner structure exposed, like a skeleton—up a hill on a kind of mini-trailer. They pushed and they pushed and they pushed.

After a while, probably out of sheer ennui, the cameraman shifted to another subject—a dog—who stared into the camera with indifferent canine lassitude. Then the camera drifted here and there to listless spectators before returning to its main attraction, which, surprisingly, was still the same sweaty men pushing the same contraption up the same apparently endless hill.

Scattered, barely audible laughter erupted in the

audience. Nobody quite laughed out loud, but one sensed a sort of suppressed merriment . . . which seemed ever less suppressed as the minutes passed and the camera persisted in recording what had rapidly become a world record in boring footage.

Eventually—I was spellbound at how long—the hardy group reached the top of the hill, and now, at last, the big moment seemed to have arrived. We were going to see The Flight.

With surprising alacrity considering his prior efforts, a thin, college-professorish man with glasses and long legs broke from the pack and pulled the contraption over his body. After a number of giraffe-like running steps he bounced into his plane's little seat, *crossed his ankles*, and for a full five seconds skimmed downhill inches above the ground.

Like everyone, I assumed when he landed the movie was over, but, no, the faithful were back to record for posterity another round of tireless pushing. And there was the dog!

The polite attention of the crowd was now gone. People talked openly, and in the row ahead of me a man threw back his head and noisily yawned. When the lights finally came on, we found we'd been watching man's oldest dream for a full thirty-five minutes—except most of it was the part nobody cared about.

"You see?" Ram crowed, "isn't that *great*?"

And then Lloyd Licher was saying, "To many of you, Bobby Wills needs no introduction."

I glanced over at Rob and saw a look of surprise.

"As some of you already know," Licher went on, "Bobby has just set a second world record in hang gliding." He paused for dramatic effect, and Rob, with question marks all over his face, whispered, "What's he talking about?"

I shook my head. It was news to me.

The president continued, "Last Sunday, at Torrey Pines,

Bobby soared continuously for three hours and three minutes!" Before he could go on, applause and cheers swept his words away.

On stage, Bobby acknowledged the tribute with a brief, solemn nod at the audience — a manner so restrained I guessed he thought a smile might be construed as bragging.

But Rob and I had no such problem and beamed openly.

Lloyd Licher was smiling, too. "I believe, Bobby, you are the first pilot to launch from Torrey Pines in a Rogallo — and also the first hang gliding pilot to land back on top. Which takes some skill, landing a craft there without tangling with the rotors. Stand up, Bobby."

Still solemn, almost oriental in his stoicism, Bobby stood. But he was pleased, I could tell. Even without a smile, his satisfaction lurked plainly beneath the surface. He exuded confidence, too, as though he belonged in the limelight and was there collecting what he knew he'd earned.

It was the first time since his piano-playing days I'd seen Bobby accepting public praise. It did him good. And it did Rob and me good, too. Leaning sideways, I whispered, "Aren't you glad we came?"

Rob turned to me and said carefully, one word at a time, "I'm not *glad* we came. It was absolutely essential."

In my mind, I was putting a checkmark by Bobby's name, *This child is making it.* After a terrible start, he was finally fitting somewhere.

I'd never have dreamed there was so much more still ahead.

16

CHRIS: When Bobby called my apartment out of the blue, I figured it must be something big. "Chris," he said, all excited, "Bill Bennett's building me a tandem seat. It'll be ready this weekend. If you can come out to Palmdale Saturday, we'll fly together — it'll be the world's first non-towing tandem flight. But we have to do it now, before someone else gets the idea."

Which is how we wound up at Palmdale together on Delta Hill, named by Bill Bennett after his kites.

When I got there, Ramsey Price was watching Bobby unload the big seat — basically two regular swing seats held together with aluminum angle irons.

Partway up the hill, Bobby hung the apparatus from the control bar and standing side by side, the two of us tightened the seat belt across our laps — a clumsy arrangement with our different heights and leg lengths. With no fanfare and only a few people looking on, we were ready to try our world-record flight.

The day was hot and the wind erratic, gusting and letting up. I wondered if we'd have a problem getting off.

Bobby turned to me. "Okay, Chris," he said, "when I say 'run' we go all out. We'll have to get up plenty of speed. We weigh a ton."

"One of us does."

He frowned. "We may drop at first."

"I know."

"Don't jump into the seat."

"Bobby," I said, "*we* taught *you* to fly."

"Well, just in case you forgot. It's going to be more like the old bamboo kites."

"Why don't we start?" I said.

So we did. Bobby ran and I ran, but not being the same size, we didn't run the same. I was faster and Bobby was longer, and it was like pairing a rabbit with a giraffe.

We ran and ran and ran and it took forever to get any lift, with the kite jerking ahead by spurts and all the extra weight and the hill being too small and the wind gusting and letting up just when we needed it. By the time we lifted off, the remaining slope was half gone. The kite hovered inches above the ground, barely flying.

Hanging ridiculously low like that, I decided to push out on the bar to gain altitude.

Nothing happened.

So I pushed harder and still the bar wouldn't move. Eventually the kite picked up speed without my help and we began flying.

But it didn't last. The hill was practically gone and we'd had no time in the air at all, so down near the bottom I decided to make the flight last longer and turn left.

There was plenty of room to the left, but we weren't turning so I pulled harder, giving the bar all my strength.

It made no sense, but the harder I pulled the more resistance I felt and the less seemed to happen. We plowed straight ahead, and then our feet were down and we were hiccoughing along the ground like a man with one short leg. We bumped and jerked to a stop. The few people down there bolted across the field to meet us.

As we were setting the kite down, Bobby said irritably, "This thing flies terrible with two people. I couldn't turn at all! My arms are exhausted! I tried with all my might to turn right and it wouldn't respond."

I realized what had happened. "It wouldn't turn for me either!"

"*You* were turning *left!*" he said, and stared at me, bugeyed. Then he started laughing. "I'll bet at the top you were pushing out!"

"Yeah," I said, "for all the good it did. You totaled me out!"

Then Price chimed in, "Don't you Willses get enough fighting on the ground?"

Bobby backed away from the kite. "Look, Chris, I don't think you and I should fly together. It'll never work. We don't fly alike. Even if we practiced, we couldn't do it. You don't know how to stop thinking."

Somebody snickered.

I said, "We can do it, Bobby. We just have to decide in advance who's pilot and he gives the orders."

We agreed to try again from the top of the hill and I said he could be the designated pilot. It worked better the second time, but instead of fighting physically we argued about the best place to go. I had my agenda and he had his, and I had to give my input. Which made him adamant about doing it his way. I finally gave in, but not without letting him know he was wrong.

The flight was about two minutes and would have been enjoyable if we'd gone my way. The kite flew well and actually controlled well. But it wasn't a perfect flight.

After we landed Bobby said, "From now on I'm going to fly with people who can't fly, and that's what you should do, too." He said it like he was developing some kind of First Principle of hang gliding.

Keeping a straight face I said, "It'll be easy getting non-flyers. But you'll have trouble digging up someone who doesn't think."

Everyone laughed, and Price said, "I'm sure you can find a moron somewhere."

Eventually hang gliding pilots all learned what we'd learned — that two equally strong pilots can't fly together. But Bobby and I discovered it first, and we needed the lesson only twice.

Every weekend Bobby and Ram and I demonstrated kites for Bill Bennett, and every week something went wrong and we didn't get any commissions. At first we were waiting around to get paid. Then when no money came, we began calling Bennett to see what had happened. I told Bennett we'd seen new kites on the hill and were wondering about our commissions, and he said cheerfully, "Let me tell you something, Chris — every salesman knows it, it's the first principle of sales. You don't make a deal 'til you close it."

When I reported back to the others, Ram said, "What he meant was, *we're* in the air flying, and *he's* on the ground closing deals."

Bobby didn't seem worried. "One of us will just have to stay on the ground the whole time, that's all."

But that didn't work either. We'd keep someone down there talking to buyers, but the new pilots would end up buying at Bennett's shop and we couldn't prove who'd talked them into it.

The money was getting to be a challenge. I said, "We'll have to outsmart him, that's all. We'll do our flying somewhere else, clear away from Delta Hill, and we'll put *our* names and telephone numbers on *his* brochures, and then we can prove who sold the kite."

By then Bobby wasn't feeling good about it anymore. "Don't say anything about this to Dad, Chris. He'll just call me a sucker like he always does."

17

MARALYS: One night Chris followed us back to the bathroom and stood in the doorway as Rob and I brushed our teeth. "I doubt that we'll ever sell many Bennett kites," he said. "So far Bobby's not doing too well. I guess he hasn't told you, huh?"

Rob held his toothbrush poised. "I've asked, but he ducks the question. I gathered he wasn't getting rich."

"Rich?" Chris laughed. "Not on *one commission*." He paused, then said offhandedly, "Ram and I have an idea. We think we should start our own business."

Rob whirled around, and we both stared at Chris. "Your own business?" I said, and Rob said, *"Making hang gliders?"*

A loud thump, two or three, and we abruptly stopped talking. Someone was banging on the wall. We looked at each other and looked at the wall.

"Kenny," Rob said. "He's trying to sleep." In a lower voice, "He gets up early to swim, so let's give him a break. It's late, Chris. We can discuss this some other time."

Chris shrugged and walked away, and I thought that was the end of it.

Late in the year Eric came home from Mt. Shasta. Life there had been more difficult than he imagined. "All I ever did was stock fish. I had to hike miles, carrying bags of slippery fish. But I never got to catch any. When winter came, the fish hatchery laid me off. Besides, our cabin didn't have any heat. Shelley was always cold."

Nobody in the family said I told you so. Eric rented an apartment with Shelley, they both found unremarkable jobs, and before Christmas Rob bought them a barbecue.

"Just like they're married," I said, feeling sheepish. "I can't believe we're condoning this."

Rob shrugged. "They live like they're married. They act like they're married. They fight like they're married. What difference does it make if they're not really married?"

"How do we explain it to our friends?"

"Who has to explain anything? Who's going to ask?"

The subject turned out to be not so difficult. In time I realized half our friends had children doing the same thing.

It was Christmas vacation, and I was in the kitchen cooking breakfast, my mind on such mundane matters as whether the mailman's gift would fit in the mailbox, when Chris strolled in and asked, "Mom, what's *your* opinion about starting our own hang gliding business?"

Just like that—as casual as dust. As though the subject had been top-ten on our list ever since that night in the bathroom. "I have no opinion," I said. "Were you thinking before or after breakfast?"

"Haven't you and Dad talked?"

"Well, no. Not about that."

"Oh," said Chris. "I thought you'd be making up your minds."

I saw that he was serious and said as gently as I could, "I doubt if Dad's interested, Chris. Nobody in this family has time to run a business, not you or me or Dad. Only Bobby has time, but he—"

"Bobby!" he cried. "Don't you see what I'm getting at? He's the one who could do it."

I looked at him regretfully. "Think about it a little more. Can you imagine Bobby running anything? He isn't organized. He's not disciplined. He's never on time. He's a dreamer. And he doesn't care about making money. In this family only you could possibly run a business, but you're taken."

Chris lapsed into silence.

In the next week he mentioned the subject a few times to Rob, who listened with his eyes and his attention mainly on the seven o'clock news.

Then one night before New Year's Rob took the whole family and Betty-Jo out for cheeseburgers, and just as we were served, Chris asked hypothetically, "If we had our own hang gliding business, Dad, what would we call it?"

Rob paused with his cheeseburger midway to his mouth. Chris had finally found the magic button. Rob finds names for everything he does: parties, games, essays — even trips out of town, explaining, "First you have to have a concept." He smiled. "Well, let's see, Chris . . ."

Until then, a hang gliding business hadn't had a chance.

Now, over cheeseburgers and milkshakes, we all pitched names to each other, and by the time we left the restaurant Rob was beaming, having hit on "Sport Kites" for the business we didn't yet have, and "Wills Wings" for the kites we'd yet to produce. And he'd said things like, "Maybe next summer."

It's hard to ignore a project for which you already have a name.

In February Bill Bennett asked Bobby to fly a Delta Wing kite in the first Canadian hang gliding championships. Then, inexplicably, Bennett's team went off without him and Bobby stopped by the house to ask for airfare to Toronto.

Rob's eyebrows went up. "You're flying for Bill Bennett, Bobby. Why should I foot the bill?"

Bobby stood in the kitchen, perplexed. "I don't know what happened, Dad . . . I called and everyone was gone.

And I don't have the money to fly."

Rob was incredulous. "Tell me why I should make up for their mistake! And yours! You should have kept better track of them." As usual, Rob's own words fanned the sparks of his anger. "No, sir, I'm not going to ship you up there at *my* expense. If Bennett wants you in that meet, Bennett can damn well get you there!"

Bobby didn't argue. He simply looked at Rob with his long face impassive. Then he turned and strode out of the room. I heard the back door slam and felt sagging discouragement. Whose fault was it anyway? And why did things always go wrong with Bobby?

Later we learned from Ram that Bennett himself was still in town and agreed to loan Bobby the price of an airplane ticket. But Bobby never called us himself. He wouldn't. He had nothing to say.

Bobby had been gone only two days when the front door opened late at night and there was Chris, looking both nervous and excited.

"Chris!" I jumped up. "Isn't this Monday night?"

It was, he said, and he'd tell me the whole story in a minute, only where was Dad?

Rob was as surprised by Chris's appearance as I and not altogether pleased. "What are you doing home, Chris — besides missing classes?"

"I have to talk to you," Chris began. "I've been giving this a lot of thought, so don't get mad until you hear it all, okay? I"— he stopped to weigh his words —"I guess I should just say it. I think we should start a hang gliding business. Right away. This month. We — "

"Is this what you came all the way home to tell me?" Rob's expression turned dangerous.

"Wait 'til you hear me out, Dad." Chris moved closer. "Price and I have discussed this in detail, so you'll know I'm not being impulsive. We figure if we're ever going to start a business, it has to be *now* — to get a head start on everyone else. At the moment there's only Bennett and one other company, but more are coming. We hear the talk. By summer we'll be tenth in line." He was literally panting. "Dad, we have to move fast."

"Slow down, Chris. Take it easy." Rob settled back in his chair and crossed his legs. "In the first place, we can't do this without you, and you're in school. I can't see Mom starting this business — or Bobby. In the second place, summer's only four months away, which can't be as critical as you think. And third, I'm not sure about such a project even then. I have grave doubts about what is essentially a fringe sport. Most people haven't even heard of it."

"I know," said Chris, "I *know*! That's why we'll have an advantage." He grinned. "We can make better kites than Bennett. Price and Bobby and I have a million ideas. Bennett used to listen to us, but he doesn't any more. He says he can't change his design every time we come up with an improvement. So we've *got* to make our own!"

Chris took a deep breath, all earnestness. I sensed he'd saved his best argument for last. "Dad, you know Bobby needs something to do — and so does Eric. What else have they got?"

Rob said, "Well, Chris. You've just presented the only important argument."

I looked from one to the other and felt Chris's energy, his boundless, irresistible zest. When Chris delivered his ideas with all that brightness in his face, his enthusiasm spilling over like popcorn exploding out of a pan, it was hard to remain calm. He made anything seem possible. Anything at all. I said, "It may be an idea, Rob."

"Except," said Rob, "he's skipped a minor detail." His eyes went to Chris. "You've told us everything except how we're going to do it."

"I've figured that out too." I could feel Chris digging in, proceeding carefully. "I'm going to take a quarter off from school."

It was like touching a live socket. I whirled on him, shocked. This wasn't what I'd imagined, not for one minute. I said, "You *can't* do that!"

Chris gave me a sharp look.

But I couldn't help it, I felt an awful premonition. If Chris dropped out of pre-med, he might never go back. You just didn't stop partway through college. The world was full of people who quit temporarily and never returned.

"It's only for *one quarter*, Mom." Chris's voice was steely. "Just one. I'll start the business and go back in the spring."

"What if you *don't* go back in the spring? You might get sidetracked and stop forever."

"Mom," he said, a little desperate, "don't get like this. I said I'd go back and I will."

"In the beginning that's what people always say."

Rob shook his head doubtfully.

The dread remained in the pit of my stomach. Even with a near-perfect record, which Chris didn't have, getting into medical school was tough. If he added complications, he might never make it at all.

I looked off into space and tried to understand my panic. Three of our children had finished high school and only one was headed anywhere, only Chris had a shot at our kind of life. All the disappointment of raising sons and seeing them grow up and fall short of what we'd accomplished seemed tolerable if one of them succeeded. But now even that one was wavering, and I couldn't let it happen.

Chris was saying, "I know what I'm talking about, Dad. I'm not taking any chances. You'll see."

Rob said, "You're wearing rose-colored glasses, Chris. You're seeing this in the best possible light, as though nothing could possibly go wrong. Like you always do." But he was wavering.

I listened, dismayed, as Chris slowly moved Rob his way, trading on that endless supply of optimism.

Gradually I began to see things differently. *Eric and Bobby* — Chris was right about them. Eric needed purpose and Bobby would find the frontiers he'd been seeking. Maybe, I thought, those two would gain more than Chris would lose.

I looked at him hard, our second son high on his own ideas, literally aglow with energy. He'd waltzed his plan into our lives and now he was dancing gracefully, trying to make us love it. Maybe he *would* make it to medical school . . . still. Listening to him, you started believing he could do anything he really cared about.

In the end Rob agreed to let Chris leave UCLA. "But just for one quarter, Chris."

"Just one, Dad. That's all I need."

For the next two days Chris was a whirlwind blowing through the house, spinning off accomplishment in all directions. You'd have thought his mission had global importance. Excitement was on his face and in his step. He moved fast, talked fast, worked without pausing. He infected all of us.

By the end of the first day he'd made extensive lists and ordered all the tubing, cable, Dacron, nuts, bolts, and tangs we'd need for a month's production. At meals he told us what he was doing, so full of laughter and enthusiasm he boiled over continually. All of us — even Tracy, Kirk, and Kenny — were caught up in his enthusiasm. The new business was all we talked about, and our conversations went on into the night.

Having compressed a week's work into two days, Chris kept saying, "I can't wait 'til Bobby comes home! I can't wait to tell him!"

Eric came over the second night and said, "Bobby's gonna be stoked. Boy! His own business!" We'd already made Eric the office manager, and he'd given notice at the motorcycle shop where he worked.

I did my usual chores with my pulse racing crazily, feeling breathless. Chris had that effect on me. Even Rob, whose money Chris was spending, had an air of high excitement. It was as if Chris had brought us all a new and glorious future, a Grand Plan. As a family we felt unified and purposeful. They were wonderful days.

Then Chris returned to UCLA to withdraw for the quarter, calling home to announce triumphantly he'd just made the penalty-free deadline. "Today was the last day," he said, laughing. "I'm clean now until spring." He'd only to pack his clothes and he'd be home to stay.

It was late afternoon when Chris phoned again — in a manner so changed I should have noticed immediately something was wrong. "Bobby called just now from the airport," he said in a flat voice. "He won the Canadian meet."

"He what?" I said, since it was obvious from Chris's tone I hadn't heard what I thought I did.

"Bobby won the championship." He made it sound like nothing.

"You mean the whole thing?" Unable to reconcile his astonishing words with his bad news manner, I added, "Are you serious, Chris?"

"I am serious. Bobby's the first Canadian champion. They gave him five hundred dollars and a hundred gallons of Kelowna wine."

"*Five hundred dollars!*" I began to laugh. "And wine, too? I can't believe it!" I carried on at some length, but I seemed to be talking to myself. "What's the matter with you, Chris? Don't you *care*?"

"I'm glad for him," he said, and now his voice literally sagged, "but Bobby's decided not to be part of our company. He's sticking with Bennett."

I couldn't adjust. Couldn't do an about-face and respond to this new set of facts. So I sat there blankly.

"Bobby was angry. He says he doesn't want our company or any part of it."

Bewildered, I tried to make sense of it. I said, "Bobby didn't understand, that's all. You didn't get through to him."

"Oh, he understood, all right. But he said Bennett's been good to him, so he's going to sell Delta Wing kites."

"But he'd be our competitor!"

"I know."

"He'd be working against us." It was all so irrational, so crazy. I sat there winding the telephone cord into a tight knot. "Couldn't you reason with him?"

"I tried. But he wouldn't listen. All he'd say was, *we* started the company, so it's ours." Chris sounded close to tears.

For the tenth time I said I couldn't believe it. I had the feeling I was part of a bad dream that would end when the alarm went off. None of it had any reality—neither the big win nor Bobby's disloyalty. This was *Alice in Wonderland*, where things appeared and disappeared without explanation. "Chris," I said, "Bobby's the *reason* we started the business. If he doesn't know that, he doesn't know anything."

"Yeah," he said. "Well, *you* tell him. He'll be home soon." With a discouraged goodbye he hung up.

Long after the other children were in bed, Bobby stalked into the house carrying the biggest trophy I'd ever seen. But he might as well have been carrying a sack of groceries. His face was expressionless, his shoulders sagged, even his blue ski jacket hung open dispiritedly.

I said, "Well, Bobby, you really did it!" trying to pretend I didn't know what I knew. This was supposed to be a moment of triumph, only he wasn't acting triumphant and my wariness no doubt showed. "What an incredible trophy!"

"It's big," he said, placing it on our family room table.

I looked it over thinking even Wimbledon didn't give such trophies. Almost four feet tall, it was tier after tier of symbolism. The bottom layer was an oversize marble base followed by a second marble slab on which rested a purple hang glider nestled among four stately doric columns. The columns rose upward to a silver chafing dish on top of which a winged goddess stood poised with upraised arms. The trophy was an extravaganza and worth celebrating if anyone felt like it.

I said, "So you're the hang gliding champion of Canada!" When he merely nodded, I decided you couldn't get into icy water one toe at a time. I said, "We've started a family hang gliding business, you know."

A dangerous light flickered in his eyes. "What's that got to do with me?"

So Chris hadn't been exaggerating. "Bobby," I began, "you're our kid . . ." and then I couldn't help smiling. "This is dumb. What do you mean, what does it have to do with you?"

"It's *your* company, not mine!"

"You've got that all wrong. Why would we start a hang gliding company for Dad and me? Don't be stupid."

His voice rose. "*You're* the one who's stupid! You did it behind my back, so it's yours."

Ah, a glimmer of light . . . Bobby's pride was involved. I said, "That's ridiculous. You just happened to be out of town, that's all, and the time was right. We couldn't ask you, so we went ahead. It's not personal. You're crazy if you think it is." I was trying to stay calm. "These last few days half our conversation has been about you — how excited you'd be, how we couldn't wait to tell you. Dammit, it's *your* company, Bobby."

"Well, I'm working for Bennett," he said, in one of those dig-your-heels-in statements that can only come from the excessively tired and therefore irrational. "You can do what you want. It's no concern of mine."

I would have saved myself agony if I'd simply stopped arguing. But I couldn't, knowing better than anyone Bobby's capacity for stubbornness. So I carried on, and in the middle of my ranting the phone rang. It was Rob calling from San Francisco.

Like a carbon copy of an earlier conversation, I put Rob through some of the same sequence Chris had given me, except I stopped before I got to the bad part. Let Bobby explain the rest for himself. If he dared.

With a listless expression, Bobby picked up the phone for Rob's congratulations. Then his face tightened. I ran to the extension in time to hear Bobby tell his father he wanted no part of our business.

A mistake.

Rob is not like the rest of us. His perceptions are sometimes greater, but his temper is also quicker, his patience nonexistent. "What do you mean you're sticking with Bennett?" he thundered. "What in hell is that supposed to mean?"

"Just what I said, Dad."

I had to hand it to Bobby. He had enough courage to tell Rob exactly what he'd told Chris and me earlier. He must have known what would happen and just didn't care.

The results were predictable. I thought Rob was going to fly home and kill him.

The rest took only seconds—Rob shouting, calling Bobby names, cursing. At the end he said, "Get out of my house! GET OUT AND DON'T EVER COME BACK!"

Two clicks followed, one after the other, then a third—mine.

As I walked back into the kitchen, I saw Bobby sunk low into the family room couch and discouragement washed over me in a slow, agonizing wave. *So this is Bobby's homecoming, I thought, this is what Bobby gets when he wins the championship for all of Canada. Curses. Rejection.*

Some great winning.

It no longer seemed important that Bobby's troubles were mostly his fault.

18

MARALYS: It was odd that Bobby didn't simply walk out of the house after that ugly phone call, but he didn't, he stood up and began pacing, and I, who am the keeper of domestic harmony and more stubborn than I care to admit, followed him around trying to stitch up all the torn family seams. We went from kitchen to family room to living room, arguing, shouting. I felt I had no choice: he might be mulish and irrational, but he was our son and I had to bring him back to the hearth.

From room to room I tried to make him understand what Chris had done, and he in turn apprised me of all the family shortcomings past and present. Over a period of hours we shouted, bellowed, talked, and whined. Had Bobby not been so tired — he'd hardly slept in four days I learned later — he might have given way a little sooner.

I asked why he wanted to stick with Bennett.

"He was good to me." Bobby's eyes drooped heavily. "He said I didn't have to pay my airfare, he intended to pay it all along."

I couldn't resist asking, "Did he say that on the way up or the way back?"

Bobby didn't answer.

By one in the morning I could no longer speak in a normal voice. What few words remained came out in croaking whispers. But Bobby had agreed, reluctantly, to be part of Sport Kites. Yet even as he left for his own apartment, he called back peevishly over his shoulder, "You shouldn't have done it without me."

Over the phone I told Rob that Bobby had changed his mind, and that was that. We never spoke of it again.

Rob found us a nice little shop in a complex of small industrial plants. It had a simple rectangular office in front and a large, barn-like room in back. There were no frills. A bathroom was our only nicety. But since Chris and I had talked of putting the business in our family garage, Rob's rented space seemed almost extravagant.

We bought a cheap blue-green carpet with tufts as sparse as thinning hair; if you looked close, you could see the scalp underneath; installed two used desks in front, one for Eric and one for me; decorated a corner with Bobby's flamboyant trophy perched atop his wine keg ("customs" had intercepted the wine at the border so all he got was the keg); and declared ourselves in business.

A few days later Eric and I sat at our adjoining desks feeling very important in spite of the fact that we had nothing to do. Eric had a title — "Office Manager" — and here I was, sitting at *our* desk in *our* company on a bright March afternoon in 1973. It had all happened so fast nothing seemed quite real. When, on our second day, we received *two letters*, which showed up magically, it appeared that Sports Kites had taken its first breath.

Since I had so few tasks, I mostly sat around being proud of my three sons. Chris's efficiency had continued unabated, Bobby for once was both tractable and helpful, and Eric had already shown some organizational ability overlaid with a strong sense of thrift.

I glanced at Eric's desk. He had begun to set up notebooks for keeping track of orders and supplies. "Did you order all that stuff Chris wanted?" I asked.

"Sure." He grinned. "I did that yesterday, Mom, when

you weren't here." (I wasn't supposed to come in every day, just one or two days a week as needed.)

In back I could hear a familiar refrain: Chris, Bobby, and Ram arguing. Ram was to help in his spare time until school was out and he could be there every day. At the moment they were setting up jigs, and now Ram's voice floated out to the front office. "If you're going to sit there and study that wire jig all afternoon, Bobby, we won't be in business for another month."

From Chris: "Come on, Bobby, *our* jigs are finished. Yours isn't even started."

"I'm thinking."

"For two days? You have to think *for two whole days*?"

Next to me Eric was saying on the phone, "If I buy a thousand of your An-22 bolts, how much can I save?" and I was thinking he had just enough wheeler-dealer in him for a good office manager — though it had its downside, such as the day before when he bought ten mops we didn't need just because they were cheap. Rob happened to see them and shouted, "Ten mops! Eric, have you lost your mind?" So Eric had to call and have them picked up.

The door opened and there was Rob — his step seemed unusually buoyant — carrying boxes of stationery, which he deposited on Eric's desk. "These are letters, Eric, and envelopes. We're going to do a promotional mailing. Go ahead and read it." He handed one to me.

The form letter, directed to advertising agencies, was an offer for one of our pilots to fly a hang glider over a populous area for a guaranteed twenty hours. Sewn into the wing of the hang glider would be a commercial slogan or product name, and the price would be nine hundred dollars.

Rob said, "It's a brainstorm — something like the Beetle Billboards [ads on Volkswagens], except better. Our kites attract so much attention we should have no trouble getting sponsors. Eric, I want you to send these letters to all the ad agencies in Orange and Los Angeles Counties."

I said, "Isn't nine hundred dollars too much, Rob?"

"Of course not. It's worth double that for the novelty alone."

Maybe, I thought.

Eric sat staring at Rob's boxes. "How many envelopes are there?"

Rob's tone became brisk. "A thousand."

"*A thousand!*" The number sent Eric right up out of his chair. "You want me to send out *a thousand letters*?"

"Yes," Rob said, "and don't be so afraid of a little work. It'll take you a couple of days, no more. Just use the yellow pages."

Eric's generous mouth became a thin line. "I couldn't finish *that* many in ten years!"

After Rob left, I looked across at Eric sympathetically. "It's not as bad as you think. You can do it."

"Why don't *you* do it, Mom?"

Eventually he opened the phone book, worked intently for a short while, and stopped. When I left to go home, he was staring into space.

The next day I found Eric fingering the yellow pages without really doing anything. In front of him was a tiny pile of finished envelopes addressed in his round, graceful hand.

"Come on, Eric," I said. "Dad wants this finished right away."

"Yeah?" he said. "Well, he'll have to wait a while, the phone book is crammed with 'em. *Nobody* could do it. Not even you."

What could I do then but help?

That afternoon, typing envelopes, I made an unhappy discovery when I realized the Carter Dunfiddle agency was also listed as Dunfiddle, Carter, and even a third time as The Carter Dunfiddle agency, and it was only because of the unforgettable Dunfiddle that I'd even noticed. How many duplicates had we already done?

As it turned out, a great many. "Oh boy, Eric, we're going to have to look up every name twice."

"That figures."

Chris happened by just then. "Don't look them up twice, Mom—Dad wants the mailing done, let Dad worry about the extra postage."

After two days of effort, Eric and I mailed a stack of 130 letters, leaving 870 to go, and I was growling, "This had better pay off."

"Don't worry," said Eric. "It won't."

Another five days of work and Eric and I were blood-brothers united against the tyrannical Rob, who kept insisting the job was nothing and the two of us were crybabies. But it wasn't all bad because we'd finally figured out systems that cut our time somewhat. Then we purchased little gadgets that cut it even more, and we carried on with a certain pride (which we wouldn't have shared with Rob for anything), knowing we were probably the champion mail-out mailers in Orange County.

As pessimistic as we were about the outcome, we'd never have guessed the project would turn out like it did. In the first week a scattering of letters came back marked "Addressee Unknown," or "Moved: Left No Forwarding Address."

At first they arrived in twos and threes, but after a while, with the mailing a third finished, they came back in quantity—some days, it seemed, faster than we were sending them out. Suddenly our volume of mail into the office had tripled, which seemed thrilling until we realized most of it was our own letters winging their way back home.

After we'd sent five hundred without a single response, I suggested to Rob, "Why don't we wait and see what happens? Five hundred's a pretty good sampling."

In one of his singularly unreasonable moments, Rob exploded, "I want you to send them all! Every one! Even a two percent return will make it worthwhile."

If we got two percent, I thought acidly, it would be a miracle right next to the loaves and fishes. I told Chris, because I was too angry at Rob, that I hoped we'd never need promoting because ad agencies seemed to have the longevity of insects: they hatched, lived, and died during a single yellow-pages season.

Another week went by and Eric and I finished the job, agreeing we never wanted to think about it again.

As it turned out, we didn't have to.

Except for our own letters returning like homing pigeons, we got only two responses. One was from a decent sort of man who took the trouble to explain that his customers would want a lot more for nine hundred dollars than we planned to give them, and the other, a pencilled note on the top of our returned brochure said, "Are you kidding?"

It was another business meeting in the bathroom.

Strangely, Rob didn't seem to mind being followed back to our bedroom wing each night, nor did it bother him to talk business with his mouth full of toothpaste. I could see why Chris found this necessary. As long as Rob was in the family room, the TV hypnotized him and conversation was impossible. I'd long since decided Rob would watch anything that moved, as long as it moved on our television screen.

Now Chris stood in the doorway and for the first time seemed at a loss for words. Suddenly he just blurted it out. "Betty-Jo and I want to get married."

I whirled around, astonished. *"Married,* Chris?"

Rob pulled the toothbrush out of his mouth. "Well! This is news! When?"

Chris stammered, "Uh, we haven't decided exactly, but . . . I guess this summer, maybe August."

I was standing at my sink smiling uncontrollably.

Rob smiled, too. "That sounds like pretty good timing,"

and I said, "Chris, I'm so excited for you!"

"Yeah," he said, "me too." Our second son stood there grinning ebulliently, the kind of shining, fresh-start look that goes with being a bridegroom. "We'd like to be married in our backyard. Think you can arrange it, Mom?"

Even as he asked, my thoughts raced ahead to flowers, lawn fertilizers, and buffet tables. "Sure, Chris. We can work miracles in six months."

"We don't need miracles," he said with a laugh. "We just need a few weeds pulled."

I was surprised to hear the rap on the wall. Thump. Thump. Thump. I didn't think we'd been that loud. Swim workouts, apparently, take precedence over all bursts of family exuberance, no matter how justified. Rob said, "All right, Kenny. All right," and waved us into silence. Holding on to our excitement, we moved the party into our bedroom.

19

MARALYS: Chris, married! I stood at the kitchen window daydreaming. It was hard to picture him in that role, but then I could hardly believe what any of us were doing these days. Only a few months ago, Chris had been just a student — a boy, really — and Bobby had been a displaced person trying to find work he cared about, and Eric was drifting, and now here we all were, running a hang gliding business and boiling over with a sense of Great Purpose — and not one of us doing a job we'd ever done before. Chris's marriage would be only another jog down an unfamiliar road.

I stood there coping with new feelings. Was I ready for this, ready to let go of the one child who'd never given us any trouble . . . the ten-year-old who'd made everyone's breakfast for weeks after I had surgery . . . the thirteen-year-old who'd built our floor-to-ceiling bookcase . . . the man whose enthusiasm for flight made all of us airborne?

Then I remembered he was also the boy who'd concocted illegal fireworks in the garage, which blew up and narrowly missed burning down the house. I felt much better.

Soon I must begin transforming our backyard into a garden.

The first month of euphoria over starting our own

business faded gradually into the reality of trying to run a commercial venture with three young males who were related to each other — which isn't the same as running a business with businessmen.

Chris and Eric grumbled frequently about Bobby: he was seldom there in the mornings; he spent too much time flying; you couldn't count on him to fetch a load of tubing in his truck until it became an emergency. On the other hand, he often stayed after hours to organize sporting events for the employees, and our shop became famous for exuberant log-rolling contests on the shipping tubes, noisy, after-dark chases across the roof, and firecracker wars.

Almost equal to the Chris-Eric complaints about Bobby was Bobby and Chris sniping at Eric, who, they said, wasted inordinate amounts of time on errands. The older boys implied he went shopping to avoid paperwork.

As for Chris, nobody could fault his work habits, but Bobby sometimes exploded, "Quit being so bossy, Chris! You're *not* my mother!"

If I escaped criticism, it was only because I wore so many hats nobody knew who I was. I was the janitor, the telephone girl, the secretary, the chief worrier, and all-around mediator. I cleaned the bathroom and picked metal filings out of the carpet. I was seldom a mother. At the shop all the usual family distinctions faded, and like everyone else I just worked there.

All of which excepts the morning I came in to find the floor near Eric's desk littered with broken pieces of white plasterboard . . . chunks and bits all over the rug, and Eric sitting there blissfully unconcerned about the mess.

"What *is* this stuff?" I snapped.

Eric pointed. Overhead was a ragged hole in the ceiling and above it all the structural rafters unattractively exposed. "If you want to know what happened," Eric said, "ask Bobby."

In back, Bobby was absorbed making wire sets and not

inclined to answer questions about the ceiling. *"I'm speaking to you, Bobby!"* I said, and he mumbled, "Oh, that . . .," and some memory made him smile. "Don't worry about it, Mom, it's nothing."

I raised my voice. "Don't tell me it's nothing. Half the ceiling is on the floor and somebody has to fix it. How did it happen?"

Chris appeared and said, "You might as well tell her, Bobby. She'll find out anyway."

Bobby shrugged. "Well, last night after we finished working, I was chasing Bill across the rafters with the fire extinguisher and his foot missed the beams and he accidentally stepped on the ceiling and" — here Bobby broke down laughing — "he fell through and came down between the desks. Boy, was he surprised!"

"I imagine," I said, trying not to see the humor in it. "Who's going to repair the ceiling?"

Before Bobby could answer, a voice floated back from the front office. "Bobby sure isn't. He doesn't take this business seriously."

"Whadya mean?" Immediately Bobby stormed to the front. "I take it as seriously as you do, Eric!"

"Then how come last night you filled all the fire extinguishers with water?"

"They were empty!" Bobby shouted. "We never got them charged!" His hands were on his hips. "What's the matter with having a little fun, huh? We don't have to work *all* the time! And I already took down the trapeze!"

Oh yes, the trapeze, I thought. There'd once been a swinging bar hanging from the rafters over final-assembly, placed there by Bobby, who'd learned to sail out over the cement floor at dizzying heights. But lithe Bill, who at every break soared across the open shop like one of the Flying Wallendas, one day miscalculated his precision spot landing atop the Sparkletts water bottle and came down on the five-gallon bottle off center. The jug flew off its stand

and crashed to the floor, sending a flood of pure drinking water mixed with glass snaking across the cement toward the sail pattern.

With lightning speed Bobby grabbed a push broom and diverted the flow, holding back the tide while Bill scrambled down the ladder. Together the two herded the water toward the back door and saved the sail pattern, but they couldn't stop laughing and Chris was furious. Eventually Bill broke his leg, and Bobby reluctantly went up the ladder with a pair of wire cutters and snipped the trapeze off at the roots.

There came a day when everyone in the shop needed Bobby at once, but of course none of us knew where to find him. He didn't show up until almost three, and when he did he was barefoot and had a friend with him — a slight man with red hair and a sharp-eyed expression.

"This is Martin Blizzard," Bobby said. "He's been spending the week at my house and I've been teaching him to fly. He's learning all the tricks. He wants to be one of our dealers some day — if we ever have any."

I could see Chris recognized him, though not with any pleasure. Martin Blizzard, I learned later, had been in one of their "training" classes — such classes conducted every Saturday by our boys who, after leading a caravan of potential customers down the freeway at ticketable speeds, commandeered a hill in the next county and taught the hardy few to fly. Blizzard had irritated Chris by taking twice as many turns as everyone else.

Now Blizzard drifted into the back, and in a lowered voice Bobby said to Chris, "Can't you act at least slightly interested in this guy? He may sell kites for us some day."

"Sure," said Chris, without enthusiasm. He watched warily as Blizzard poked around the shop.

When I went back there, Martin had stopped and was looking down at the sail pattern on the cement. "This is pretty inefficient, you know. Most sails are cut on raised wooden platforms, so the guys can stand instead of kneel. It's a lot faster."

"Hey," said Bobby, "that's a good idea!"

"And why are all the wire measurements written on the walls?"

Bobby looked at Chris, and Chris answered, "The walls keep the measurements handy."

As Blizzard looked around, shaking his head, I knew he was seeing our shop for what it was—amateurish—and I was both defensive and annoyed. The boys made excellent hang gliders, most pilots said the best, and what did it matter if we didn't look like General Motors?

I was wishing Martin Blizzard would take his officiousness elsewhere when Rob happened by. Bobby introduced Rob to Blizzard, and they talked—or mostly Blizzard talked and Rob looked at him—and then Blizzard left. Eyes narrowed, Rob watched him go. "I don't like that man," he said, and I wondered how Rob had judged him so fast.

Bobby stiffened. "Why not, Dad? You don't even know him. He's got a million ideas. Even Chris could see he was trying to help. He knows manufacturing"—Bobby was trying to keep the whine out of his voice—"and he looked around the back, pointing out stuff that—"

"You let him in back?" Rob was incredulous. "You let him study our jigs and the methods we've taken weeks to develop?" Out came a flood of words about the stupidity of giving away secrets, about Bobby's lack of judgment when it came to business. "I don't trust that man," Rob finished, "so you'd better keep him out of my way." With that he left.

Bobby held on to himself and for once said nothing.

In April Ram's grapevine carried news of an informal fly-in to be held in Northern California's Coyote Hills. All that region's flyers would be there, most notably Dave Kilbourne, an early disciple of Bill Bennett's who was famous both as the first man who'd ever foot-launched a hang glider and the first to soar over an hour. Until Dave, gliders had been launched entirely behind boats.

Ram said, "Sport Kites has gotta be there, Bobby," so he and Curt Kiefer and Bobby went.

When the three arrived at the site, nobody was flying, thanks to a strong and capricious wind blowing up the hill from the sea. Hundreds of spectators waited on the grassy slope, but the wind was a near gale and the local pilots knew better than to launch a craft as wind-sensitive as a hang glider.

To the amazement of those who gathered closer to see what fools were about to risk their necks, Bobby, Ram, and Curt began assembling their kites. For them, the veterans of Palmdale, such winds were routine.

Bobby was ready first, and with his kite nose down into the wind, he got under the buffeting sail, slowly lifted the glider, braced himself to hold it as steady as he could, and in a dramatic moment suddenly lifted off the ground and rose straight up.

Everybody stopped what they were doing to watch. Carl Boenish, a photographer who'd come to film Dave Kilbourne, now trained his camera on Bobby.

The wind was fierce and erratic. Bobby's sail rattled, his shirt filled with air and puffed out around his body, his hair blew into his eyes. For long seconds he made no headway but threatened to blow backwards. To the watching spectators, he was a madman.

With everyone standing around in awe, Bobby at last managed to penetrate and flew by himself down the coastline, a lone pilot in a private confrontation with the wind, an adventurer to be watched but not emulated. When, after a time, he returned to head out over the bay, Ram and Curt launched and flew out to join him.

After a while Bobby tired of soaring and returned to impress the crowd. He flew poetically, putting the kite

through maneuvers he'd worked out on other hills—
swooping toward the ground, flying in tight circles, roller-
coastering out to sea.

The photographer had found his subject. Carl Boenish
made his movie a one-man story—the story of an airborne
daredevil who rode the air currents like a surfer riding the
waves until he seemed to own what he rode. And then
Bobby did the unthinkable: in late afternoon, with the
flying somewhat steadier, he let go of the control bar and
dropped backward, hanging by his knees. It was a third-act
climax to a good show.

Nobody who saw him that day at Coyote Hills ever
forgot what he did.

When Ram got home even he was impressed and still
raving. "Bobby was incredible," he said to Chris and
me. "Carl Boenish says he's never seen anything like him.
He wants to follow him around and photograph every move
he makes." A wry grin. "Like he's some kind of flying
god."

"So how did the trip help Sport Kites?" Chris asked.

"Are you kidding, Chris? Those guys are way behind.
Even Kiefer and I impressed them. But Bobby put us on the
map. He just became the best-known pilot in hang
gliding."

Who'd have thought fame would have its downside?

The problem sprang up suddenly, when Carl Boenish
followed Bobby down from Coyote Hills about the same
time Ramsey Price saw an award-winning short on television and by diligent sleuthing discovered the photographers
lived in nearby Laguna Beach. Price persuaded Greg Mac-
Gillivray of MacGillivray-Freeman Films, noted action
photographers, to come out to our hills.

Almost simultaneously, Bobby was spotted near San
Diego by Mike and Frank, filmmakers who began talking
with Bobby about a major project.

Nobody wanted to share him.

Bewildered, Bobby asked his dad what to do. "I never thought I'd have this problem. Some of them say they won't film me if anybody else is there, and I don't know who to choose."

Rob said, "I don't see any problem. Why should you be put on the spot? Let them work it out."

"They won't agree to that. Can I bring them all over, Dad? Will you talk to them?"

Rob didn't answer immediately. When he said yes, it was mostly because another idea occurred to him. "Bring them next Friday. We'll have a film party."

Thus it was that I first met Carl Boenish, and Mike and Frank, and Greg MacGillivray, and we started a party-giving tradition that would go on for years.

Not only the four photographers came. So did a few of *our* friends and a dozen or so flyer-friends of the boys and various hangers-on. Our couch and chairs overflowed and people sat on the floor. The four showed their movies in turn, a kind of Battle of the Photographers, and after the movies I served refreshments. Eventually all the spectators went home, leaving only us and the filmmakers.

There followed a long, awkward period of fragmented conversation and averted eyes, when nobody, including Rob, seemed willing to mention our dilemma.

Finally I couldn't stand the tension any longer. "Bobby tells us there's a problem here," I began. "He says he has to choose who will film him and who won't."

Bobby looked embarrassed.

Greg MacGillivray said, "We didn't mean to make this awkward for Bobby." MacGillivray, who looked like a boy himself, was slim, curly-haired, with a quick smile. "But you'll have to appreciate that it would be a waste of my time to photograph him with two other photographers standing at my elbow getting all the same shots. In the long run, duplicate footage will be cut out of all the films."

Rob said he thought it would be rare to find more than one photographer at a flying site at once, and Greg smiled and said it had happened already.

Then Tracy was at my chair telling me someone wanted to see me in the family room. The San Diego contingent had slipped away and now whispered urgently that Bobby should refrain from making any commitments because they'd already chosen him to be the star of a full-length film and they had his Europe trip all arranged. I was giddy with excitement. Europe? Full-length movies? Bobby a star? How had this dazzling array of possibilities come upon us so suddenly?

"Tell me more about Europe," I said, and the two men said they hoped I understood they were making the *Endless Summer* of hang gliding and were paying all his expenses but no salary and they'd need Bobby for at least a year.

My mouth fell open and I just sat there. Then the implications sank in and the excitement faded. Bobby didn't have a year to give. We couldn't spare him that long. Besides, people were calling me back to the living room.

Rob finally gave his views: "I don't see any conflict. Why should anyone have exclusive rights? I say those who want to make a film, go ahead and make it. If Bobby's busy in one place, he won't be available in the other, that's all." As always Rob took the pragmatic view.

MacGillivray said he simply didn't want to film Bobby followed around by two other photographers, and Carl Boenish—diffident, almost shy—said that was all right, he'd take whatever part of Bobby's flying was left over.

They all departed with nothing much decided except Bobby didn't sign anything and I was wondering aloud if we'd been hasty about discouraging the trip to Europe. But Bobby said, "I didn't want to go anyway. It's too long."

In the end, only the San Diego group dropped out of our

lives forever. Carl Boenish and Greg MacGillivray eventually brought Bobby's flying to millions, and because of
them I am forever seeing Bobby where I least expect to find
him.

The business was underway, and to my relief Chris
returned to UCLA as promised. Bobby and Eric and I were
on our own, haltingly trying to make the place run without
Chris's energy and his internal sense of order. But I didn't
care. UCLA was where he belonged.

With Chris gone and Martin Blizzard no longer living at
his house, Bobby worked longer hours. They were still
erratic hours — afternoons and nights and seldom mornings, but he did seem to be trying to expand into Chris's
jobs. And Eric had stopped looking for excuses to duck out.
The way he was going, he could soon run the office alone.

One Friday just before quitting time, Eric announced
offhandedly that he was going flying on Saturday.

I looked at him curiously. He hadn't flown much and I'd
never asked why. Now he sat at his desk holding an invoice
and staring into space. "The guys have been bugging me to
go out."

"You don't have to do it, Eric."

He gave me a look. "Yeah, I do. How can I keep selling
kites when I don't know how to fly?"

"*I* don't know how to fly."

"That's different. You're a mother."

Sensing his reluctance, I should have urged him to forget
the whole idea. Flying wasn't for everybody, though I
didn't know it then. Was he afraid? If so, he hid it well.

I studied him as he sat nearby, wide skinny shoulders
hunched forward over his work, long hair falling in wavy
strands down the sides of his face. In spite of the hair,
which I thought ridiculous, he was still good-looking. And
now I was getting to know him, thanks to our adjoining
desks and his frequent people-observations: "That cus-

tomer'll never be back, Mom—we offered him too much free stuff. . . . If he brags like that, he probably can't fly. . . . The guys who say they'll buy ten kites don't buy any"—insights of a type he'd never bothered sharing with us before. As a teenager, Eric had disappeared into an underground of his peers, and we, his parents, were left out.

The Eric I knew best was a boy: selling lemonade at the curb; clipping coupons for *free* samples whether he wanted them or not, the key word being free; looking for ways to "trade up" among his friends for ever more valuable possessions (which we heard about only after the fact, usually from some angry parent: "Tell your son to bring back my son's surfboard and he can pick up his Prussian sword"). Since boyhood Eric had been waiting for the Big Deal, the stroke of luck that would drop riches into his lap—riches like a hang gliding business.

"So who are you going flying with?" I asked.

He toyed with a paper clip on his desk. "Bobby, mainly. Chris and Ram might be there, too." Then, looking toward the windows, he smiled. "But it might rain. I don't care if it does."

It didn't rain, but the rain we'd had the week before undoubtedly saved Eric's life.

Maralys (above) and with husband Bob.

The whole family showing its affinity for heights (and hats).

Chris astride the Red Baron.

Bobby on his "high-bike."

Another version of the "high-bike" with Ramsey Price on the second story.

Bobby surveying his domain.

Back row: *Eric, Bobby, Tracy, Chris, Kenny*. Front row: *Kirk and Betty-Jo, Chris's wife*.

Bobby in his role as dirt-bike champion.

Chris and Bobby on their "bamboo and aluminum" prototypes.

Bobby figures out the hard part: getting the hang glider back up the hill.

Richard Jenks

Eric

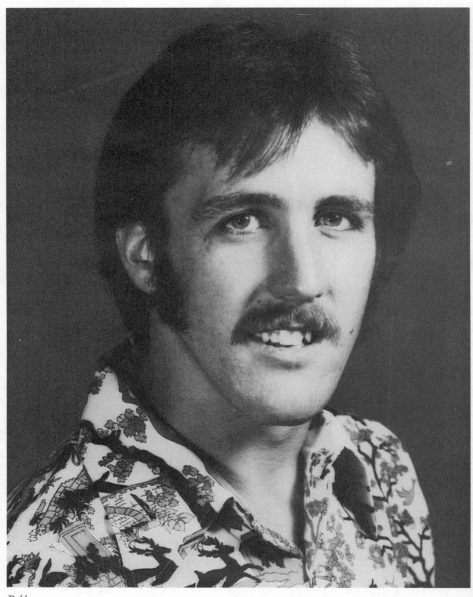

Bobby

Betty-Jo and Chris

Bobby and Suzette

Bobby on his flying motorcycle.

Chris after winning the first U.S. hang-gliding championship.

Bobby (left) and Chris giving their sponsor a double shot of publicity.

Chris recovering from a bad cliff-launch on Hawaii as Eric scrambles back from the edge.

Bobby landing on the bull's-eye during U.S. championships.

George Uveges

20

MARALYS: The phone rang at eleven-thirty at night while Rob and I were reading—an ominous sound in a quiet house and never good news. I jumped up to hear Shelley say, "I'm worried about Eric. His neck hurts and he doesn't look good." Her voice was anxious. "You know he crashed on the hang glider today," and I said Chris had told us briefly about an accident but not how bad it was. I asked, "How does Eric feel, besides having a sore neck?" Before she answered Rob took the phone away.

While Rob asked the important questions—was Eric throwing up, were his pupils dilated, had he been unconscious—I remembered a similar occasion only a few years earlier when I was just coming out of a grocery store and a neighbor called across the parking lot, "Maralys! I've been looking for you! Eric's had an accident!" and how it felt when the day changed suddenly from good to bad and complacency became laced with fear.

The memories came rushing back—Bobby pacing outside Eric's curtained-off cubicle in the emergency room, saying in bewilderment, "I don't know how it happened, Mom. Eric was riding one of my hot rods pretty fast down this empty street and he just kept going and crashed into a wall. I—I don't know why he didn't slow down . . . unless the brakes failed . . ." Eric, pale and motionless and unaware that he was in the hospital—unaware, too, that he'd been convulsing when the ambulance arrived . . . a neurological exam . . . and then a sudden, miraculous recovery that allowed him to go home the next day . . . Eric sneaking outside that very afternoon to shoot baskets with Chris in a game of Horse. . . .

Now something similar had happened again, and for the same reason — Eric had been trying to keep up with his brothers. I listened to Rob telling Shelley to watch him closely and call us if anything changed.

Then Chris happened into the room and Rob turned on him. "You didn't tell us the whole story, Chris! You didn't tell us how bad it really was — about the furrow Eric dug with his head and how he could have broken his neck! You and Bobby downplay things like this. I think you deliberately keep us in the dark so Mom and I won't shut you down. Well, Eric's in bad shape — we don't know how bad yet. He could be critical!"

Chris went white and sat down.

Suddenly I felt weak. "Rob, maybe we should take him to the hospital!"

Giving Chris a venomous look, Rob growled, "We'll wait. But Eric had one helluva crash, and they *knew it!*"

That night on his way to bed Rob said, "This sport isn't as innocent as it seems. Sometimes I get the feeling there's a wolf lurking right outside the door."

Rob had overstated his case, as he often does. At least I thought so then. Eric's sore neck soon went away and no other symptoms appeared. He seemed unbelievably tough. But he stayed away from flying for almost a year.

I had tears in my eyes, I who have never considered myself sentimental or weepy. But I couldn't help it, and I suppose another time on a similar occasion I'd weep again. It was Betty-Jo, standing on the lawn next to Chris in the sweet, simple wedding dress she'd made herself — her beauty, the grace with which she became a bride, as naturally as she did everything else. And our son, Chris, manly in his tuxedo, beaming his happiness . . . smiling across at Betty-Jo and then out at the audience gathered on the lawn, smiling continuously because he was unable to stop. And it was the two of them together, holding hands, laughing.

As they said their vows, the daylight faded, and the lights Chris had installed in the garden glowed faintly and then stronger and brighter, illuminating the trees and shrubs and creating magnificent shadows. A hush came over the August night in the moments before the crickets started. While nature held its breath, our minister declared them man and wife.

How could I not weep for the beauty of it?

At my side, Rob cleared his throat, and later, when he tried to talk, his voice was husky.

The party swirled on until midnight, an evening of laughter and boys who seldom wore shoes strutting around all dressed up. Everywhere I looked one of my offspring graced the party, and I felt like a queen with six royal children.

From time to time I caught glimpses of Chris and Betty-Jo entertaining their friends as if it were an ordinary day and the wedding was merely an excuse to get together. Less serious now, Chris, Bobby, Ram, and a friend, all in tuxedos, threw themselves into a "keep on truckin" pose and held it for the photographer.

Tucking away my memories for another time, I intended to pull them out later and savor them. There'd never before been such a wedding, I was sure of it.

After the wedding Ramsey Price took charge of the business, and Chris and Betty-Jo flew off to Hawaii. The rest of us packed to join them five days later, though not without reservations on my part. Even with a head start it seemed like excessive good sportsmanship for newlyweds to let a whole family come along on their honeymoon.

Not everyone wanted to go. Kenny decided to swim instead, at a national meet in Louisville, Kentucky, and Eric declined for his own, unstated reasons — finally admitting he didn't want to go without Shelley.

Rob thought about it briefly and said, "Why don't you bring her, Eric?"

Eric said, "That would cost a fortune, Dad," but Rob shrugged and said the trip was already costing a fortune and since he was going broke anyway he might as well go broke in style. So Shelley came, a decision Rob and I have never regretted.

On the day of departure Bobby showed up with a ratty suitcase and two hang gliders in round yellow canvas bags, all of which he began tying to the luggage already on top of our car — over the objections of Rob, who said he couldn't believe Bobby was trying to take *hang gliders* to *Hawaii*, and didn't he know they'd never fit on the plane?

"Sure they'll fit," Bobby said.

Once we were on the freeway, the kites thumped the roof, and the red flags tied to the ends flapped in front of the windows. But it was the suitcase that came loose and fell into the fast lane, with Bobby groaning, "Wouldn't you know it's *my* case that went?"

Inside the airport Bobby created a scene threading his way through crowds with two twenty-one-foot tubes on his shoulders, and another when he dropped his load on the floor near the ticket counter, blocking a considerable area and making it impossible for customers to get at the counter except by straddling the yellow tubes.

The ticket agent did a double take. "You're not shipping *those* . . . they may not fit in the baggage compartment. . . ."

Bobby said cheerfully, "Try it, you'll see."

Pessimistically, Rob and I watched the kites disappear down the luggage conveyer, and I kept wondering what we'd do when they were spit out at the last minute and we had to leave them behind. To our surprise, that didn't happen. And Rob wasn't charged extra, perhaps because the things didn't fit any category then known to the airlines.

Maui was warm and festive. Our condominiums were right on the beach, all windows and bright furniture in yellows and greens.

Chris and Betty-Jo were as glad to see us as we hoped they'd be, and we all relaxed on the beach in the daytime and at night toasted them from a magnum of champagne graciously donated by the landlady. For a couple of days the hang gliders lay untouched across one end of our living room. Then Bobby and Chris began talking flying and Bobby, with a wistful eye on Maui's dramatic ten-thousand-foot crater, Haleakala, said they ought to fly off the top and set an altitude drop record, and Chris asked, "How? The top's always covered in cloud!"

"Maybe there's a time when it isn't," Bobby observed. So they went off to the weather station at the Kahului airport and gathered wind, cloud, and topography data, discovering among other things that the mountain was clear every morning at dawn.

"Which isn't what we had in mind, exactly," Chris said, "but I guess we can get up early for a world record. We'll have to be airborne by six."

They planned their assault like explorers working out a new route to the North Pole. But they never said exactly what day they'd do it. Instead, Bobby and Chris loaded up the gliders, and we all drove to Haleakala midday for a look at the terrain. From partway up, the two made a series of mini-flights from one bend in the road to the next, like birds hop-flying across the lawn.

We soon attracted a crowd. Few people had ever seen hang gliders before and here they were, colorful prehistoric birds, whooshing by just over our heads. I kept feeling we'd brought along a wonderful traveling show to share with anybody who happened by. Our spectators became a caravan of cars that followed us down the mountain from one curve to the next.

But the fun ended when Bobby's wallet popped out of his pocket over a meadow. He felt his empty pocket, and his face turned gray. "It's gone," he said, "two hundred dollars — everything I had."

"*Why* did you carry it with you?" Rob asked.

Bobby had no answer, so Rob quizzed him until the two narrowed the area of loss to an enormous meadow, which the family then searched for hours, nine abreast.

Rob's attitude about lost things is that they aren't lost, they're just out of sight waiting to be found, which has worked in the past for contact lenses and misplaced documents, but failed with a wallet hurtled into a square mile of meadow. In the end Rob went to the ranch owners and gave them our name and address and that was that.

Two days before we were to leave Maui, at almost midnight with the family spread out in the living room in various somnolent positions, Bobby suddenly cried out, "Hey, we've gotta fly off the top of Haleakala tomorrow. It's our last full day!"

No reaction. The family had all but forgotten the world-record business and was on the verge of going to bed.

Only Chris looked interested, but he said doubtfully, "Dawn is five-thirty, Bobby, and that's sorta early — we'd have to get up at four."

Bobby stiffened. "But Chris . . . when else are we going to do it?" Searching the room for support and finding none, he implored, "We can't give up now. We'll *never* get another chance!"

"Bobby," Rob interjected, "you should have thought of this days ago. It's late, and I assure you nobody's going to get out of bed after four hours' sleep and drive across this island in the dark and all the way up a ten-thousand-foot mountain." He yawned a loud, squeaky yawn. "You'll just have to let it go."

Bobby jumped to his feet. "*I'm* getting up. It's important! Are you coming, Chris?"

From a room full of silence, Chris looked back at him, and I assumed that would be the end of it.

I assumed wrong. Bobby was not an ordinary person. He never had been ordinary and what happened next demonstrated the difference between the handful of people in the world who climb Mount Everest and the rest who go to Las Vegas and lounge by the pool. He positioned himself squarely in front of his brother and said, "We agreed to do it, Chris. We went to the airport and got the data and made our plans. It has to be tomorrow. *You can't back out.*"

What could Chris do but say yes?

The rest was harder. The boys needed a driver, and nobody there was so inclined. I could almost see the gleam in Bobby's eyes and hear the deliberation whirring through his brain: *I've got Chris. I only need one more.*

I suppose I have been and always will be the easiest mark, which explains why he started with me. "Mom, will you drive us?"

No, I said. I just couldn't.

"Please, Mom?"

"It's too late. I'm sorry."

A quick pivot, and he was looking at Eric. "How about you, Eric?"

"Naw. No way."

Bobby's eyes flicked over Rob and didn't pause. And then he was looking at Betty-Jo. "Betty-Jo?" he asked.

Betty-Jo glanced at Chris, and Chris shrugged and smiled sheepishly. But she hadn't said no, and Bobby was quick to notice. "*Please*, Betty-Jo? We can't do it without you."

Again she darted a look at Chris, but he wouldn't urge her. She said, "I don't know . . ."

Bobby's voice became a soft wheedle. "You'll do it, won't you, Betty-Jo? We *need* you, Betty-Jo. Please help us. If you don't drive, we can't fly."

Betty-Jo blinked tiredly. In a voice that was almost inaudible she said, "All right. I guess I will."

I don't know what snapped in me then, whether it was the small, frail look of Betty-Jo or Bobby's intensity or just my usual overloaded conscience. But words suddenly popped out of my mouth for which I attached no conscious thought. "If you're driving, Betty-Jo, I'm going with you."

A quick look of gratitude from Betty-Jo, and I was glad I'd said it.

Rob came fully awake, furious. He glared at me. "If you're going to do this hairbrained thing in the middle of the night, you damn well better not wake me. I warn you, you're not setting any alarm clocks in my bedroom. In fact, why don't you sleep somewhere else?" But there was nowhere else to sleep. I looked at the boys helplessly.

Chris said, "Don't worry, Mom, I'll sneak in and wake you up."

Once in bed, I couldn't believe I'd agreed to go. But I had, and I spent the rest of the night waking up every half-hour to make sure I hadn't overslept.

Life deals us funny cards, always the hand we aren't expecting. Looking back, I see that getting out of bed that morning was one of my better moves. At first I did it for Betty-Jo, then for Bobby and his idiotic dream of setting a world record. But in the end my small sacrifice seemed tiny indeed, and it wasn't for either of them. It was a gift to myself.

How silently the four of us drove up the cool mountain in the Hawaiian dawn, arriving just ahead of the peak's faithful cloud. We gathered on a rocky formation of black lava, casting anxious glances down the slope at the cloud bank that was even then creeping stealthily up from the sea. Before long it would envelop us, and the boys would be unable to leave. Clouds and hang gliders don't mix. Inside a cloud, the pilot loses orientation and, having no sense of direction, is apt to turn back and fly into the mountain.

With half an eye to the west, Bobby and Chris hurriedly set up their kites.

Betty-Jo and I, arms wrapped around our middles, stood on the flinty rock and gazed out toward other islands. The air up there was cold. It might have been Hawaii, but ten thousand feet is ten thousand feet. The ocean was miles away.

Betty-Jo, echoing my thoughts, said, "Where are we going to find you?" We couldn't see the bottom, of course. When the boys flew away, they'd just disappear.

Bobby was too busy to answer. With a bolt in his mouth he worked feverishly over his wings, and I could see he didn't *care* whether we found him. That was distant stuff. Getting off quickly was now.

"It's a big island," I said.

Chris gave us a fleeting glance and pointed. "We'll be down there."

Betty-Jo and I exchanged looks. What a ridiculous answer. Down *where*? He'd pointed to an area that encompassed about forty square miles, and I could see Betty-Jo and I were thinking alike, for she persisted, "*How* will we find you?"

Grimacing as he snapped closed a quick-release turn-buckle, Chris said, "We'll be on a road somewhere. Down at the bottom."

Well, if he wasn't worried, why were we? Sighting down the mountain, I saw our real enemy creeping closer. The mist was now two-thirds of the way to the top.

I kept trying to put the next phase — the "finding" phase — out of my mind, but ignoring the problem seemed cavalier . . . like, shouldn't we decide all this *now*? This was a very big island, perhaps a hundred miles around, and I remembered our taking a small, twisting road once, to a place called the Hana Ranch, a journey that took us half a day through forests and over mountains, and even then we'd traveled only partway around the island. If we had to search for them via the Hana ranch . . .

As if reading my mind, Chris said optimistically, "Don't worry about finding us. You know which direction we're taking off, and you have a map."

Oh really now, I thought, they've put you on the map?

"Gotta hurry," Chris said, and Bobby offered his first comment. "Come on, Chris, the cloud's comin'!"

His kite ready, Bobby stretched tall on the rocks scanning the far horizon, a pioneer, an adventurer. He said nothing, but I saw him dramatically silhouetted against the sky as he waited for wind, a stance that spoke words he never uttered: *Hurry up, wind. We have to take the record now.*

His words were unremarkable: "See you at the bottom," and as casually as he'd ever flown from the smallest hill, he gripped the kite in his big hands, ran long-legged over the lava boulders, arrived at the edge of solid earth, and plummeted out of sight, straight down.

I thought he was gone. Dead.

For an eternity of two seconds Bobby was missing, and then he reappeared with his sail billowing full. I breathed again, and Bobby gently floated away.

Chris handed Betty-Jo the camera. "Don't worry, B-Jo, you'll find us," he said cheerfully, and he, too, took the few running steps that carried him into space — and, like Bobby, he stalled over the edge.

Serenely, with only a suggestion of motion, the two figures under their great rounded canopies drifted away toward the ocean. Between us and that purple-blue haze they call the sea, the land was a stranger, too much of it even to contemplate.

For a long time, as long as we could still see them, Betty-Jo and I stood quiet and awe-struck. The silence. The drama. The starkness of dawn on a mountaintop. A mixture of pride and fear filled my throat so I might have cried, except I didn't want Betty-Jo to see. Instead, I took deep breaths around the tears and watched my two sons grow smaller and smaller until I wasn't sure I saw them any longer and they disappeared against the horizon.

"Maybe we'd better start," said Betty-Jo, and we followed the spiralling ribbon that led down the mountain.

At the bottom we had impossible choices. Should we go left or right? In either direction a high road and a low road offered options. But which was most likely? After discussing the road to the right which led to Hana Ranch, and how it was so long and tortuous, we agreed to go left.

I can't say how long we followed the curves of that island, but it seemed hours. From time to time the terrain changed. The winding, pot-holed road took us through cane fields, boulder-strewn outcroppings, inlets from the sea filled with rocks, past an occasional house. But generally we were in wilderness, and most of what we saw was inhospitable ground, too rough for landing hang gliders.

We met only one other car coming the other way.

Betty-Jo drove and we spoke very little. We were on an impossible mission, but neither of us wanted to admit it. How, on that enormous island, could we expect to find two specks who'd disappeared hours before from the top? From time to time I glanced skyward, knowing it was pointless. The boys were long since gone. We had no choice but to keep wandering in the direction we had arbitrarily chosen.

The wind came up and gusted across the island.

I looked up again and studied the peak. Haleakala was once again wearing its fuzzy white cap pulled down over its eyes. When we spoke, we agreed we had little hope of finding them that day. It would probably be the next, yet what else was there to do except keep driving?

It was in this resigned, contemplative frame of mind that I looked up at Betty-Jo's sudden cry, "Maralys, what's *that*?"

Something was out there, a car coming our way. No, not a car, but a kind of truck . . . a Jeep? . . . and then I saw two objects on top stretched across the roll bars and pointing at us like rifles — two round things that couldn't be anything except rolled-up hang gliders!

Behind the driver, standing up and waving, laughing triumphantly, were Bobby and Chris!

After the Jeep had gone and Bobby was fitting himself into the backseat of our car, he grinned across at me. "Ya done good," he said, "finding us so fast."

Given the fact that either they or we could have started off in the opposite direction, I thought we'd done miraculous.

"How'd you know which way to go?" Bobby settled back against the vinyl, plainly tired.

"It wasn't that hard," Betty-Jo said, smiling. "Neither of us wanted to go to the Hana Ranch."

They set the record, the first hang gliders ever to descend ten thousand vertical feet. Hang gliding records were informal then — if you had a witness or two you were believed. And though the flight was easy for them at first, the boys said, at the end it wasn't. They landed near the ocean in a wind so stiff it blew them backwards. Instead of coming to a running stop, they had to look behind them and pick out a spot to land among the rocks, "like backing into a parallel parking space," Chris said.

Their feat made the newspapers, then the hang gliding record books, and finally hang gliding history. It was Rob who called all the newspapers and proudly touted his sons' accomplishments and I who exulted in a private pleasure — that for the price of getting up before dawn I had a front row-seat.

Until late that night Chris described the flight, the excessive winds, the way they shouted back and forth to each other on the way down, the odd and crazy thoughts that ran through their minds.

Rob poured champagne. "Well, they did it!" he exclaimed, smiling and holding up his glass.

"Yeah," Bobby said, and he didn't exactly smile; he just looked enormously satisfied.

That night, when feelings of triumph warmed us like a spring sun, it was as though we'd all become part of the record. It was a family thing, everyone showered equally with importance, and we conveniently forgot how the previous evening we'd been hostile, discouraging Bobby all the way. I will always contend that the record came about mostly because Bobby fought for it late one night in a rented living room.

Sometime during our celebration, lost in the laughter and general ebullience was a quiet, offhanded statement from Bobby. "Day after tomorrow, on Oahu, we're going to set another world record."

21

MARALYS: From our rented house on Oahu, Chris called Ramsey Price, full of excitement about the altitude drop record, knowing if we wanted the news spread, we didn't have to tell the media, we just had to tell Price.

Afterwards, Chris was more excited than before. "The first U.S. hang gliding championships got a sponsor while we were gone, Bobby—Annie Green Springs Wine—and they've got big prize money now and they're expecting all the major TV stations!" Chris was literally breathless. His words tumbled out on top of each other, and he was laughing. "Price thinks whoever wins will have it made."

"Maybe so," said Bobby, "if he's right about all that."

Ah, Price, I thought . . . who always finds so much to be excited about—whose enthusiasm infects us even across the Pacific Ocean.

"Does he have it made *now*?" Rob asked. "Is he selling kites?"

"Well, no," Chris said, retreating a little. "He's only sold one. But right now it's stinking hot over there."

By some mysterious means Bobby and Chris found a group of local pilots who flew off tiny local hills but who'd long been eyeing the sheer cliffs above Sea Life Park. Which is how we found ourselves following two cars up a small, locked construction road to the cliffs of Waimanalo.

Up top we pushed through weedy shrubs to a small plateau thirteen hundred feet above the sea and stood looking down at the ocean spread out below like a shimmering purple cloth. We felt like gods overseeing the world. The wind blew a gale up the rocky face as though some jealous spirit were trying to force us back, our hair whipped sideways, and loose sand peppered our faces.

The other flyers stood watching us, waiting to see if Bobby would take off. They said no one had ever flown a hang glider from those cliffs before, and they seemed to be daring Bobby to do something which they, in their wisdom, would never try. I saw them whispering among themselves, trying to guess if he'd be fool enough to do it.

Bobby didn't say he would and he didn't say he wouldn't. Having carried his kite through the hedge, he stood with his hand shading his eyes, just looking.

Nobody said anything, and after a while, no doubt satisfied that looking was all we would do, the other flyers left.

Absorbed with the wind and the stunning beauty of the ocean, whose purple gave way to aquamarine then to green, I didn't notice what Bobby was doing until I turned around and found him with his kite assembled ready to fly. I was quite surprised. He hadn't said a word.

Rob was more than surprised; he was shocked. He said, "You're *not* going to take off, Bobby, not in all this wind . . ."

"Sure I am, Dad. It'll be great!" A whirlwind of sand dusted our skin, and Bobby's hair blew sideways across his face and a strand went into his mouth, which he had to spit out.

Rob turned to Chris. "Is this safe?"

Chris shrugged and gave us a dubious half-smile, which said it wasn't safe, but you know Bobby.

Rob said, "This looks treacherous to me, I hope you know what you're doing."

Bobby said calmly, "I've flown in wind before, Dad. I know how to handle it."

Whether Bobby flew or not seemed out of my hands, an issue to be settled by our Overseers of Safety. What did worry me was the precariousness of the cliff and how there was nothing to keep you away from the edge and if you happened to take a misstep you'd fall a thousand feet and that would be the end of you. I kept saying to Tracy and Kirk, "Careful! Stay back! Don't get near the edge!" which, thinking about it later, was probably the last place either of them wanted to be.

As for Bobby, I could see he'd come up there to fly, and nothing, no words of mine or Rob's or Chris's, would deter him, any more than the wind. Bobby said, "You know what to do, Chris," and in growing apprehension I watched Chris back warily toward the precipice, followed by Bobby carrying his kite nose down against the wind.

Much too close to the drop-off, the two stopped and faced each other in a frozen tableau. Eyes locked onto Bobby's face, Chris stood grim and poised, his hands holding Bobby's flying wires, while Bobby, legs braced hard under his shorts, gripped his silver control bar in huge hands and tried to steady his kite.

While I held my breath, they waited for a moment only they understood.

The sail cried to get away, protesting with a loud and angry flap, flap, flap, the sun struggled to reach us through the gusts, the wind blew and blew.

Suddenly the moment came — a brief lull when the wind steadied and the sail momentarily quieted. Opening his hands, Chris dropped to his knees and Bobby, released, went straight up. All we could see were his legs hanging down and above him the sail billowing full in two rounded mounds.

Everything changed. Silence replaced the insistent rat-a-tat-tat. Bobby's legs grew smaller. The kite rose steadily, smoothly, quietly, as languid as any bird riding an unseen air current. Up. Up. Up. In moments Bobby was gone.

With everyone else, I stared into the sky. The kite went higher and farther away, like a disappearing balloon, until the sail lost color and was nothing but a dark, triangular shape. Not part of us any longer, nothing to do with us, a speck in the wind, so high it could hardly be seen.

"I can't believe this," Rob said. "Incredible!"

I was too overwhelmed to speak.

For a while we all stood on the cliff ignoring the wind, almost forgetting where we were. Heads back, we followed the tiny dark form that was someone we knew — someone we thought we knew — a triangle that drifted one way and then another and finally moved next to a cloud and sat there, motionless.

"When will he come down?" Tracy asked nervously.

We all looked at Chris. "When he wants to, I guess."

"*How* will he come down?" It was Kirk.

"He'll have to fly out of the lift, away from the cliff. Head out toward the ocean a way."

"You mean *land* in the ocean?" I asked.

"No, he won't have to do that. The lift gives out somewhere over the land." Suddenly Chris was the resident expert, our only link to that speck up there near the cloud.

For almost an hour we watched Bobby-the-dot as he flew out a little, came back to the cloud, flew down the line of the cliffs and went back. Nobody said very much, but a thousand questions burned in my mind. What was he thinking? What was it like up there?

The sun, deep orange and large as a beach ball, crept down to the horizon and started to sink. The light faded fast and the wind grew colder. Rob growled, "He damn well better come down now . . .," but the wind grabbed his words and blew them away.

Bobby chose that moment to cut away from the cloud.

High overhead he began circling — one circle, two, a third — big, wide 360s, one after another. Bobby had decided to come back to earth.

He was traveling down an invisible staircase. Each 360 made him larger, brought him closer, until he became a living man again on a life-size hang glider. We saw the distinctive pattern of his sail — red, yellow, and blue with a big orange dot like a monarch butterfly. Waving, he signaled toward the ocean. "The beach!" he shouted, "Pick me up on the sand!"

It was all we talked about that night. Hours later in our temporary home a few miles from Waikiki beach, we relived Bobby's flight and thought it might be historic. Actually, we *knew* it was historic. Hang gliding was a limited sport in 1973, just a few flyers in one small part of the world, and our boys knew them all. We could safely say no hang glider had ever risen as high as Bobby, two thousand feet above takeoff.

But Bobby wasn't satisfied. "We'll never get winds like this anywhere else, Chris. I've never been in lift like that before. Never. You won't believe it until you're up there. We have to set the time-aloft record while we're on Oahu. Both of us." He grinned triumphantly, a man letting us in on a secret too good to keep. "And you know what, Chris? It won't even be hard."

22

MARALYS: There was a feverishness about our preparations that next day, as though the world were waiting for what we were about to do and if we didn't move fast all those breathless people would be let down. Which was nonsense, because *nobody* knew what we were up to.

Almost every family member had a role, though most were unspoken and largely self-assigned. Betty-Jo, Tracy, and I were "kitchen." Rob saw himself in charge of media, and called the *Honolulu Advertiser* and Channel 9 television, which was CBS. Eric and Shelley went out to rent a second car. And Bobby and Chris were busy making their kites endurance-ready, which meant borrowing a couple of Rob's undershirts as padding for their swing seats, and finding rubber bands to anchor the shirts, and checking cables for frays, and similarly bolts, nuts, and turnbuckles for proper threads and the right number of turns.

Bobby said, "Think what they'll say, Chris, when brothers set another record! This will put us on the map for sure!"

Chris said, "We haven't done it yet. I kind of wish Dad wasn't having everyone show up *before* it happens." He stopped working. "Three hours and forty-five minutes is a long record to beat. Maybe too long."

Bobby came over to him. "Don't think like that, Chris! Setting records is all mental. You have to divide it into parts.

Do one part at a time and it won't seem so bad." He grinned. "We'll just stay together."

"Sure," said Chris. "That'll make it more interesting."

I could see realism entering the picture—at least with Chris. Privately, I wondered how anyone could do it—sit on a tiny swing seat almost long enough to cross the country—with no chance to stretch, no way to change positions. I couldn't endure that kind of confinement in an airplane!

Up on the cliff we found our plateau crowded with people. A man with a CBS shoulder camera pointed his lens at Bobby and Chris, and men with notepads and Kodaks slung around their necks waited for interviews. Even a few curious spectators had found the action and were wandering about waiting for something to happen.

Dick Yomura from the Honolulu Advertiser—round-faced with an ample belly—began asking questions. How old were Bobby and Chris? Where did they live? How long had they been flying? What sort of record were they trying to beat? And then . . . Why were they doing this?

For heavens sake, I thought, if he didn't *know*, why was he there?

For a second Bobby looked past Dick Yomura's round face, then *he* asked why balloonists tried to cross the Atlantic or men climbed Mount Everest, and Yomura said he couldn't figure out a lot of the challenges people took on.

Yomura put his pencil away, and others pressed closer to pepper the boys with questions. All that time they were being polite but also trying to assemble their kites because time was getting away, and it was now past noon, which was supposed to be the moment of takeoff. Meanwhile, I was getting nervous that Rob, who'd gone out for drinks and candy, hadn't yet appeared. Was he going to blow everything, including the takeoff?

Suddenly we all heard him. "Juice!" Rob cried, pushing

through the hedge. "Candy! Looky here!" He was waving a small white plastic bottle. Ebullient and full of energy, he walked fast, talked at a movie-director's clip. "Well, boys" — he had to shout over the wind — "I got every kind of candy, plenty of drinks, kite string, these little bottles, the perfect size to carry." He began pulling his treasures out of a bag.

Chris took over. "Here's how we'll do the juice," he said. Working fast, he filled one of the little bottles with apple juice and tightened its lid, then tied kite string to the handle and the other end to a loop in Bobby's pants. "Can you reach it okay, Bobby?"

Bobby felt his pants. "Sure. Easy."

Chris did the same for himself, then filled his pockets with Snickers and Baby Ruths, leaving the M&M's for Bobby, who loved them.

Betty-Jo came over and touched Chris's arm. "Good luck, Chris!"

From somewhere Rob produced a rope. "Nobody's backing up to that cliff again without something around his waist. Yesterday was a nightmare." He circled Chris with a long length and gave Eric one end to hold while he took the other. "Don't let that end get away from you, Eric, whatever you do."

Bobby picked up his kite and Chris backed slowly toward the edge. I felt a jab of something wonderful — a thrill. The beautiful kites! The awesome cliff! The cameras! The crowd! It seemed like a historic moment, and inside I was all trembly and jittery. I wouldn't have traded being there for being anyplace else in the world.

CHRIS: As I backed up, I felt the rope around my waist, the wind on my arms. The crowd followed, pressing close. Cameras pointed at us. Betty-Jo stood near Mom, gripping her arm.

Grabbing Bobby's wires, I watched his face and waited for a signal. He was calm. Dead serious.

Before I had time to think, Bobby nodded and I opened my fingers and ducked. Off to one side, above the noise of the wind, a voice yelled, "He's up! Set your watch!"

Bobby went up fast, even faster than the day before, and people stared and pointed.

Behind me, the CBS camera whirled to catch him. The man was having a hard time focusing on a fast-moving kite.

Bobby faded fast. When you could hardly see him, the crowd starting looking at me.

I said, "You going to launch me, Eric?" Suddenly I wanted to be up there too. I was filled with nervous energy.

Eric took a quick look behind him and his eyes got big.

"You don't have to back up so far. It isn't necessary."

Eric grinned. "'Preciate that."

Dad was back in action, tying the rope around Eric's waist, wrapping one end hard around a bush and taking the other end himself. I picked up my kite and moved forward into the wind, trying to make sure Eric was okay. He was too thin for the job — not dense enough — and he was scared, too. "Stop right there," I said.

He grabbed my wing wires and I faced him. His job was to keep the kite on the ground and steady. Mine was reading the wind.

It was the ultimate concentration, ignoring the way the wind hammered my body and threw my hair around — focusing only on the way it shaped itself over the nose. I waited for that split second when the kite was in balance and stable enough to fly.

Just when I figured it wouldn't happen, the wind smoothed out and the kite leveled. "Now!" I yelled.

Eric let go, but he didn't let go evenly. One hand stayed on the wire a fraction too long, and instead of releasing me to go straight up, he sent me sideways into the wind, so one side was flying and the other wasn't. The kite turned, and I was in trouble. I found myself flying back toward the cliff, about to go over the top, headed for a crash in the rotors.

I fought the wind, threw my weight to the right, leaned, pushed out. My muscles knotted. The wind pushed against the sail. I pushed back. Time passed. A lot of time, but maybe only a few seconds.

Slowly I won.

As I rose above the cliffs, the wind smoothed out and the lopsided pressure eased and I gradually turned into the wind again, headed away from the rocky face.

I took a deep breath. God, that was close!

Eric should have known better. I'd have to talk to him.

Gradually I noticed other things—a deep, sudden quiet. My sail no longer flapped. Instead of a violent wind in my face, there was the gentler side, a warm, easy breeze that billowed out my shirt and flowed over my arms.

I was still rising, surprised at the flow of air that carried me up with so little effort, then exhilarated by coasting in an unseen current that rose and rose. Defying gravity, it sent me up, ever higher, until I lived one of my dreams, soaring higher than eagles. I'd reached a different world. Like a bird, I could move in any dimension—rise or dive or turn sideways, or spin in endless circles if I wanted.

It was the ultimate freedom.

The view was spectacular. Clouds drifted below the kite like pieces of white cloth with frayed edges. Waves outlined in shaving cream formed into long lines, broke apart and joined again.

I was almost out sight when I remembered the photographers. They weren't getting good footage, so I flew out of the lift, lost altitude over the ocean, and flew back over the cliff as low as I dared. The cameras pointed upward, catching the white stars on my blue sail. There was no point in setting a record where it couldn't be seen.

Five or six times I buzzed the cliff. People waved. So I flew up to Bobby and yelled for him to join me. We both went out to sea and came back and buzzed the crowd in perfect formation. But it was work. That kind of flying took energy. If I was going to last five hours, I had to save something for later. Bobby and I stopped showboating and cruised, letting the wind take us up where it wanted.

There was nothing but time now, a lot of time. My watch said I'd been up only an hour and ten minutes. The swing seat began to get lumpy. I'd done a lousy job turning Dad's undershirt into padding. Figuring I could rearrange it, I loosened my seat belt, lifted off, and pulled the shirt around, but it wasn't easy and didn't seem to help much, so I gave up. Plenty of time to do that later.

For a while I flew carelessly in the incredible lift. And then I looked at my watch again. Only two hours gone! Time moved slower when you *had* to fly.

I was having less fun now than I'd figured. It wasn't the actual flying that got to me, but knowing I had to stay up no matter what. In a crazy way I felt confined because I was bound to the kite and couldn't get out of it. I'd never thought of flying that way before. Flying had always meant freedom.

The kite drifted upward to a thousand feet above takeoff. Higher, the air was cooler.

I looked at my watch. We'd burned up only two and a half hours. How would I make it to five?

Still colder. Not three o'clock yet, but the wind no longer felt good. It was like a chilly fan blowing across my skin—a fan you couldn't shut off. I shivered. I was beginning to discover what we would later call a fundamental rule of hang gliding: You can never be dressed too warmly when flying in the open wind.

How much longer could I stay up?

Then I thought, Don't concentrate on the negatives, think about when it's over and what this means, that two brothers are making history and it's going to help the business and you'll both be in the record books forever.

I couldn't think any more. I was too busy shivering.

Exercise, I told myself, do some 360s, so I banked into a turn and did about eight circles before I realized it wasn't working, I was too far gone for exercise to help.

The minutes wore on. I could no longer deny I was miserable.

About then Bobby flew next to me and yelled, "Are you as cold as I am?"

"Yes!" I yelled back, and it hit me how I could get out of this gracefully. "Hang on! I'll fly down and try to get you a jacket!"

He shouted back, "I can last a while longer! But hurry!"

Turning toward the ocean, I lost altitude at a pace that seemed to take forever. Luckily, people were still there when I buzzed the cliff. I yelled as loud as I could, "I'M GOING DOWN!"

Someone waved like they'd heard.

Then I headed for the beach—the solid, *warm* sand of the beach.

23

MARALYS: We found Chris on the sand working frantically to fold and bag his kite. "I had to come down," he explained with a hint of apology. "I was freezing up there."

Suddenly I was a tangle of mixed emotions, sorry he'd been cold, but let down that he'd given up . . . then angry at myself that I could be so callous, like a stage mother for whom glory counts more than the welfare of her child. I said, "You were up a long time, Chris, longer than most of the records," and Rob said as he helped boost the kite onto Chris's shoulders, "Don't worry about it, I understand perfectly." We set off across the sand. "It's Bobby I don't understand."

"It isn't the flying that's so bad," Chris said, "*that's* just monotonous . . ." His voice trailed off as we reached the car and he lifted his hang glider to the roof. "Bobby's cold, too. He may not stick it out unless we do something. He doesn't have much on."

Just a T-shirt and cutoff pants, I thought dully. And no shoes, of course. Naturally he'd fly half naked. But when had *that* ever mattered?

While the two tied the glider down with bungee cords, Chris asked where everyone was, and Rob said Eric and Shelley wanted to be by themselves so they took one of the cars, and everyone else was back on top. But the news media had all left. "They told us to call when you'd set the new record — especially if it happens before the evening news."

Chris nodded and scooted into the car. Inside, he shivered and rubbed his hands together. "Oh boy, I never thought an overheated car could feel this good!"

As we wound up the grade, words floated back to me from the front seat about the need for getting Bobby a jacket — to which I hardly listened because it was obviously impossible.

Out on the cliff once more we found Bobby flying slowly seaward and then back again, not far overhead. Bare arms. Bare legs. Bare feet. As a group we stood silently staring up at him, wishing we could communicate — at least let him know we were trying to figure out a way to help. But Chris had already told us words from the ground couldn't be heard.

Surveying the group, Rob asked urgently, "Does anyone have a jacket?"

A few shrugs, no answers. Of course there were none. This was Hawaii. Also August. Even back at our rented house I doubted there was one jacket among the lot of us. On other island vacations we'd learned wraps of all kinds went round trip without ever leaving the suitcase. "If we had one," I said, "what good would it do? He can't come down to get it."

Rob grunted and I wandered off by myself feeling dispirited. First Chris, now Bobby. The day had started with such promise, so much excitement. All those people involved — newspaper reporters, television cameramen, spectators. Everybody anticipating a momentous event. Only it wasn't going to happen. What idiots we'd been, collecting all that publicity before the fact!

Odd that with all our meticulous planning, nobody had foreseen the only problem that mattered.

Damn! I thought, why was I feeling so bad about a stupid record when it was the boys I should be feeling sorry for. Yet it seemed a personal loss, nevertheless. Failure spoke with such a sour breath.

I leaned back to look up at Bobby. He made me feel guilty . . . all drawn together, his back hunched like an old man, his legs pulled in tight, only one hand on the control bar. With his free arm he was hugging himself.

Why was he still up?

While Rob and Chris huddled with one of the onlookers, Buzz Truitt, a schoolteacher with a feathery beard who'd been there both days, I walked over to Kirk, thirteen, who stood a few yards from the edge throwing pebbles into the wind and watching them return, like boomerangs. "You getting tired?" I asked.

"No. Bored. How much longer is he gonna be up there? I want to go to the beach."

"Tomorrow," I said absently. "We'll go tomorrow."

He shook his head. "Both days we've been on this dumb cliff, and tomorrow Bobby'll think of some reason to come back. Wait and see. And then we'll be here again."

I couldn't deny it. Bobby's role in the family was changing. More and more we seemed to follow where he led.

"I wish he'd quit. He won't make the record anyway." He tossed another pebble and froze, his expression shocked. "Hey! Where did he go?"

Following his pointing finger, I almost stopped breathing. The kite was empty. Bobby was gone.

Fear must have made me half blind because all I could see was emptiness where he and his seat should have been—and a yawning space below. "Bobby!" My hand went to my mouth and horrible images flashed through my mind . . . Bobby falling out of the kite . . . a flailing body plummeting into the sea . . . people trying to find him under the water . . .

Heart pounding, I wheeled toward the others. Just as I did, Kirk shouted again. "Oh, *there* he is!"

I turned back and, good Lord, he was there after all! But he was up inside the control bar, squatting in the triangle with his big knees under his chin and his hands gripping the sides of the triangle like a gibbon in a cage.

"Look at him!" I yelled at Rob, but I was laughing at the same time because whatever cockeyed way Bobby chose to fly the kite was okay, in fact, wonderful.

Rob shook his head. "How the hell did he get up there? What's he doing, anyway?"

Chris explained quickly, "It's nothing, Dad. He's done it before. We all practice—just in case."

"In case of what?"

"In case we forget to hook in some day. Everyone should know how to fly standing in the control bar. We saw a guy almost get killed, forgetting to hook his seat into the kite, so Bobby says that'll never happen to him. It's probably coming in handy now, a way to rest his legs."

Rob growled, "I wish he'd get back on that seat. It's nerve-racking."

When I searched the sky again, Bobby and his seat were back where they belonged. Twice he'd done something spectacular and I'd missed it both times. I glanced at my watch: three hours now. Impossible. Feeling ever worse about him and his shivery nakedness, I wished he'd give up and come down.

And then the atmosphere changed abruptly, because Buzz Truitt, who'd hung in with us so faithfully, was saying he might be able to get a jacket from a friend who lived at the bottom of the hill. And Rob pointed and said urgently, "Tell him, Chris, give Bobby a signal! Here he comes! NOW!"

Bobby flew in low, and Chris cupped his hands and bellowed up at him in a voice so loud his face turned red: "WE'RE GETTING YOU A JACKET!"

Incredibly, as the kite passed overhead, Bobby nodded. It was the first time in three hours we'd been able to communicate ground to kite—and just that little bit of contact made us all feel unreasonably warmer.

"How are you going to get it to him, Chris?" I asked, envisioning a pole, something very long and very stiff Chris could poke up at him—which there was nothing even remotely similar to up there on the cliff.

"Can't talk now, Mom—gotta hurry . . .," and Chris ran after Rob and Truitt, who'd started for the car.

Much speculation ensued from those of us who were left. My "long pole" theory, however, didn't survive the first minute as Betty-Jo and Tracy thought it went beyond impossible to hilarious. "But I still don't see how they'll do it," Betty-Jo said. "Sometimes Chris is too optimistic."

Twenty minutes later the men returned—with not one jacket, but *two!*—and Chris was wearing the second. Hurriedly they explained that Buzz Truitt's friend hadn't been home, but they'd knocked on the door of Friend's neighbor, and Neighbor—a very trusting man, I thought—had handed over his nylon jackets to a bunch of total strangers.

Chris began working fast. He rolled the spare jacket into a sausage and wrapped it with kite string, all the while debating with Rob and Buzz Truitt the relative merits of doubled string versus quadrupled. Or, more to the point, Bobby's ability to break the string versus the jacket's likelihood of ending up in the ocean.

In the end Chris doubled the string, tied the sausage to his belt loop, and zipped his jacket up over the works.

I still couldn't envision what was about to happen. "How will you get it to him, Chris?

"Fly it out," Chris said. "You'll see."

I didn't see, really, but I saw that *he* saw, and I presumed he had some solution for the problem of two hang gliders being unable, safely, to fly close together.

"Okay," he said, "I'm ready to go." Looking around, he realized, just as we all did, that he had a problem. There was no one to launch him. Eric was gone. Bobby was in the sky. Rob was needed to hold the rope.

For a moment we stared at each other in disbelief. We'd come this far . . . and now? In the silence that followed we heard a lot of wind and not much else.

To our astonishment, Buzz Truitt said, "Why don't *I* do it?"

And that was how, a few minutes and some detailed explanations later, Chris once more lifted off and headed out to sea.

Even as Chris rose dramatically, questions burned in my head. How could Bobby possibly know the game plan? Since kite-to-kite communication was nearly impossible, I guessed he'd have to read Chris's mind.

And what *was* the plan?

Like the others I stood on the cliff mesmerized, every muscle straining toward the two hang gliders, until all awareness of the wind and the ocean and the cliff and the people around me ceased.

The blue kite with the white stars flew seaward and, using techniques I didn't understand, managed to stay higher than the butterfly kite . . . two silhouettes flying together, one above, one below.

Then slowly, almost imperceptibly, the higher kite moved ahead of the lower.

A voice shrieked, "He's let down the jacket!" and Betty-Jo pointed to a small dark object trailing the forward kite, a bundle so tiny and disconnected it seemed to have no relationship to the kite at all. I thought, You're wrong, Betty-Jo, it's too tiny, it's . . . nothing. But my eyes were glued to the speck.

The thing wasn't actually down either. It flew straight out behind Chris's kite like a tail, and Rob said nervously, "Chris'll have to slow down. Bobby can't get it back there."

Even as he said it, the bundle dropped lower, now trailing Chris's kite at a sharp downward angle. The two kites flew tandem, one above and ahead of the other with the little bundle seemingly on its own between them. The seconds passed and nothing changed except the tableau traveled slowly from left to right.

They've done all they can do, I thought nervously. These are non-powered craft, they're using the same wind, the same source of lift. Nothing will change. They're finished.

But I couldn't speak and I couldn't look away.

Then something happened. Catching us off guard, the lower kite suddenly streaked under the higher, an event that happened so fast you wondered if you saw it. When it was over, the little black object followed a new master.

"He's got it!" Betty-Jo screamed, and she grabbed my arm and together we yelped and jumped up and down and laughed like kids. Rob just stood there shaking his fingers repeatedly in that odd gesture of his.

I thought it was over. But it wasn't. The small dark dot that trailed Bobby's kite merely followed and I thought, Oh Lord, he doesn't have it *yet* . . . the jacket still hung out in space. It could still fall into the sea.

We grew anxious again. Bobby flew on and the bundle followed, just trailed aimlessly, and none of us could figure out why. Rob muttered darkly, "For God's sake, reel it in!"

But something was happening, only we were slow to see it. The bundle's position changed. One minute it was a long distance from Bobby's kite, the next somewhat closer. And abruptly it was gone. Bobby either had the jacket or he'd dropped it, we didn't know which.

The wind blew a sharp, warm blast across our heads. Sand drummed our cheeks, but nobody noticed because out over the sea Bobby's silhouette changed. Around him, billowing cloth suddenly burst forth like a parachute, material that flapped and ballooned. Then we saw an arm extended, an arm reaching for a jacket that writhed and shook, trying to get away. Inside my head a voice cried, "Hang onto it, Bobby! For God's sake, hang on!"

While we watched, the cloth waved and wriggled and fought, refusing to be possessed. And then stopped.

Bobby was wearing the jacket!

We cheered and screamed into the wind.

Moments later Chris flew by low and yelled "Pick me up!" and for answer got a great, ebullient, pent-up yell, a collective roar of victory.

He smiled as he flew by, raised both hands in triumph. Rob and Tracy and Betty-Jo and Kirk went down to pluck Chris from the beach.

I couldn't imagine how Bobby did it, how he gauged his flying so perfectly that he was able to trade altitude for speed and attain the exact height he needed to intercept the kite string. God knows, it was a big ocean he flew over, and the string was two thin filaments, like two human hairs in the scheme of things. Bobby had to find those hairs out in space and grab them and break them loose and fly the kite and hang onto the string all at the same time. Yet somehow he did it.

For us it was anti-climactic after that.

Bobby flew on, literally into the sunset like the hero walking away at the end of a Western. He did nothing unusual, just meandered down the length of the cliff, turned around, came back, went the other way again and returned. There was nothing special to see or anything to talk about, except he endured. It was dramatic for its very lack of drama, that solitary figure sitting there above us through the fading afternoon, his coming and his going and his lasting beyond what anyone ever would have imagined.

Soon after he'd broken the record and we'd all cheered again and pointed to our watches, Rob said he wanted to find a phone and call CBS, and afterwards he meant to find a television. Betty-Jo said she was getting tired, so Rob and Chris and Betty-Jo and Tracy and Kirk drove off.

Then Eric and Shelly came back and heard the news, laughed about the jacket transfer, asked Buzz Truitt if he'd mind taking me down the hill, and also left.

Buzz and I settled down to wait, wondering how much longer Bobby would stay up. We tried to make ourselves comfortable on adjoining rocks; we talked a little, stared at the ocean, stared at Bobby, and one way or another passed the time.

Bobby flew on for another four hours.

When it was almost dark he finally yelled down at us, "Come get me!" and Buzz and I jumped up, waved, and drove rapidly down the mountain.

Before Buzz quite stopped the car I jumped out to race after Bobby's kite as he flew in over the beach. Though I was no match for a flying kite, I dashed across the sand, pouring everything I had into the run. I wanted to be there when he landed.

It didn't happen though. I wasn't fast enough, and there was something ironic about the ending that you could understand only if you'd been there. While I was still running, Bobby came in low, turning across the sand, at the end flying over people who were eating their dinners at picnic tables near the ocean. He whistled as he passed over their heads, trying to attract their attention because he didn't know I was there.

I understood what he was doing: he wanted his time official, which it would be only if someone saw him and verified the hour. But nobody looked up.

Bobby redoubled his efforts, whistled louder, but still in vain. Not one head turned because he wasn't expected. Nobody would have imagined a human was up there, swooping over their heads like a bat in the dark. Out of context and out of phase with their normal world, Bobby passed by unnoticed. It was almost as if, after all that time and all that enduring, nobody really cared.

When Bobby touched the sand, I was the only one who saw him.

He stepped away from his kite and looked around and then he noticed me, stumbling and panting across the beach. Too far back for him to see in the dark came Buzz Truitt, and together we made the flight official. But I might as well have been elsewhere. Bobby stared at me blankly as if I were a stranger.

I caught up with him, lifted my arms to give him a hug, and put them down again. Something stopped me: the haggard look on his long face, the fatigue that mattered more than celebrating. Dull and spent, he circled his kite once, testing his stiff legs.

Knowing my words were inadequate I said, "That was wonderful, Bobby. What you did was . . . was really something."

Finally a smile, but it was thin and weary. He hadn't enough energy left to look happy. I wondered if he even knew what his record really was — that he'd stayed up, in the end, eight hours and twenty-four minutes.

Our celebration went on for hours. Bobby was television's big news that night, and to our surprise the newspapers kept the story going for days.

Even as Bobby was still drifting above the cliffs, Rob and the others had found a bar and seen him on the TV news. Thanks to Rob's calling CBS minutes before they went on the air, viewers living near Makapuu were able to rush outside and see the kite silhouetted against the sky.

Later that evening we gathered Buzz Truitt and his wife and friends from California and all our clan, and Rob led us to someone's house to watch Bobby on TV a second time. It was Bobby they talked about, but Chris we saw on the screen, his white stars on the blue sail flashing by dramatically.

Rob bought everyone pizza and champagne, and the next day he was ready to celebrate all over again because when we plucked the newspaper off the front porch, there was Bobby's kite flying across page one! A Monarch butterfly with wings spread, dominating the page. The house reverberated with excitement, everyone laughing about our record which could never be beaten.

Our record — oh yes, it was our record, a family thing, as if every one of us had been up there flying above the cliff. I think we believed it, that the record belonged to all of us, that without the jacket Bobby never would have gone the distance.

But when I thought about it later, I wasn't so sure: it's just possible Bobby would have made it without us.

24

MARALYS: It was the last thing in the world I ever expected to do — fly a hang glider off an eleven-hundred-foot cliff, even with Bobby as pilot. A hundred times since then I've asked myself what came over me that morning in our rented kitchen when I broke down and said, "Okay, Bobby — I guess I'll do it."

The idea had seemed ludicrous at first. There was Bobby hovering over Rob and asking casually, "Why don't you and Mom fly tandem with me?" And Rob saying, "*What?*" and lowering his newspaper to stare at Bobby as though his son had, as the kids say, "flipped out."

When it seemed Bobby might argue, Rob said, "You can't be thinking about those cliffs, Bobby — about Mom and me flying off a mountain you and Chris only tried for the first time a couple of days ago. Don't be ridiculous."

Bobby said, "Come on, Dad, the cliffs only scare you because they're high and because there's so much wind. But don't you see, that's what makes it easy. Hawaii's the easiest place in the world to fly tandem."

"When I fly — if I ever fly — " Rob said emphatically, "it's going to be from some place low and soft. Like a sand dune. I'm keeping my body within ten feet of the ground at all times. As for Mom — " his look of skepticism bordered on naked disbelief, "can you see Mom doing that?"

I said gently, "He's right, Bobby. For me it's impossible. I was born scared. I've only been on one roller coaster in my life and I hated it. All these years nobody's ever gotten me on the Matterhorn or Space Mountain." I thought back a long way. "Once when I was a kid somebody made me go on the Teacups, and I cried so hard they finally stopped the machine and let me off." I shook my head. "Believe me, you wouldn't want me up there."

He obviously hadn't been listening. "I've taken lots of ladies." And then he was standing close to me and looking right into my eyes with this warmth, this eagerness. "I've even taken grandmothers." He went on talking softly, all the time watching me intently, quite serious, as if the subject were still open, and I began to feel I was dreaming. The idea was absurd, too ridiculous for discussion, yet we were discussing it. I would turn into a princess any minute or I'd eat a mushroom and become smaller. None of those things seemed any stranger to me than flying off that cliff and I wanted to tell him so, but he managed not to let me. He stood there arguing gently as though it were simply a matter of time and his persistence.

"I love you, Bobby," I said finally, "and I'd do anything for you, but I simply can't fly off that cliff. I can't, and you'll have to accept it."

"And you, Dad?" He turned to his father hopefully.

Rob just laughed. "Bobby, no. It's a great idea, but you've got the wrong people."

Bobby shrugged. "Well, think about it anyway."

I didn't think about it, not at all. In fact, I was making a point of *not* thinking about it. So what happened when he asked me again a few hours later?

I'll never be sure. Bobby's outlandish idea must have snuck up on me, simmered away in my subconscious until his will quietly overpowered mine. Anyway, I found reasons: here I was selling hang gliders every day, yet I'd never flown one; flying tandem would be *really different*, and maybe one ought to do something extraordinary in life, just once; the cliffs were safe he'd said, even easy.

After I said I'd go, he grinned and said, "You'll be glad, Mom," and I shrugged and refused to dwell on the idea any further until we were back on the hill and he was setting up his glider.

We stood side-by-side in the awful wind, Bobby and I, waiting . . . our senses assaulted by the insistent flapping of the sail, which seemed a hundred times more threatening now that I was the launchee. For a brief interval my mind had been diverted by minutiae: the buckling of our two seat belts, making sure the seat was wide enough for both of us. But all that was over and now we delayed until the right moment to walk toward the cliff, I quietly trembling inside. The wait was rife with agony. What in God's name was I doing there?

Bobby said casually, "Okay, Mom, let's go," but just as we started forward a squall blew over, dense cloud mixed with rain, and we had to postpone the flight. It was like the electricity breaking down on the electric chair. Divine intervention! I laughed, childishly grateful for the reprieve. The sail blew and blew, and after ten minutes of hearing it up close I got used to the sound and it didn't seem so sinister.

About then, Rob, who'd capitulated after I did and agreed to his own flight, came over and asked sympathetically if I wanted him to go first and I said no, I would have to be first. What I meant was, you can only gather that kind of courage once. My bravery was a blind leap across a deadly crevasse, and if I waited or looked down, it would balk and back away and be gone forever.

The squall passed, and Bobby gave me a sideways glance. "Ready, Mom?"

I did not break down and laugh hysterically and ask if he was kidding. I just nodded.

Slowly we started forward. The tandem seat was one long metal piece, meaning when Bobby walked, I walked.

Together we gripped the aluminum control bar, together we moved our legs—in my case, wooden—together we faced Chris, who waited for us at cliff's edge like a minister waits for a bridal couple. He reached out and grabbed our cables.

I looked over Chris's head at the sky beyond and my mind went blank. It was as though I were going into surgery and this was the final moment of consciousness before I surrendered to the anesthetic. A vast calm settled over me. Fear vanished. I was past worrying. From now on my fate was in another's hands. If I died, I died.

From somewhere I heard Bobby's voice say, "Now!" and my eyes focused momentarily just as Chris's fingers released the wires. At the same moment my left foot flew out for no reason and caught Chris in the chest.

Chris staggered backward and disappeared.

Bobby yelled, "CHRIS! Are you all RIGHT?" . . . and a faint reply came as from another world, "Yeah . . ."

Then everything was gone.

It happened so fast I didn't react to our takeoff, didn't feel anything except an acute awareness of Chris's having survived at the edge of the cliff.

Then my perceptions changed, and I realized we were rising, though there was nothing to tell me so, only that the world was dropping away and silence had taken over. No wind rattled the sail, for it billowed full. Yet there was still a wind that pulled at my clothes, and particularly my shoes. I looked down. For the moment my feet were still inside.

Nervously I said, "Bobby, my shoes are going to blow away." If the shoes went, I'd never see them again.

Bobby laughed. "They won't blow away."

How did he know? *He* wasn't wearing them. But I half believed him and, anyway, like everything else, the shoes were beyond my control.

We'd been up only a minute or two when the precariousness of our situation struck home. Besides my legs dangling in space, there was nothing to lean back against, nothing to rest my feet on, nowhere to put my hands. In fact there was nothing, anywhere, for security, just that narrow seat the width of a Kleenex box and the seat belt sitting across my lap. I tried not to dwell on how easy it would be to topple backwards into eternity.

My hands . . . what did one do with the hands? All too often I'd heard stories of people "freezing" on the control bar and Bobby wrenching it away from them, nearly losing control of the kite. By no act of mine would Bobby lose control of the kite! I might faint, but I wouldn't freeze on the control bar.

Where to put my hands then? There were only the yellow nylon ropes supporting the seat, very thin and not too handy. Tentatively I gripped the ropes, but since they tended to tilt me backwards, I rested my hands once more on the control bar and sat as motionless as a picture.

The moments passed. Instead of growing calmer, I grew steadily more tense. The kite was now so high I could hardly find the cliff where we'd launched, much less see anybody on it. I felt cut off. Alone. Precarious. Barely supported. It was the ultimate insecurity.

A wave of terror swept over me, and I could feel myself going white. In a voice I could barely control I asked, "Bobby, can we go down now?"

He turned to me in surprise. "*Why*, Mom? We just got here."

I shrugged, not wishing to discuss it: one did not go into the subject of panic while dangling at two thousand feet.

But Bobby was sensitive to my mood. "You'll be okay, Mom, relax. It's smooth up here. The air is unbelievable. Can't you tell how smooth it is?"

Well, actually I couldn't, as I'd never done it before, either rough or smooth — and smooth, or the lack of it, wasn't what was bothering me. I hated to dash him by saying smooth meant nothing, that *down* was what I wanted. Instead I said, "There's a plane, Bobby, and it's *below* us!"

"Sure." He grinned. "Lots of 'em are below us."

"But that's not safe!"

"It is if you're not in their way."

"How can we be sure we're not in their way?"

He said soothingly, "I can *see*, you know."

Funny, I couldn't. Until now I hadn't been able to see anything. It was as if my eyes were glazed over and I was blind to everything except my immediate, perilous environment and the frailty of the craft holding us up. Almost from the first I'd felt it necessary to sit absolutely still, and now, if I hadn't been so sure he'd laugh, I'd have asked Bobby to sit still too. The kite's chances of holding together seemed better that way. If we both stayed motionless only the wind would disturb our craft—and if I took shallow breaths I might not weigh so much.

I had drifted into split personalities: one of me believed this was the world's strongest kite and Bobby the world's best pilot; the other wondered how it would feel when the ropes parted from the sail and we went our separate ways.

My face must have betrayed me, for Bobby kept looking at me sideways, trying to read my expression. When he spoke again, he was quite solicitous. "Look, Mom, if you can just relax a little, you'll enjoy it. It's great up here, you know. You can see everywhere." I could almost feel him reaching out to me. "Try to enjoy it, huh?"

I nodded and said I'd try, though I had no idea how to go about enjoying what I didn't enjoy.

Intent on distracting me, he exclaimed, "Look at that view!" and I thought, You don't understand, Bobby, I don't *care* about the view! . . . but I forced myself to look down and saw clouds blowing toward the cliff—clouds moving *below* us! Then, with no warning the cliffs spun past and suddenly there was the ocean, then the cliffs again and then the ocean, and though I *felt* nothing, visually the impact was sickening. The world stopped spinning and I turned to Bobby suspiciously. "Did you do a 360?"

A hint of a smile. "Two of them."

Oh my God! I thought. He's running through his whole act like I'm not even here. He doesn't realize I'm just a mother and very fragile and hanging on to myself so I won't faint out of sheer terror. What if he does it again? I clawed through my mind for reasons to dissuade him. "Please don't do any more, Bobby, they're making me sick."

"Okay. I won't." Yet in my current schizophrenia I was glad we'd done it once, that I could say, if I ever lived through this, that we'd done the dreaded 360s. Besides, for brief moments they'd taken my mind off the fear.

We had come to the west end of the cliffs. In his best tour-guide voice Bobby explained, "We're going down to Makapuu now," and he pushed the control bar a little—the amazing thing was how little—and the kite turned imperceptibly and we headed back toward Sea World Park and Makapuu Beach.

Bobby became my host. "Look at those big waves! There, Mom, over there, that's the beach we're looking for. Makapuu." With his arm near my nose, pointing. "Do you see Makapuu?"

I looked hard and said I thought I did, though from two thousand feet all the waves and all the beaches looked alike. Anyway, I couldn't forget where I was long enough to care which beach was which. In an airplane, with seat, seat belt, backrest, floor, walls, and windows I can study the coastline. Dangling by a thread above the clouds, I am not concerned with landmarks, I'm concerned with reaching the ground.

I hated to bring up a tired subject. "Can we come down, now?" and I heard my own voice and thought, Good heavens, I sound like a child! And I glanced at his strong profile and thought, This is his world, and I *am* the child and it's affected everything, even the way I speak to him. He's a different Bobby, and I'm not the same me that once ordered him to clean up his bedroom. How conversation changes when the roles are reversed!

"We're already headed down," Bobby informed me. "Look back, Mom. You'll see we're below the cliffs."

I looked and it was true. The cliffs now loomed above us, which meant we were less than a thousand feet off the ground, though it had happened without my noticing. Daring to glance below, I saw that houses, trees, cars, the beach had taken on near life-size proportions, and I felt better, as if I were once more part of the world.

Then even this changed and I felt more than better, in fact, strangely euphoric, which was out of proportion to the sudden realization I would probably survive after all. The feeling was positive joy, a wild, carefree kind of joy, and it burst forth like a living dream. I realized I wasn't asleep, I was here, awake, living those moments of breathless flying we've all known in dreams.

It was me! And I was flying!

I couldn't get enough of it, the sensation of floating over tree and chimney alike, of feeling all-powerful, all-magical. I was omnipotent, superhuman, and I wanted to shout, Hey, everybody! Look up! Look up, I'm *flying*!

With a glance at Bobby I thought, What a gracious pair we are, what a freewheeling twosome, Bobby and I! Is there anyone down there who wouldn't wish to be us?

But it ended so quickly . . .

Suddenly we were over the beach and coming in fast.

In urgent tones Bobby issued instructions: "Listen, Mom. Push the bar out when I tell you." A pause. "Okay! Now!"

We moved into a large, graceful turn, pushing together on the bar, though not very much. Abruptly the kite stopped flying about four feet up and we hung momentarily, suspended as if by a giant hand holding our kingpost. Then we dropped on our bottoms in the sand.

"Sorry about that," Bobby murmured, embarrassed. "I stalled kinda high."

From my sprawled position on the beach I looked at him and smiled. We were too high? Really? I hadn't noticed, and what did it matter, anyway? We unbuckled our seat belts, and I picked myself off the sand and brushed at my clothes. Then, without knowing I was going to do it, I threw my arms around Bobby and hugged him like a long-lost son. And words poured out, a whole flood of them. "You were wonderful, Bobby, incredible, the best." He drew back and gave me a strange look. "Thanks for taking me. You were right to talk me into it. I'm glad I went, it's one of the best things I've ever done. I wouldn't have missed it for the world!" I was babbling out of control.

He stared at me, incredulous. All this coming from someone who moments before had been speechless with fear, begging to come down. Absently he patted my shoulder. "Yeah, Mom," he mumbled, "you're welcome." Then he began folding up the kite, but over his shoulder he kept stealing little puzzled looks.

The odd thing was I meant every word. He'd been terrific. The definitive pilot. A master. The experience had been a highlight of my life. Because of him I'd accomplished the unthinkable, lived through unbearable panic and survived with most of my dignity intact. It was an experience few people like me would ever have, and I was insanely grateful to be one of the few.

One last thought lingered in my head, an idea I dared not express, which Bobby would never know as long as we both should live: I'd done it and I was glad.

But now I never had to do it again!

I saw Bobby in a new light after that—he seemed older, infinitely more mature. Our relationship shifted subtly, from mother-son to friends, and I doubted I'd ever tell him what to do again. Which must be what happens when you hand one of your kids responsibility for your life.

25

MARALYS: While Bobby wrapped bungee cords around his folded kite, I sat in the sand dreamily, the euphoria still with me as I exulted in the knowledge that I was the bravest person alive. I was brave as only a devout coward can be brave, reasoning it is no victory when the naturally bold do something daring. Bravery is a matter of where you started from. Without Bobby, I'd still believe merry-go-rounds were all the ride I could manage.

Then it occurred to me that the next person up would be Rob, and all my euphoria came to earth with a thump. Rob! Had we all lost our minds? Rob is afraid of heights, always has been, can't look down from a tall building without quivering knees and a sensation in his stomach he describes as a "very funny feeling." If I, who have absolutely *no* fear of heights, had found two thousand feet of space so unbearable, how would Rob find it?

My musing carried me further. What if fear made him faint? I shuddered, seeing a terrible scenario: Rob falling over backward, unconscious, Bobby grappling with his father's two hundred pounds while trying to control the kite . . . Bobby either losing his dad overboard, or the two of them plunging to their deaths on an out-of-control hang glider.

It was unthinkable: they had to be stopped.

"You'll have to forget about Dad, Bobby," I said abruptly.

"This won't work with him. He's afraid of heights." I assumed that would do it.

But Bobby went on stuffing his kite into its bag, hardly listening. "It'll work," he said briefly.

"Bobby, you don't understand . . . you'd be in real trouble if Dad passed out!" I didn't want to sound melodramatic, but he might as well know.

Bobby's back was to me and his shoulders went up in a silent shrug, perhaps because he was thinking he'd already had the worst passenger he could possibly have.

"Bobby—"

"Dad'll be okay," he said firmly, and I glared at his obstinate back. A stubborn, blind kid who thought he knew it all.

It wasn't the kind of thing you take chances on. Two human lives were at stake, and they happened to belong to me.

I decided to work on Rob.

"Don't be silly, Babe," Rob laughed off my entreaties a little later, "I don't need you turning into a worrywart."

"Rob—" I glared at him, "you haven't been up there! I have! You'll be scared out of your wits!"

"Babe"—his tone was faintly derisive—"if *you* can do it, I believe I can."

Twenty minutes later he stood beside Bobby preparing to buckle in. I was just angry enough to be thinking, Go ahead, you idiot, and fall overboard if that's what you want!

By then, though, Rob's mood had changed. He stood next to Bobby at the back of the cliff, and the wind beat against the sail in a tattoo of sound and Rob was no longer laughing.

"You buckled in, Dad?" Bobby glanced over at Rob's waist. "You're not," he said. "Buckle the seat belt, Dad."

Like a sleepwalker, Rob obeyed. But it seemed that was as much as he could do. When Bobby started to walk forward, it quickly became apparent he wasn't going anywhere because over on Rob's half of the kite someone had "dug in," apparently for eternity. Rob's whole body was directed backward, toward land and safety; his thighs bulged against his corduroy shorts, his calves formed huge knots, and his shoes had a death grip on the ground. He was an unwilling jackass, braced to remain exactly where it stood.

Remarkably patient, Bobby took a couple of steps, moving his half of the kite by brute force. Pulled along, Rob's feet moved, but in quarter-inches. He did a kind of shuffle, keeping his soles flat against the ground. Carried thus unevenly, the kite turned almost sideways to the cliff.

Chris, taking movies, began to laugh.

Rob, on the other hand, didn't so much as smile. Grim faced and white, his lips were two thin lines, his eyes fixed at a point just beyond his shoes.

Bobby didn't try to coax him. He just kept a steady pressure on the kite, slowly moving it forward while his passenger alternately skidded and shuffled. At this rate, it was going to take them half an hour to cover the distance from the back of the cliff to the front. The fools!

Eventually Bobby dragged them both, to the edge, and we had a last look at Rob standing there staring at his launcher, Buzz Truitt, like a doomed man — a man facing a firing squad. Truitt released the wires, and the kite bloomed and rose over our heads.

In dismay I thought about the terrors still ahead for Rob, the traumatic moment when he realized how high he was, with how little around him. He was going to hate it! But who could tell those two stubborn men anything! No wonder they fought with each other like religious zealots. They were both born knowing everything.

Craning toward the sky, I waited for their first pass over the cliff, anxious for reassurance that Rob was still aboard. In a whir of color they flew over high, and Rob was there, all right, but I thought I heard something, a noise of some kind that defied identification. Another pass, this time lower, and I recognized the voice: it was Rob's.

Rob was *cheering!*

Exuberantly he shouted out a great YAHOO! and then another, the kind that goes naturally with "Heigh ho, Silver, away!"

Across the top of the cliff the rest of us exchanged looks of disbelief before we started to laugh.

"Can you believe Dad?" Chris hooted. "Can you believe what he's doing?"

"I can," I said petulantly. "He's doing it on purpose. Just to irritate me. I know his rotten tricks. He's up there hellbent on being the most unpredictable man alive!"

The *Honolulu Advertiser* ran several pages of text about Bobby two days after they ran his picture, and Rob decided to abandon the cliff temporarily while he took Eric and Shelly and me to the Dole pineapple cannery—with a stop first to scrounge in the bins behind the *Advertiser* for extra copies of the newspaper.

"Rob, that's undignified," I said as he came puffing over to the car with his arms full of papers. "Would you want any of your lawyer-friends to see you back here with your head in a trash barrel? Why don't we just *buy* copies?"

"Nonsense!" he said. "These are going to waste. Why should I buy them?"

"Which reminds me, Dad," Eric said, "I've been meaning to tell you how much Shelly and I appreciate your bringing us here to Hawaii. We've had a blast."

Shelly's dark eyes sparkled. "Yes we have, Rob. Thanks."

"Well, I'm glad you both came." Rob grinned. "I'm always happy to contribute to a blast."

We were once more headed for the pineapple cannery. The day was bright, the air clean as always. The whole place seemed perpetually on vacation—just like the girl I saw pedaling toward the crosswalk on her bicycle.

Rob stopped the car to let her pass, and the four of us

watched her progress. Then something struck me about her as I realized, first, that she wasn't a girl but a forty-ish lady, and, second, that she wore a rather peculiar outfit, in that everything she had on was green. She wasn't going very fast so I had time to observe that her shorts were green, her long-sleeved shirt was green, and the green repeated itself in her knee-length stockings, her hat, and the hat-scarf tied under her chin.

She was, actually, a rather startling sight when you thought about it.

I was too spellbound to comment, and Shelly, Rob, and Eric seemed equally caught up with her, for a hush fell over us as we watched her pedal by.

It was Eric who finally spoke, his head turning to follow her progress, and what he said was so offhanded at first you had to be listening to hear. Starting the sentence softly, he apparently gathered his thoughts as he went, for he finished in a virtual explosion of sound. "It's . . . ahhhhhh . . . LIZARD!"

The last word went flying right out the window.

Whether the lizard heard or not we never knew (she pedaled on without looking back), but *we* certainly did, and Rob and Shelly and I all but fell out of the car laughing. We continued to laugh for a full twenty minutes, all the way through downtown Honolulu.

A day would come when Rob, Shelly, and I would repeat the story to each other with tears in our eyes.

26

MARALYS: It wasn't the kind of phone call you get every day.

Home again, I was sitting at my desk paying bills and trying not to listen to Ramsey Price holding forth on the hang gliding championships when the phone rang and a long-distance voice said, "This is *Sports Illustrated* calling."

Sports Illustrated? For *us*?

In cool tones, very New York, the lady asked if she'd reached Wills Wing (our new name), and I said yes, more surprised than anything else, and a moment later I was talking to Coles Phinizy, senior writer.

"We're thinking of doing a piece on Robert Wills," he said in a gruff, impersonal voice. "When would be a good time to come?"

A story on Bobby. Suddenly my head was spinning and I could hardly think. I managed to ask, "Did you know the first U.S. hang gliding championships will be held in this area two weeks from now?"

To my surprise, he didn't know. But I could tell I'd hit the jackpot. "That should work out about right," he said, a little less gruffly. "If you can get me a hotel reservation, I'll be out the Wednesday before the contest."

We said goodbye without my revealing (I hoped) that I actually believed the story would change our lives and Bobby would soon be rich and famous.

Sports Illustrated! I was trembling with excitement and couldn't wait to reach Rob and Bobby and tell them how Rob's recent press release about the eight-hour record had paid off. None of us had expected anything, of course. Being somewhat more sophisticated now, we'd supposed Rob's brief bulletin to the country's major magazines would be as fruitful as his Great Promotional Campaign with the thousand advertising agencies.

Two weeks to go, and everyone was excited except Bobby, who, ever since we'd returned from Hawaii, had been out of the shop more than in and more absent-minded than ever.

One day he brought a girl to the office. "This is Jeremy Tanner," he said proudly—and no wonder. She was a beauty, literally glowing: bright, intense blue eyes, a wealth of curly brown hair, radiant smile.

Just then Ram came in from the back and gave Bobby a disgusted look. "Why aren't you out at Sylmar, practicing?"

Ram had been there often, and Betty-Jo laughed that Chris had her on the mountain every afternoon counting his 360s and timing him with a stopwatch. "And he eats his meals," she said, "with the rules propped on the table and a calculator next to his plate."

Ignoring Ram's dyspepsia, Bobby said, "I'm teaching Jeremy to fly. She's really good now. She's a natural. You should see her run, Price. She'll be flying with us soon."

Jeremy smiled up at him. "It's because you're such a good teacher, Bobby."

Ram had had enough. "Bobby, you've gotta take this contest seriously, man. If this company's ever gonna be anything, we have to win!"

"Sure," Bobby said, and took Jeremy on a tour through the shop and a few minutes later led her out the front door. Through the window I saw her leaning against a small blue car, smiling, and Bobby looming over her. His eyes never left her face. When she finally drove away, Bobby stood motionless in the parking lot watching her go. Even after it was certain he could no longer see her, he stood staring in the direction she'd gone.

Ram came in from the back shop scowling. "I can't believe what he's doing," he said in waspish tones, "right now when we need all of us. Why does he always pick the wrong time for things?"

"Maybe this is more important for him, Ram," I said. "In the long run it probably is."

Nationals. Nationals. It was all anybody talked about down at the shop. Who was going to win? What were our chances? How did the rules favor us — or not favor us? What were the other manufacturers doing?

Excitement ran so high that even I was getting twitchy. Ram was on the phone to Chris whenever he could catch him. "We gotta win it, Wills . . . Bennett, Chandelle, and Seagull are practically jumping through hoops. With all that TV — oh, man. . . ."

Two days before the event, Coles Phinizy arrived.

There he was, walking into our family room as though he came every day, and there I was, trying to pretend it was nothing special. He was a gruff man, unsmiling, looking at me over the tops of his horn-rimmed glasses. His face was deeply seamed, and he had an aura about him — of authority, of vast experience. He never seemed like "just anybody." Phinizy was from New York; he represented Big-Time News. I kept telling myself he was a normal human being, while never convinced he was.

We sat right down and got to work. Phinizy set a tape recorder on our dining room table and listened intently as Rob and I talked, bombarding him with stories about Bobby. We would later learn he'd caught not only every word we said but every nuance too.

The longed-for day finally arrived. From a client, Rob had gotten the use of a huge recreational vehicle for a week, and with "The Hog," as he dubbed it, filled to capacity with friends and family, and also soft drinks, cookies, crackers, apples, nuts, candies, wine, potato chips and cheese, we lurched gaily down the driveway—or almost gaily—because I knew we were late and said so. "We didn't *have* to buy all this food, Rob, and miss the contest."

However, Rob's good spirits were unassailable. He wore a black chauffeur's cap and sat on the elevated driver's seat as though on a papal throne, dispensing bonhomie in all directions. From time to time he livened up the trip by whistling—a peculiar, piercing emission, half bird-scream, half cheer.

One glimpse of the contest area, and Rob began shaking his fingers excitedly. The parking lot was jammed with cars and RVs, and as we reached the flying site, colored pennants formed into long lines and cheerfully waved at the crowd. Cameras were everywhere: carried by hand, slung around necks, and the oversized variety, bearing the letters NBC, CBS, and ABC, riding sidesaddle on human shoulders. When I wondered aloud why so much attention was being lavished on a hang gliding championship, Rob said, "Commercial sponsorship, Babe—what else?"

Thanks to an obstinate cloud that perched on the mountain top like a furry hat, the flyers were still below, so of course Rob crowed, "Do I ever miss anything?"

We looked everywhere for Bobby, Chris, and Ram, only to find them so deep in reporters it was impossible to get near them. In a quiet spot next to a temporary building, Coles Phinizy, pencil in hand and head cocked, interviewed Bill Bennett.

Eager to see everything, I went off to find the booths set up by the fledgling manufacturers. All but Bennett and Seagull had started their businesses after we did, but when I got to "manufacturer's row," it was hard to feel much pride. Side-by-side along a dirt path were a series of nice little enclosures—wooden structures with professionally painted signs and literature displayed in containers.

And then I saw ours. We hadn't even the beginnings of something you could call a booth. In fact, it hardly qualified as an *area*. Instead, Ramsey Price had hastily hand-lettered a small, crude sign—Wills Wing—which Bobby had nailed to a flimsy post, which someone had then pounded into the earth, though not very far. The ground was so hard and the post so insubstantial that the thing had a drunken tilt and threatened to fall over. Even standing properly erect it would have been insignificant. Leaning like that it looked merely dangerous.

I stood there shaking my head in disgust. Among those swans we were certainly the ugly duckling.

Then Eric came up dragging a folding chair and table and I realized things weren't going to get any better. Rob had given him an old, somewhat rusty, collapsible display table, emphasis on the collapsible, I realized when Eric leaned against it momentarily and one of its legs buckled inward. But at least the table didn't have to hold much, I reasoned, only our literature.

"Boy, this isn't too wonderful," I said.

With a grimace Eric unfolded his chair, then looked up and down the row. "How come all those other companies have such fancy set-ups? How come nobody told us? Ram and Bobby weren't even going to make a sign 'til Chris called them up."

"You call that a sign?" I laughed. "It's a menace."

"Well, I've got the literature, anyway," he said, and laid a few pamphlets on the table, where they promptly blew away.

As it worked out, the table never quite collapsed, but then it wouldn't because the literature was gone about half the time. No matter how often Eric replaced the rocks holding it down, some bystander always came along and took a brochure and forgot to re-rock them, and each time Eric had to jump out of his seat and pursue the flying leaflets, which took off like a covey of frightened quail. In the gusty winds blowing across the site, our literature was airborne about as often as our kites.

I thought it remarkable that Eric was so patient about his job. For most of the competition he sat in the rickety chair behind our even more rickety table and told everyone who paused near our "booth" about the wonderful kites we built, and, with his usual cool, he never acted as if our credibility were in any particular danger.

While Eric and I were still settling into our spot, Bobby, looking somewhat more animated than usual, appeared with Martin Blizzard, whom I hadn't seen since before we went to Hawaii. In bright daylight his red hair seemed a shade too bright and his critical expression verged on hostile. "Hey, Mom, Martin's going to be our Western States dealer. He just told me today!" Enthusiastically, Bobby clapped the man on the shoulder. "I told him we had this setup and you'd be here by now and he oughta get some new brochures."

If he'd thought Martin would share his enthusiasm for our efforts, he'd misfigured. Martin looked like he was smelling something bad. His eyes flicked over our table once, twice, before he said, "Is this . . . this is it?"

"Sure, this is it."

"Oh." Martin glanced upward and his eyes narrowed even further. "You should have had a professional paint that sign."

Eric spoke up. "We didn't have time, and signs are expensive." He knew we were lucky to have any sign at all.

"Yeah," Bobby agreed, "we were in a hurry."

"Perhaps you should have taken the time . . ." He glanced down manufacturer's row. "*They* all did."

Bobby's face grew resistant. "Their kites aren't as good as ours. We do what's important."

Chagrined, I patted the brochures into a neater pile, but that only revealed more of the rusty table.

"It's your image," Martin said, "it's impressions I'm thinking about. A lot of people judge you by these things. Well, we'll have to do something about it later."

A flinty look crossed Eric's face and Bobby said distractedly, "Maybe we'll get a better sign next time. Martin, I've gotta go. They're calling the pilots' meeting."

Eric watched them leave. "He's a jerk," Eric muttered. "I don't see why Bobby wants him for a dealer anyway. Who's gonna like that guy?"

"Unfortunately, Eric, people do judge you on pretty stupid things."

"Yeah," said Eric. "People like him."

An hour later the cloud cover still hadn't lifted. The pilots' meeting was over, and the pilots milled near the road wearing the black-and-white numbered vests that proclaimed them contestants. I found Chris with a big 33 on his chest and for once not all tied up in conversation.

"You nervous?" I asked.

"Not exactly nervous, but I'd like to get started. Hey, Kas!" He waved at a small, energetic man who trotted toward us with his hand out. Once a professional clown, Kas de Lisse hadn't entirely given up his saucy trappings, as one could see by his baggy clothes and his face almost buried under a large pancake of a hat.

"Chris!" the man boomed, and while they shook hands, Chris introduced him as the meet director.

"All right, Chris," Kas asked with a sly grin, "who's going to win this meet?"

Chris smiled. "I am, Kas."

The man drew back, surprised. "You sound serious."

"I am."

With a grand gesture, Kas swept the pancake off his head. "If you're going to win, you'd better autograph my hat." He pulled a pen out of his pocket.

In bold letters, Chris wrote, "Chris Wills, Champion. 1973," and handed the hat and the pen back, smiling. "Just remember: I wrote it *before* the meet."

Then somebody called Chris. Cloud or not, the first heat was going up.

From time to time my thoughts returned to that moment. It hadn't been like Chris, he never bragged about anything.

The cloud still hugged the mountain, and Rob and I and our two youngest sat down to wait on a small ridge that circled the landing area, a dirt field with a series of concentric circles outlined in chalk. Outside the largest circle, four judges sat on folding chairs. Farther out still, a line of pennants marked the boundary.

Except for the cloud, Sylmar was a logical choice for the contest. Not far from metropolitan Los Angeles, the mountain was both accessible by paved road and relatively free of civilization, with a number of alternative, empty fields for pilots who couldn't reach the designated area.

Wills Wing had been lucky in the drawing for heats: in the first round neither Chris, Bobby, nor Ram had to fly against each other. In general, the rules had been given much thought. Designed to include all the capabilities then known to hang gliders, the contest tasks measured skill at staying aloft, ability to execute 360s with a minimum loss of altitude, and accuracy in spot landing. But judgment was also involved because the three tasks tended to work against one another: stay up too long and you'd lose the altitude necessary for 360s; do too many 360s and your altitude loss would deprive you of options for a decent landing. It was a contest of trade-offs, of knowing the point designations well enough to decide when points should be relinquished in one area for greater gain in another.

I shifted position restlessly: the long wait had made me nervous. How odd, I thought again, that Chris had opened himself to ridicule on Kas's hat. The expression on Chris's face replayed itself in my mind and suddenly I understood: *Chris wasn't bragging.* He intended to win. For the first time I'd seen a different Chris, a Chris whose resolve was as hard and fixed as Bobby's. Well. This was going to be interesting!

Back at our shop when ours were the only flyers I saw, I'd somehow imagined them flying without much competition.

But today I'd had glimpses of thirty-two other men, all of whom looked as confident and capable as Bobby, Chris, and Ram. It was well and good for our three to feel they had an edge. But I knew now it was the same edge felt by every man in the contest.

27

CHRIS: We were going to the top too early. I *knew* that mountain — sometimes it was clouded over half the day. But they loaded us in the truck anyway, and, sure enough, higher up the driver had to crawl around the curves ten miles an hour.

Up top we unloaded in the fog. After a while the truck came back with the second heat, which included Bobby — who nodded and went off by himself. Nobody felt like talking. The pilots found trees to lean against and sat alone, psyching themselves up.

About two o'clock the fog blew away, and we could see out over the valley. The man who'd drawn the first slot waited at the edge, and at a signal from the launching judge, he ran a few steps, wiggled into his seat, and was gone. Out over the steepest part of the hill, which was mostly brown grass, he made a turn and headed left. I watched the top of his sail, trying to see where he was finding lift and where sink, mentally flying the course.

He didn't have a good flight — only one 360 and a lousy landing. Coming down in brush yards from the field wouldn't be anyone's first choice.

Before the second man could go, the judge put up his hand and pointed. Between us and the target were two kites, and they weren't just flying, they were doing radical stuff — full-out dives and hairy pullouts. I looked again. I *knew* those sails . . . the Sizemore brothers. They'd bought our first two kites.

Bobby came up, frowning. "They're way too good for the alternate list, Chris, everybody can see it! They should be up here right now."

"*We* didn't make the list, Bobby."

"But we should have done something. I *told* you to call Kas."

We were whispering, trying not to be overheard. "Up at UCLA I don't think about things like that. Why didn't you do it?"

"You know Kas better than I do. You blew it, Chris."

"Look, Bobby, forget it. We can't do anything now." I turned away. This was the wrong time to be arguing.

He called after me, "They'll be on your conscience, Chris."

I resented that remark. Swinging around, I caught the expression on his face. No belligerence, just tiredness—black circles under his eyes like he hadn't slept for a week. So now we had a new problem. Bobby was a zombie.

The Sizemores were finally gone. The launching judge announced on his walkie-talkie that pilot number two was ready, but the man shook his head. He didn't want to fly until the wind picked up.

"That's the purpose of heats," the judge explained, "to give everyone the same time slot and the same conditions."

Still the flyer refused to go.

He finally launched after a lot of arguing, but now every man who followed him stalled until conditions suited him or he was talked into leaving, whichever came first. It was almost three o'clock. We'd never finish our three flights apiece.

Eventually they called my name—fifth in the heat. There was no point in delaying. The wind was always a variable. I ran off.

It all came back to me, everything I'd been practicing. Heading out toward the right, I circled twice, then turned left for three more circles. The lift was out there, right where I expected it.

Too low to try for maximum time aloft, I went out wide, setting up my landing. I was flying the way Bobby and I had agreed—conservatively—aiming for maximum points but never taking chances trying for a few extra. Bobby, on the other hand, would go all out, shooting for maximum. Whatever the conditions, one of us would have an edge.

At the end, the lift gave out. The pennants still pointed up the hill, but they angled off to the right, changing my final approach.

No mistakes, I thought. I measured the distance, judged my last 180 turn so it brought me into the wind, came in high, adjusting all the way, and finally put my feet down.

I was dead center in the bull's-eye.

People shouted and whistled, and I couldn't help grinning, knowing the flight was good, probably better than I hoped for. I couldn't wait to call Betty-Jo.

The whole family stood at the edge of the landing area, laughing.

"You can't beat that," Dad said.

"Betty-Jo should have come," Eric offered. "Why didn't she just hang up her classes?"

I laughed. "*I* almost didn't make it—and wouldn't have if my chemistry professor hadn't let me take my midterm early."

Coles Phinizy was there with his hand out. "Not a bad flight, Chris." He squinted down at his pad. "How many points?"

I told him.

"Hmm. Nearly maximum." He wrote something down and looked back at the hill. And then he frowned. "Isn't that Bobby?"

I swung around. We'd forgotten to watch for him and there he was, his kite silhouetted against the mountain, just starting down.

But things weren't going right. Bobby started a 360 and gave it up, started another and barely completed it. After that he came straight down. I wasn't sure whether he didn't know the mountain well enough or he just plain blew it, but in seconds he was over the landing area, grabbing the uprights of his control bar and shaking his kite.

Phinizy asked, "Is that the way he normally lands?"

"When he's trying for a bull's-eye, it is."

"Different," he said.

But it worked. Bobby shook his kite, hovered, flew again and shook the kite again, like someone coming down stairs—always on the edge of a stall—until he was exactly over the smallest circle. He flared and hung there. Then he dropped straight down. A lousy flight but a perfect landing.

The crowd cheered.

Bobby stood there only a second before he lifted his kite and walked away. It was obvious he didn't want to hear the points.

"Well," said Dad, "so much for Bobby!" He looked disgusted. "He told me he got no sleep last night, and I can see what it's done to him. He never did know his priorities!"

Mom said, "It isn't just any girl, Rob . . ."

But Dad wasn't listening. "*Why?* Why the whole damned night before the competition? That's idiot behavior."

I wished he'd stop. The more Dad talked the angrier he got, and he was already so mad it was embarrassing. I glanced at Coles and saw *he* was listening, all right, and I thought, Why does Dad have to say all this crap in public?

"Wait, now. Wait. He isn't finished yet." It was Coles sticking up for Bobby. "Give him a chance, Dad. He has two more flights today. He'll redeem himself."

Dad just shook his head, and that was when Bobby came over, not in a mood to talk. He didn't try to explain, but it wouldn't have made any difference if he had. Dad had already counted him out.

It was Coles Phinizy who kept track of the scores in Bobby's heat.

"Look, Chris," he said, showing me his numbers, "the second man is out of it and the third too. Here comes number four." We watched the pilot make a poor landing, heard the score announced. "Bobby's still ahead."

The wind died as the hour progressed, and though Bobby's score was low, all the other flyers in his heat finished lower. None of us felt good about it, just relieved.

Late in the afternoon the wind picked up again, and Ram started his heat by spinning off three 360s, his red kite with the yellow thunderbolt spectacular as he came in to land. He was way out ahead in points, more than any flyer in the last couple of hours. I ran to the field and pounded his back. "Way to go, Price!"

"Shoot," he said, grinning, "I almost coulda done another 360. Conditions were cooking up there, lift everywhere. Right now I'm ready to fly again. I'm feeling lucky!"

"It wasn't luck, Price."

"Yeah, well . . .," he said, with this big grin as he moved his kite away. "So Wills Wing is in there solid. I've been telling you for weeks we could do it!"

But it wasn't over. The last man in Ram's heat had just left the mountain, and without a worry Ram and I turned to watch his flight. The pilot was Mike Larson, making the last flight of the day because time had run out and it was too late for another round.

I saw right away that Larson was high. In fact, he had so much altitude his kite was just a speck. I swear, he was finding lift and going up!

He started turning, a couple of 360s one way, then two more another—and he'd already done one more than Ram! He still had enough altitude left for a good approach to the field. Disappointment started creeping up on me.

And then Larson did it, landed square in the bull's-eye!

The crowd cheered him like a hero.

Ram and I just stood there. Larson had had incredible conditions, even better than Ram's. But he'd flown well, too. What could you say?

So Price was second in his heat. Maybe that would be good enough and maybe it wouldn't. Neither of us felt too great any more.

That was when Bobby found us. "Don't worry about Mike Larson, Price. They're taking two from each heat for the finals. And nobody else in your heat is even close. You've got no worries. You'll beat him next time."

Then Dad was shouting, "Come on, everybody! Wine in the Hog!"

and he marched away, with all of us following in a celebrating mood because overall Wills Wing was looking good.

The second day the wind blew from the wrong direction, down the hill instead of up. The press and the crowds and the flyers all showed up, but there was nothing to do except stand around and wait for the wind to change. Which it never did.

Lloyd Licher, president of the USHGA, spent the day giving interviews. So did Bobby, talking about his eight-hour record.

Pretty soon a writer came over to interview me. Just about everybody seemed to be writing a book, or working on an article, or making a movie, or reporting for a newspaper.

By late afternoon Bobby was bored, so he came looking for Ram and me. "Let's go fly," he said.

"Downwind?" asked Price. "It's blowing pretty strong down the mountain."

"Hey, you know we can do it, Price. We've launched like that plenty of times. We'll take off in the rotor and hang on."

"I will if you will," Ram said, and picked up his kite, and I thought, What the heck, we might as well. "But let's not smear ourselves in front of all these people," Ram said, and Bobby just grinned.

The three of us got off by running as though our lives depended on it, and using the rotor—the wind that curls over the top of a mountain—for lift. Our flights were short and extremely bumpy, but we all hit the bull's-eye for good effect. A couple of spectators told us our flights were the only interesting things that happened all day.

At four in the afternoon Lloyd Licher called a pilots' meeting. "We're in trouble," he said. "Because of our sponsor and the media, we have to finish this contest tomorrow. I'm sorry, but we've had to make a tough decision." His expression was sad, like he really *was* sorry. "We've done the only thing we can possibly do. We're taking the top man in each heat and going on. So tomorrow, will the top seven men please report back?"

A gasp went up from all the flyers, and Bobby and I turned to look at Ram. His face had gone red. He was madder than I'd ever seen him. Not knowing what to say, he stared straight ahead and then he walked off fast, almost running. As he went by, we heard a loud, "Shit!"

Bobby started after him, but I grabbed his arm. "Leave him alone. He won't feel like talking."

"But he's been cheated. It isn't fair."

"I know . . . yet what else could they do?"

Bobby's jaw went out. "It's rotten, Chris, you know it's rotten. Price had a higher score than I did. We should talk to the committee, try to make them see—"

"Leave it, Bobby," I said. *"Whatever* they do will be unfair to someone. We can't change anything, not this late. You tell me some good way to shorten this contest."

Bobby was only half listening. "Boy, I'd be mad if I was him. There's got to be a better way, Chris. I'm going to find Kas and talk to him. Price got the shaft."

I nodded. Third-highest score in the contest—and then out. Ramsey Price was just plain screwed.

Bobby disappeared, but it turned out Ram found Kas de Lisse first. I saw them over by the judge's shack. Ram had him pinned, shouting, and both Kas's hands were up, trying to fend him off. Yet Kas de Lisse seemed as upset as Ram.

It was embarrassing. There was no point in hanging around. None of us could do anything. A couple of seconds later Ram went running past, head down and going sixty. Ducking among the parked cars, he disappeared.

He didn't come back to the contest again.

28

MARALYS: October 25, 1973: the final round of the championships. To ensure they would finish in one day, the seven remaining men would make only two flights apiece. And they'd begin with a clean slate, no scores carrying over from the first day of flying — which was good for Bobby but not so good for Chris.

Bobby flew early in the first round, his flight accompanied by excited hype over the loudspeaker from an announcer who'd apparently boned up on Bobby's past accomplishments. As he started his 360s, Rob and I were certain he'd make up for his bad first day.

But it didn't happen. He wasn't up long, and he completed only two of the maximum five 360s. His landing, however, was perfect, and the crowd went wild over his kite-shaking stair-step performance. When the score was announced over the loudspeaker — a discouraging lack of points — Rob muttered acidly, *"Twice now!"*

Ready to defend Bobby, I saw the uncompromising expression on Rob's face and gave up. Besides, I was disappointed too. How often, these days, I fought an inner war between my natural competitiveness and a mother's imperative to offer unconditional love.

A short time later Chris came off the top. Right from the beginning we knew it would be a good flight. Two 360s spun off in each direction, reasonably good time aloft, then his feet down on the inner circle. Not Bobby's dramatic landing style, just a steep slow glide that carried him where he wanted to go. But a bull's-eye is a bull's-eye. When Chris stood on the field afterwards you *knew* how he felt: his features were all but lost in his expansive grin.

Betty-Jo, who'd come for the last day, rushed up to him laughing and grabbed his arm. Chris had collected so many points he'd be hard to overtake.

Then Mike Larson flew, and I knew the first day hadn't been a fluke; he was real competition. While his score fell short of Chris's, it was considerably better than Bobby's. After the first round, Chris and Mike were far out in front, but surprisingly, Bobby was still a distant third. The rest of the field had done even worse than he.

The order for the second round changed. Chris flew first and had only begun his third 360 when he unexpectedly aborted midway.

Watching from his usual vantage point, Rob couldn't believe what he was seeing. "My God!" he cried, "*now what?*"

"He must have run out of lift," I said, which seemed to be the case, because within seconds Chris was down and setting up for his landing.

But he was too far from the field.

With virtually no altitude left, Chris made a slow quarter-turn, came in low, floated endlessly, and somehow stretched out the flight until he reached the target. Just. I never knew I could hold my breath that long.

Rob shook his head as Chris waited in the inner circle to hear the score.

And then Chris ran up to us, winded. "Boy, I barely made the field. I got let down that time. There was no lift at all."

"You gave up on a 360," Rob accused.

"I had to," Chris said. "Remember what we talked about, Betty-Jo?" and she nodded. "Well, it happened. I had to make a choice. There was no way I'd sacrifice the landing for one more circle. Pointwise, Dad, I couldn't play it any other way." He shrugged. "With those conditions I did about as well as you could do."

Rob said, "You know the scoring better than we do."

Good old Chris, I thought, as he and Betty-Jo left for the concession stand. He always finds the right words for Rob . . . a skill Bobby would never have, not if he lived to be a hundred.

Four more flights and the last round was almost finished. Only Bobby and Mike Larson still remained on top. None of the four intervening pilots had come close to Chris's total score, but Mike could still beat him with a great performance. Bobby was a question mark. Depending on what he did on his next flight, he could wind up anywhere from fifth to third, with second only a distant possibility. But Mike Larson's lead was probably insurmountable.

"Bobby's off!" someone cried, and I looked up. Bobby was in the air, still close to the top.

Anxious and tense, I watched the butterfly kite begin a slow circle, then another, and this time Bobby's flying was near-miraculous. Even from that distance I could see the way he was performing, his 360s slow, perfect, kept almost level so the kite stayed high. From a hill on which there was very little lift—judging from the flags—he was managing to wring out one 360 after another, four altogether, all in excessively slow motion. His flight seemed to take all day.

Around us people exclaimed, fingers pointed. The announcer kept asking, "How long is Bob Wills going to stay up?"

Then at last he was large and close, nearing the bull's-eye, setting up for the spot, shaking the kite again—and down. It was the single best flight of the day. Cumulatively his points were fewer than Chris's, but he could no longer do worse than third.

The top-three standings now hinged on Mike Larson.

Mike had his choice — first, second, or third.

We all watched the last flight of the Nationals, hardly breathing. From the minute he came off the top, Larson seemed to be going for the gold. He completed his first 360, his second, his third. Then he turned in the opposite direction and slowly rounded through a fourth . . . then a fifth! He was on his way to first place.

I was sick at heart. After all Chris's efforts — his determination, his confidence, his hours on the hill — he wasn't going to win after all. He was going to be beaten, and Mike Larson would be the first United States champion.

Well, I thought, trying to swallow the bitter pill, Chris had performed well and flown smart, and what more could he do? But the knowledge didn't slow a creeping, gnawing disappointment as I watched Mike coming down toward the landing field. In the beginning it hadn't mattered very much, but now it did. Once I'd seen Chris in the lead, blind parental optimism took over and I imagined he would win. Larson's flight had the feel of stealing.

Mike started a long, slow turn, setting up for his landing. And we all stood there numb, unable to do anything but watch.

But I couldn't watch. I looked down, unwilling to see him finish . . . still staring at the ground when Rob cried, "Look!"

Eyes up again, I realized something had changed. Larson, in his final approach, was suddenly losing altitude too fast. In a flash of recognition I knew he was dangerously low and still too far from the landing area. He would have to fly his kite with superhuman skill even to reach the field.

I was suddenly overcome by mixed feelings — hope that Larson would land short, revulsion at thinking such mean thoughts. As I watched him struggle, conscience and self-ishness wrestled for supremacy.

The kite went lower and lower.

Then came new feelings, a sudden admiration for Mike,

who was refusing to give up and set down. Lying out flat and straining in his black harness, he skimmed across the weeds, almost down, not quite, trying to wrest a few yards, a few more feet out of his kite. The effort seemed endless and heroic. As long as he could, he floated inches off the ground, on and on.

Bobby stood at my elbow. "He won't make it," he said, but his tone was without elation.

Then it was over.

When Mike lowered his feet at last, he hadn't quite reached the official landing area. He walked away in silence, and even the announcer was quiet.

Together Rob and I turned to the boys, saw Bobby nod solemnly at Chris and lean across Betty-Jo to lay a hand on Chris's shoulder. "You're the champion, Chris!"

Congratulations all around, and Betty-Jo threw her arms around her husband. But Bobby still had something to say. "I knew you had it made, Chris, the way you were flying. None of us could have caught you, you know."

Chris looked up. "*He* almost caught me," nodding toward the landing area and Mike.

"Naw," said Bobby. "It looked like it for a minute, but he went for too much there at the end. It was yours, and it was always going to be yours." Casually he strolled away.

People rushed up to shower Chris with kudos, and now Rob and I and the younger children stood by ourselves.

I said, "They haven't announced Mike's score. Who's runner-up, Rob? Can you guess?"

He shook his head. "I can't. They've each had one good flight and one bad. The point distribution is scattered all over the map. Who knows whether landings outrank 360s."

Tracy said confidently, "*I* think Bobby's runner-up."

"Good," I said. "We'll tell the judges: Tracy Wills thinks Bobby Wills is runner-up."

She smiled. "Well, he should be."

Too nervous to stand in one spot, I wandered off by

myself. Mentally, I tried to balance Mike's and Bobby's flights, tried to decide how the judges might be scoring, but it was hopeless. There were too many unknowns — points for form, subtractions for distance from the field, varying points for time aloft. Whatever wasn't announced simply wasn't known.

It was when I was standing alone, thinking, that Coles Phinizy found me. His voice at my elbow startled me out of a reverie. He smiled, a faint, craggy smile. "How much are they giving for second place?"

"Two hundred dollars."

"I see," he said, nodding toward the judges' hut. "I just saw a check in there for two hundred dollars. Bobby's name was on it."

They took the boys' pictures for hours, it seemed, standing under Chris's kite with the big black 33 showing above their heads. Chris and Bobby shook hands; then Eric wandered up and all three shook hands.

Eric backed off and Chris and Bobby stood alone, trying to please the photographers as they shouted demands. Look up. Turn this way. Look over here, please.

Finally somebody asked Bobby how it felt to have his younger brother win the contest, and Bobby turned to Chris with a slow grin. His answer would be the first time I heard swearing on television. "I'm glad as hell," he said.

The fallout from their winning one-two in the first hang gliding championships brought the boys some of what we'd all hoped for: a lyrical essay from Coles Phinizy in the December 10, 1973, *Sports Illustrated*; queries about a possible hang gliding movie from a major studio; a burst of inquiries about our kites.

Oddly, Coles Phinizy predicted an end to all this. "In a sport so young and booming," he wrote, "the preeminence of the Wills brothers is apt to last about as long as the head on a glass of ginger ale."

I'd been reading the article excitedly. Now, as I came to his ending I drew in my breath, feeling an almost-superstitious sense of a curse having been laid on us. Instinctively, I fought it. You're wrong, Coles, you're dead wrong, those boys will go on and on, you'll see. They'll last in this sport until they're old.

29

MARALYS: It wasn't a good way to start a Saturday. Though I hardly knew the voice that called our home that November, I recognized distress when I heard it, one of our flyer-friends saying urgently, "Can you find Bobby, Mrs. Wills, and have him come out to Sylmar immediately? There's been an accident on one of your kites."

My heart began a frightened pounding. "Who is it?" I asked, afraid to find out.

"Dave Sizemore."

The pounding got worse. "Oh, no! How bad is he?"

The man hesitated. "I'm not sure. I was flying over him when his kite folded up. He was struggling, trying to wrestle it open, but . . . when he went down, it didn't look good. I didn't wait to see how he was, I landed and found a phone. I figured Bobby would want to know."

"He would," I said. "I'll make some calls."

As I stood with my hand on the phone I saw him clearly—Dave Sizemore, the merry youth with straight, jet-black hair, and mischief in his blue eyes. From the beginning our shop had been a boys' club, and Dave was one of the boys. In fact, he was one of *us*.

Feeling scared and worried, I began dialing. When I reached Bobby, he listened solemnly, as the head of a family would listen, and within minutes was on his way to Sylmar.

The news reached us hours later: Dave Sizemore was dead.

An aura of gloom settled over the shop. Death on a hang glider was chilling enough, but death on one of our kites had awful significance, made worse when it was someone we liked as much as Dave.

Knowing what happened didn't help very much. When Bobby returned, he told us grimly, "A wire broke. A piece of bailing wire that Dave put in himself." He looked away and tried to get himself together. "Glen Sizemore was waiting for me out there, and you know what he said? 'Bobby, your kite didn't kill Dave. Dave killed Dave.'"

Silence. Then Ram said, "It's strange, but I'm mad at him for dying. I feel like shouting at him, 'You idiot, why did you get yourself killed?' But he's not here to yell at."

The conversation died away after that.

For days Bobby looked terrible. We learned that the Sizemore brothers had been out at Sylmar often since the Nationals, sometimes flying radically, other pilots said, which only made Bobby feel worse. "I *knew* we should have gotten them into the contest. They wouldn't have had to keep proving themselves."

The aura of sadness was hard to shake. And sales dropped off, which we hadn't expected, so we had to let people go. One of the few men we kept on was Steve, who had three children and said he needed the money. Why a married man worked there in the first place, I never understood because our pay scale wasn't exactly McDonnell Douglas. We owed Bobby more money for commissions than we could afford to pay him, and we had to trim back on Eric. My salary would have been cut except I wasn't getting paid.

As the holidays approached, I could see Steve looking desperate. One day he pulled me aside. "Is there any way I can get a small raise? Christmas is coming, and things are kind of rough."

"Trouble is," I said, "we're not selling any kites. All the kites we're making are going into inventory."

"I figured that was the case. Well, it's okay, Maralys." He started to walk away.

"Look, Steve . . ." I pulled my wallet out of my purse. "What if I lend you fifty dollars? Would that help? Just pay me back whenever you can."

He said it would help and tried not to thank me too much.

Sometime later when Eric and I were discussing Steve, Eric said, "Bobby offered him a hundred dollars yesterday—to help out until his next paycheck."

"That's nice. Steve can use another loan."

"It wasn't a loan, Mom. Bobby told him to keep it."

After Christmas we all imagined kite sales would pick up again, but they didn't. The only person making any money was Butch Hibbs, a flyer-friend who earned twenty dollars an hour giving hang gliding lessons on Saturdays, because the original three no longer wanted to do it. As Chris explained, "We just burned out."

By late January Chris stopped fooling himself that he was needed at our shop and concentrated, instead, on sending applications to medical schools—which happened in stages because the first few went out to the California schools and they all turned him down. So he decided to go national, and when I asked where he meant to apply, he said, "Every school in the country where I have a chance."

Before long Betty-Jo was helping. For two months she spent every spare minute studying catalogues and filling out forms, and Chris spent his time writing essays and getting transcripts and filling in personal data. It took both of them until April because in the end he applied to forty-two schools.

Like the Nationals, Chris was playing the odds.

Nobody complained anymore when Bobby took Jeremy flying during the week. Then Bobby went off to Canada for his second try at the Canadian championships. He came back four days later with a check for five hundred dollars, which he casually laid on my desk. "Put it in my bank account, Mom."

A quick glance at the check, and I jumped up to hug him. "You won!" I cried. "Oh, Bobby!" And then I looked around. "Where's the trophy?" He'd had to take his life-size winged goddess back with him, and for a week now our wine barrel had sat in the corner abandoned and lonely.

"I didn't win it all, just the towing portion."

I looked at him blankly.

"But I got the biggest check. I just didn't get the trophy."

He wasn't making sense. "You got the most money, but they gave the trophy to somebody else?"

He shrugged. "That's the way it came out."

It was Ram who later explained. "One of the judges was a manufacturer who persuaded the other two judges to wipe out the day that Bobby won the foot launch, and they never gave him another chance to do it. So all he won was the towing." Ram grinned. "But the Canadians didn't like what happened, and *they* decided where to put the money."

Sales continued to slump through February—which is when I happened to call the office on a Friday night and Bobby happened to mention that Eric was there working and his kite was almost finished.

"That's interesting," I said, "since I didn't know he was building a kite. Why does he need one?"

"Didn't you know? He wants to learn to fly."

"No, I didn't know."

An edge of pride crept into his voice. "It's a good one,

Mom, I've looked it over. Eric's done a great job."

"Why didn't he just take one out of inventory?"

"We all build our own. Besides, he's proud of it. He used mostly scraps, so it didn't cost us any money. Tomorrow he's going out flying with us. He'll learn fast. I just have to teach him right."

It wasn't my first choice for Eric. But I supposed under Bobby's tutelage he'd be okay.

Chris and Betty-Jo were there when Eric walked into the house one Saturday night looking smudged and exhausted. He'd gone flying with Bobby, and now it was after nine and he'd obviously been out longer than he intended. His long hair was a tangled mess and his shoulders sagged.

"Not a good day, huh?" Chris asked.

"No," said Eric, making a face. "I landed in brush up to here"—pointing at his waist—"and it took three hours to hike out. The kite's still there. Tomorrow I've gotta go back through that junk to get it. Whatever I do, I'm never going to land in brush again." He plopped onto the couch and his expression softened. "I can see why you and Bobby like this sport, though. As long as I'm flying, it's great. But I always goof up."

Chris was calm. "Everybody goes down in brush sometime or other. We've all done it."

"Yeah, but I never fly without making a mistake."

"Then maybe you shouldn't have started again."

I was astonished to hear Chris say such a thing.

Eric slid onto his spine, sending his lanky lower half off the couch. Offhandedly he said, "In a few weeks I'll be as good as Butch Hibbs."

Chris and Betty-Jo exchanged knowing looks.

So that was it, I thought. Money. Eric the coupon-clipper—running hard after Butch Hibbs's hang gliding lessons and his twenty dollars an hour. I should have known.

At the end of February Greg MacGillivray arranged to take Bobby to Hawaii to make a film, but Bobby went a week early so he could bring Jeremy. I drove them to the airport, Jeremy looking lovely in a belted blue dress and Bobby dressed in a tan open-necked shirt and dark brown slacks — and wearing shoes, for once.

Jeremy and I watched Bobby swinging through the airport with a yellow-bagged kite on his shoulder, and then he was back to swing her off the ground, one-handed. Laughing, he said, "This tiny thing, weighs nothing, would you believe she's going to be one of the best flyers you'll know?"

She said, "We'll be flying tandem off the cliffs on Oahu. I decided if you could do it, Maralys, so could I."

But I was terrible, I wanted to say. Instead I said, "The view is amazing — if you're not too scared to see it."

We all laughed and they headed for the plane-arm-in arm. Their week had been a long time coming.

Some time after Jeremy returned home, Bobby called us from Oahu late one night. Rob and I ran to the two extensions.

"We're on Kauai," Bobby said, "making a film for the Smithsonian called *To Fly*. It's going to be great. They're getting fantastic footage." He was feeling expansive. "We're on a part of the island you can't get to except by helicopter. But I'm glad I'm through with my part." He hesitated, as though unsure whether to continue. "For the last few days I've been flying the gaps, which are tall rock formations with space in between — barely enough for one kite to pass through. A couple of feet on either side of my wings, that's all I had. You have to fly it exactly right. There isn't room for a mistake."

I could hear Rob suck in his breath. "How much are you getting paid?"

"Enough."

"You should be getting a thousand dollars a day for stuff like that!"

"Yeah. Well, I'm through with the hard part now."

"Through risking your neck."

"Don't *worry*, I did it fine. I guess I shouldn't have told you."

Rob said, "You're a fool, Bobby, people take advantage of you. They always have."

Over the long-distance wire I heard a faint expulsion of breath. "*Nobody's* taking advantage of me. This has been the best two weeks of my life."

"Good. I can't tell you what to do any more."

"No, Dad, you can't." And he was gone.

"At least it's over," I said to Rob as we met in the family room.

"Maybe it's over and maybe it isn't." Rob was skeptical and angry.

"You don't believe what he says?"

"Not when he's talking about risk, I don't. If Bobby says something's dangerous, it's so dangerous he shouldn't be doing it."

With that he snapped on the television. Before the sound came up he said, "It's just possible, you know, to be happy *without* risking your life!"

It was Shelley, stopping by the office to drop something off for Eric, who made me realize abruptly that our boys had found some astonishingly beautiful girls—though no two were even remotely alike. Betty-Jo was blonde with pale green eyes and an alert, collegiate look. Jeremy, with her masses of tan curly hair and eyes so bright blue they were riveting, seemed practical and mother-earthish. Shelley was an Indian princess. Her hair was long, absolutely straight, and as dark as obsidian. Her eyes had that same intense darkness—the cliché would be smoldering—and she had prominent, aristocratic cheekbones and an aura of mystery, enhanced by the fact she didn't talk very much. Which made her perfect for Eric, I thought. Together they were a complete enigma.

That day Shelley changed the pattern and opened up a little. "Eric hasn't seen me yet, but I'll bet he knows I'm here. I've noticed something funny about him — he always knows where I am, even when I haven't told him where I'm going."

I nodded. As a child he'd had the same sixth sense about us.

"Sometimes I see his station wagon in my rearview mirror — in funny places, when he didn't know I'd be there!" She smiled. "But I don't mind. It's sort of like he's watching over me."

Eric appeared from the back and held out his hand. "Come watch me work, Shelley." They stayed together for an hour or more.

After Shelley left, Eric came to lean against my desk. "She wants me to come live with her again." A few months earlier he'd come home to stay.

"You going to?" I looked him over thoughtfully. His face had filled out over the last year, and he was better-looking than ever. I was even getting used to the long wavy hair. Not loving it — just accustomed to it.

"I dunno, I'm thinking about it. I don't know if I like being a married man. And she's got that little girl. Twenty's too young."

"It is young, Eric." I'd married at nineteen, but it seemed older then. He was dead serious, and I was trying not to smile. "I suspect she'll give you a few hours to decide. Maybe even a few months."

"She thinks we're old enough now. Depends on how bad you want to. She wants to more than I do, I guess."

"Nobody says you have to live with her. You do have a choice."

"That's just it. Maybe I really want to, but I'm scared of

getting trapped."

"Well . . . it's you who have to decide."

"Seems like I can't make up my mind about lots of things. Maybe it'll be easier when I'm twenty-one."

"Maybe," I said.

I thought about him as I drove home. Two years earlier Eric had dashed right into homemaking with Shelley, but it must be a function of growing up that he was now pondering his moves.

He'd changed in many ways. Just in the last six months he'd taken on jobs he'd balked at earlier — disagreeable jobs like taxes and social security. Best of all, Eric handled our customers as well as I did. I'd hear him talking on the phone and feel one of those bursts of pride indigenous to parents. That's my kid you're talking to — my kid who's almost a man.

Eric was solid, headed somewhere.

I rather hoped he wouldn't live with Shelley again. Better to wait and be sure. And then do it right and marry her.

A few days later Bobby called again, this time to the shop. He was still in Hawaii, he said, and wouldn't be home for another week. All the film of his flying through the gaps had been ruined in the developing, and he had to do it all again.

A premonition swept over me and I shook my head. "Oh, God, Bobby. I wish you wouldn't."

"Yeah. I'm not happy about it either. But they need the footage. I can't let them down."

Fear crept into my stomach and stayed there. I felt an ominous foreboding, different from anything I'd felt about Bobby before. "Bobby . . . tell them you can't. Please."

He hesitated. "It'll work out. It did before." His good cheer seemed forced. "Besides, I don't have any choice. I said I'd do it. A couple more days of flying and I'll be through."

So it was predestined, I thought. Out of my hands.

"Don't tell Dad."

"I won't. But if he asks, I'll have to."

"I'll be home before he asks."

Rob didn't learn about the second go-around until much later. But by then he was past reacting.

30

MARALYS: I couldn't shake my uneasiness about Bobby.

I kept trying to picture him home again, safe, with the gaps finally behind him. Three thousand miles between us, and no telephones on his cliff, so there was no way to contact him, nothing to do but wait. Fortunately Rob had lost track of his schedule and never asked why Bobby wasn't home.

It was Saturday again and Eric hadn't moved back with Shelley, but he was still thinking about it. In the meantime he was going flying for fun. A banana grabbed off the drainboard, a fast stride through the room, and he was out the door. Casual, without overtones or shadows; I hardly gave his leaving a thought.

How could I know I'd been worrying about the wrong son?

Late Saturday afternoon. With company coming soon, my attention was on minutiae: dusting, setting the table — doing mundane chores with a sense of peace that came out of deep contentment with the family and my life. The last two years had been something of an ongoing spectacular . . . all the world records, championships, hang gliding movies, and media attention. For our family the hang gliding had become a wonderful, unifying force. Only three months earlier I'd written facetiously in our Christmas letter, "It is all too good to be true. Superstitiously, I find myself looking over my shoulder — have I turned the stove off, removed the skateboard from the driveway, locked the back door? I keep hearing this small voice, 'When your cup runneth over, looketh out.'"

It was just a little joke. I was too happy to looketh out. And then Danny Wilson, Eric's friend, called to tell me Eric was dead.

The shock. The sense of having slammed into a wall at ninety miles an hour. For a few minutes I reeled, too horrified to think.

But no! cried an inner voice, Impossible! Eric wasn't dead, I could see his face clearly, he was at the next desk, looking at me with his blue eyes and his calm expression, he was talking in that laconic, relaxed way of his. *You are my son . . . my friend. You can't be dead.*

Grief is like a storm at sea, washing over you in great waves that come, recede, and come again, sometimes growing larger and increasing in intensity even after the first moments have passed.

Oh, Eric, the voice cried again. Eric. Eric. How did it happen? Did you suffer? Oh, God, did you *know*?

Our neighbor, Ed Buster, took charge. He called San Bernardino, reported that Eric had been taken out of the hills by helicopter and was now at the coroner's office. He said gravely, "I spoke to the coroner. He said there was never any hope, Eric's neck was broken."

Another wave washed over me. I was drowning in tears. Never a chance for him . . . oh, Lord.

"Rob," I said, "I want to be with him."

Rob stood. "I want to be with him too."

Quickly our friend Tom offered to drive. Tom, father of seven and a doctor, had arrived before the news was ten minutes old. But Ed put a restraining hand on Rob's shoulder. Don't go, he said, it wouldn't be wise, you might not be able to see him anyway. You'll see him tomorrow — tomorrow Eric will be brought home.

I sat down again. Brought home. Eric wouldn't *come* home, he'd be *brought*. It was true then. He was dead.

For a while we all sat in the family room staring in different directions — at the floor or out the window. We were like riders in an elevator, passing time until we got off.

Chris came. It felt like I'd been holding my breath until he got there. And our friends kept coming too, hugging us, making us talk, even briefly forget.

Then Danny Wilson arrived and brought it all back. Unemotionally, Danny sat by the window and described Eric's final moments: a first 360 and Eric's initial exhilaration, then disappointment that it was too high to be seen; Eric's going up again and this time, too much the novice to understand that a 360 can become a spiraling dive, starting lower and circling until the ridge rose to meet him. And landing in brush — brush everywhere.

On foot his friends raced up the mountain, fearful of what they'd find. It was worse than they'd expected: Eric, neither dead nor alive, but dying, gasping away his life. They tried to revive him and couldn't.

Rob and I listened in horror but didn't cry, not until Danny said offhandedly, "Both his legs were broken." It was more than I could bear.

What did it matter that an already-lost son should also have two broken legs?

I don't know why it mattered. It just did.

Chris went to call Bobby, and some time during the evening Shelley came and stood briefly in the doorway, eyes dark and wide like a frightened doe, literally quivering. Later I found her in Eric's bedroom, huddled on the bed with Kenny sitting beside her. Their heads were close and his arm was around her shoulders, and that's where they sat most of the night.

After everyone had left, after Rob and I had gone to bed, I got up, sleepless, and went into the bathroom to cry. I sat down in the only place you could sit and felt myself coming apart. Oh Eric, Eric, I loved you. I loved you and I was proud of you. You'd come so far this year, you were on your way, it was going to be great from here on. And now . . . *Eric, why did you have to do it?*

Rob found me there and put his arm around my shoulders.

"Rob, it's so unfair. All this time it was Bobby I worried about."

"I know," he said gently. "I know. Come to bed, Babe." He pulled me to my feet and led me to our room.

Ours was a bed of nails. After Rob fell asleep, I got up again and spent the rest of the night writing about Eric's bittersweet life, not knowing the minister would read what I'd written at the funeral. It was just easier to write than lie there crying.

Chris went out the next day to the scene of Eric's crash.

He went alone, climbing the hill to find the place where he'd landed. It wasn't hard: scuffled places in the brush, a torn-up look to the area. He stood there and could see how little extra space Eric had needed, a foot at most. Down on his hands and knees, Chris searched the ground — why, he didn't know. And that was when he found the pennies that had fallen out of Eric's pocket. He didn't leave much behind, Chris thought — a couple of pennies to mark the spot.

Bobby came home. Safe.

The days blurred, became fleeting images which I recall with effort until they fall out of memory to blend into one sadness-shrouded period.

But one image remains, starkly clear: Eric lying under a sheet at the mortuary.

Why do we go, yet how can we not?

Rob and I crept into the room fearfully and saw him lying there, his face as sweet and calm as we remembered, unmarked by trauma. He seemed only asleep.

His wavy hair fell on the pillow, looking as I'd always known it — too long. Eric, I thought, too long is all right, I don't mind your long hair . . . wear it down to your knees if you want.

His shoulder — cold to the touch, like wax.

Only traitors would walk out and leave him there.

CHRIS: I keep remembering all these details about how it was after Eric died. Like Bobby coming home. He stood on our front porch in a wrinkled shirt. His chin was dark—probably days since he'd shaved—and his eyes, which normally drooped some at the corners, seemed to droop more than ever. All I could think was how tired he looked. He said, "Hi," but I could hardly hear him.

Mom flew at him and hugged him, then grabbed the suitcase out of his hand. But he just stood there, slumped. Six-three and all of it discouraged. He said, "Why couldn't Eric wait, huh? I could have taught him right. Why couldn't he wait—just another three days?"

What could I say?

The next day Saddleback Mortuary brought Eric back to our town, and by myself I went down to the funeral home to see him. Then I couldn't do it, couldn't bring myself to look at him that way, so I wandered into the casket room instead because Dad had said if I was going to be there I might as well start helping him choose.

The place was a joke. They called it the Slumber Room. All those decked-out boxes, satin and stuff and little cards with prices, like we were choosing one to go in the living room. I wandered around. Copper. Silver. Burnished steel. Gray. Varnished wood. Even a plain wooden box, which they kept kind of hidden. Yuck. I felt someone in the room and turned around. It was Bobby. "Ridiculous, huh?" I said.

He stood in the middle of the room with his hands in his pockets. "We're supposed to pick one of these things?"

"Somebody has to." I shrugged. "I'm not gonna do it, though. It's stupid. A big waste of money." I pointed to an ornate job in bronze. "That's seven hundred dollars!"

A funny look came over Bobby's face. "Remember the way Eric used to clip coupons and send away for all the free stuff? Wonder what he'd think of this."

"Not a whole lot. He'd think it's stupid, too."

Bobby leaned over a dull silver casket fitted out like a battleship. "You know what, Chris? It's sick. This whole business is a rip if you ask me." He began strolling around the room peering at all the price cards, and then under his breath he said, "A big fancy box for one day, just to look good at the funeral, and after that, who cares?" He shook his head and then he started with this little smile, a barely noticeable glint in his eyes. I knew that look, but I'd never expected to see it there. "I've got an idea, Chris." He tried to suppress the smile. "Maybe we oughta try rent-a-casket."

I didn't mean to laugh. I knew it wasn't something you do in a funeral home. But I did. Right there in the Slumber Room I started to laugh, and once I began I couldn't stop. And Bobby's being there made it worse, his laughing under his breath in his typical low-key way.

I wanted to go into the next room and apologize to Eric, tell him we weren't being disrespectful—which I think Eric would have known if he'd been there. But we'd turned on something we couldn't turn off, and the more we tried the worse it got, the two of us choking and making noises that didn't belong anywhere in the building. I could hardly breathe, trying to hold it in. Boy, if anyone had heard us, we'd have been thrown out for breaking up all that hushed quiet. Between us, we nearly blotted out the piped-in organ music.

When we finally calmed down, we edged toward the door like a couple of burglars, sneaking looks to see if anyone was watching. I peered around the door jamb. Bobby was right behind me.

"Nobody in sight," I said. "We can go."

He stood poised, throwing one last look back at all the coffins. "Seven hundred bucks to impress people at the church—and if you asked Eric, all he'd want is the money!" He gave me a shove, laughing again. "Make a run for it, Chris!" A few fast steps and we exploded into the California sunshine.

The funeral was a big surprise. None of us knew Eric had so many friends. They were all ages and they kept coming and coming—until the line in front of the church was a block long and people were left standing outside.

I suppose we could have guessed. Eric was one of those guys that just never told you everything he was doing. And part of what he was doing, it turns out, was making a lot of friends we never knew about.

MARALYS: We bought a pine tree for Eric's grave and Rob ordered a plaque which read, "Gentle Man of Mirth, We Miss You." Our family went alone to the cemetery, listened to the words of our minister, stared at the flowers heaped over Eric's coffin, and afterwards walked slowly toward the car.

I found myself looking around for him so we could go home. I never could count to six — I'd driven off quite a few times without one or another of my children. For a moment it seemed I'd done it again.

31

MARALYS: Our world was on hold, a fork in the road where we all stood doubting and torn, waiting to see which path we'd take. It was odd, I thought later, how we remained there a full four days without anybody saying a word — without so much as a question raised. Would we go on with our hang gliding business or not?

The problem was, the question was obscene.

After Eric's death, how could we talk callously and calmly about the sport that killed him? How could we go back to the shop, pretending that it was business as usual? This wasn't war, where people drop and the war goes on. It was our son. Our family. The core of our lives.

But it was more. It was also Chris and, to an even greater extent, Bobby, whose love of flying superseded all that he did.

So, when we gathered in our living room after we returned from the cemetery, our thoughts were separate, yet all alike. What were we going to do next?

In the end we had to go on — for Bobby's sake we couldn't do anything else. As a family we recognized a simple truth: to pull Bobby out of hang gliding would be to shred up a new and hard-won life. Bobby had finally found a career that fit his talents, and he had nothing else to fall back on.

When I finally looked in on the shop again, Ram was sitting at Eric's desk, and it gave me a start. He looked up and smiled. "So here I am." It sounded like an apology. I thought, *You can't help it if you're not Eric.*

Our checkbook was in his hands, and in front of him was a page filled with columns of figures. "Looka here, Maralys, what do you make of this?" He pointed to a column, and I shook my head. Of all Ram's quirky and interesting qualities, his handwriting ranked near the bottom. Right next to his spelling.

"What are you trying to tell me, Ram?"

"Only that a thousand dollars is missing." He squinted down at his numbers and picked up the page for a better look. "I've been working on this all day. And a check is gone too. I don't know if Eric had it or what."

"How could we lose a thousand dollars?"

"I dunno. Our check register shows we have it, but the bank says we don't."

Preoccupied, I sat down and glanced idly through the checkbook, then looked over the deposit book. I was thankful Ram couldn't see my face because I felt it happening again, tears filling my eyes. Damn! It was hard enough, Eric's being gone, but now this problem, too . . . and we couldn't even ask him about it. The mocking cruelty of death struck me again as I sat there looking at Eric's work. With what suddenness death removes its victim from your questions — so discouraging that whatever he carried away in his head you could never get back. Neither him nor anything he knew.

When I was silent, Ram said, "Well, maybe the answer will turn up."

"I hope so." I stood up, feeling old. I couldn't stay any longer, I said.

"Will you be coming back?"

"I suppose I will."

He said he'd hold the place together until I got there, and

I realized it had already been more than a week. March 16, 1974, it happened. How well I knew the date. Sometimes I'd had to stop and remember the children's birth dates. I never thought I'd have to remember one of their death dates too.

As I walked toward the door, I tried to summon concern about the missing check and the missing thousand dollars. But what did they matter . . . really?

Routine was comforting. When I went back to the office, I found myself swept quickly into the mundane chores I'd done before. I cleaned the bathroom, picked metal filings out of the shag carpet, talked to customers on the phone, answered the mail.

Ram took over Eric's job as office manager. But it was a struggle. As brilliant as he was in other ways, Ram had simply never learned to write. Whatever he scribbled onto paper nobody could read, including himself. Clearly his forte was not bookwork. But for now he did it without complaining. Bobby did most of the jobs in back, and up front we talked of improving our systems so Ram's handwriting wouldn't matter so much. Meanwhile, we continued to stew about the missing check and the missing thousand dollars.

Then, about a week later, the mailman brought us a parcel. I opened the small package, unthinking, though I should have suspected something from the postmark—San Bernardino. When the lid came off the box, tears welled in my eyes. In it lay Eric's wallet, a scruffy thing without much inside. Just a picture of Shelley and a dollar. And also the missing check with a stub which showed a deposit—a thousand dollars. We checked the date, then the check register, and suddenly the mysteries were cleared up. Eric had simply written his thousand dollar deposit twice.

"So it's not lost," Ram said.

"No," I said, fingering Eric's wallet. "It isn't lost." But you are, Eric. How long will everything remind me of you?

285

We kept the business going, waiting for Chris to finish his quarter at UCLA and come back. Gradually, with warmer weather, people bought more hang gliders.

We asked Shelley to come work for us, which she did for a short time, answering letters and keeping records as well as I. But she soon left again. "I can't hack it, Maralys. The memories are too much."

One day in early April, Chris called. "Did you hear about Pat Conniry?"

"What about him?" I asked, dreading to hear. Pat had flown in the Nationals against our boys.

Chris said grimly, "Killed. Yesterday, on an experimental hang glider."

"Oh, God." It began to seem like war.

Soon afterward Rob suggested that the U.S. Hang Gliding Association form an accident review board, and at the next monthly meeting they voted to make him chairman. For the next eight years all the tragedies of hang gliding would pass through Rob's hands.

As dismal as the job was for him, Rob had a definite effect on the sport. The more he wrote about the trends and causes of accidents, the more the accident rate went down. Through Rob's articles in *Hang Gliding Magazine* went a steady, insistent drumbeat: Read this and learn.

People did. And gradually the sport became safer.

It was late April. Bobby worked in the back somberly, not flying very much.

I hadn't seen Jeremy since the funeral when she sat in the pew with Bobby, her fingers lightly touching his hand. She'd come back to the house afterward, staying only a short time. Now I supposed he saw her in his spare hours, though it was just a guess. His thoughts were unreadable in a face that was set in hard, drawn-together lines. He worked long hours but without zest, coming and going without any of his usual games. I sensed that he and Ram were almost ready to let the business go, though neither actually said so. I still came in, but sporadically.

Our paperwork deteriorated. Ram proposed some of the formal bookkeeping systems he'd learned in college, which I, for one, didn't understand. I said, "Let's just keep our records like we've always done, okay? We seem to get by."

"Do we?" he asked with raised eyebrows.

"Well, we would if we could decipher more of your work."

Finally Rob drew the obvious conclusion that we ought to give up trying to turn Ram into an office manager, and Ram told me frankly he hadn't liked it anyway. He was bored with talking to all the idiots on the phone.

"Really?" I said. "I thought that's what you liked most — collecting gossip."

"That's not what we get on our phone," he said shortly. "We get dumb questions."

So we hired someone else to replace Eric — thin, curly-haired, quick-thinking Roy, who ate Twinkies and Cokes for lunch — Ram called them "Roy's vitamins" — and was apt to burst into a singsong wail whenever our dealers annoyed him, which they did frequently.

Soon after he'd taken over, Ram took me aside. "Now that we know Roy is slightly nuts, I think he'll fit right in."

Ram returned to doing wire sets in back, and we all settled in to await the return of summer and Chris.

June came, the bright warm days of late spring coaxing forth the scent of orange blossoms to permeate the long evenings. One day the postman brought us a parcel from Hawaii. Even before I opened it, I noticed an odd smell emanating from the brown wrapping paper — an odor of something musty and old, which intensified as I pulled off the wrappings. When the last layer came off, the smell was quite unbelievable, but I hardly noticed because I was holding something I never expected to see again — Bobby's lost wallet! He'd had it last flying over a meadow on Haleakala, nine months earlier.

I was dumbfounded. Not only was the wallet reasonably intact, but all the money was inside — two hundred dollars in limp, mildewed bills. It was the worst-smelling money I'd ever encountered. The enclosed note named the cowboy who'd found it, and to that honest man we sent an enormous package of all the California goodies we could gather.

In a way I associated that wallet with Eric — as though *something* precious from those good days had come back to us. God sending us a little message: you haven't lost everything; this is Hope, and it's from Me.

Chris came back, bringing a sense of order to our place. And his boundless optimism — that was back too, infusing us all with new energy.

In the weeks before school was out Chris had been approached by Twentieth Century Fox for consultation on a hang gliding movie. He reported confidently, "It's just a matter of time until Wills Wing gets the flying assignments." Meanwhile he went to meetings in Hollywood, discussing feasibility with producers and the chosen cinematographers, Jim Freeman and Greg MacGillivray.

How Eric would have loved this, I thought — Eric, always looking for the Big Deal.

Gradually Bobby's grimness faded, and he drove himself to design a new kite to fit the radically different sail design Ramsey Price had sketched on one of our brick walls. As though his energy had been too long pent up, Bobby worked into the night designing a frame for the kite, developing new cable sets, even dreaming up extra supports for the leading edges in case the kite went inverted.

One morning Ram found him sitting on a chair in the middle of the sail floor, staring at his new sail pattern as though in a trance. He didn't turn when Ram came in.

"Christ, Bobby," Ram said, "that sail pattern's a whole different shape since I saw it last. You been here all night?" He'd been sitting in the same chair when Ram left the evening before.

Yes, Bobby said, he had.

In the ensuing weeks, arguments once again raged in back: the new kite needed different wing posts . . . it was too large . . . it wasn't large enough . . . it needed better hardware . . . the sail panels were being cut wrong.

After the others had left one night, I said to Ram, "You and Bobby and Chris sure argue a lot."

He gave me one of his impish grins. "Yeah, we do. But we've got this theory about ourselves: if any one of us can convince another he's right about something, then those two have the answer and the third has to go along. It works every time." He laughed. "Together we're a genius."

Just before he flew the new kite for the first time, Bobby sketched the design for Rob on the back of an envelope. Rob said, "It looks like a swallowtail butterfly."

Bobby burst out laughing. "Thanks, Dad! That's just the name we've been looking for!"

And then Bobby took his kite out for its maiden run and later that day pulled his green truck into the back alley with a monumental squealing of tires. He exploded into the office yelling in a way I hadn't heard since before Eric died, his arms and legs all on the move at once. "You shoulda been there, Chris. You guys are gonna love it! Price, it's got so much performance you won't believe it! Performance! Boy, it's about twice as good as anything we've ever had before!" No competition win had ever elicited such excitement. It was as though while he was telling us about this wonderful machine — how long he'd stayed aloft, how much farther he'd gone, how easily it handled — he'd had a vision of flying revolutionized. To Bobby, that kite transcended any of his other triumphs.

For hours, laughing excitedly, Bobby extolled its virtues

to Chris and Ram, and when they'd heard it all, he got on the phone and called other flyers.

The next day when he came into the shop he had Jeremy in tow. She smiled at me happily. "It's good to see him like this, isn't it?"

For a short while we moved into a solid lead ahead of our competitors. With a naivete born of having a competent man to support me, I supposed we'd be instantly profitable, even rich enough to pay the boys decent salaries at last. I pictured us replacing Bobby's old green truck, which had cost us five times its original price in repairs. The Swallowtail kite was going to change everything.

But it didn't happen. And Bobby, with his trusting nature, was partly to blame.

32

MARALYS: We should have known. Anyone but us would have questioned the wisdom of Bobby's giving Martin Blizzard free run of our shop — especially once we'd developed the Swallowtail . . . and more especially when we saw the way Blizzard examined our jigs in detail and asked questions no dealer needed to know. Full of enthusiasm, Bobby walked him around the back. But there was an air of condescension about Blizzard while he picked up this tool, examined that half-finished kite, as though he were the final judge of everything we did.

All the time Blizzard was prowling around, Chris ignored him, but Ram kept looking up from his wire sets and jabbing at Blizzard with small, pointed questions. "So what're ya gonna do, Martin, go home and build one?"

Blizzard gave him a quick, hostile look.

"Well, it won't do you any good, even *we* mess up about half of what we build!"

Bobby literally rounded on him. "What did you say a dumb thing like that for, Price?"

Ram was sheepish. "Well, we do mess up a lot of sails . . ."

"A few," Bobby said indignantly. "Not half."

Ram shrugged. "I just don't want any of our dealers getting ideas."

Angry, Bobby looked toward Chris for support, but

Chris stayed determinedly busy.

I watched from the doorway as Blizzard strolled to Ram's workbench and picked up a wire set, turning it over speculatively. "There's nothing you can do if someone wants to copy your stuff, Price. They can do it any time they want."

For once Ram didn't say anything.

"So you might as well cool it."

When Bobby and Blizzard reached the front office, Roy was gone, so they asked me to gather up some literature.

Hands full of our brochures, Martin paused to say one last thing—in a tone so deceptively casual it took Bobby and me seconds to know we'd been shot at. "Spitfire's been copying your standard kites, you know."

We went on closing up, and then Bobby stopped dead in the middle of the room. "Who's Spitfire?"

I stopped too. What was he getting at?

"Oh . . ." Blizzard waved his hand, passing it off. "They're nobody. I've sold some of their kites."

I said, "You're selling for them too?" Supposedly he sold exclusively for us. That was Bobby's understanding also, and he stared at his friend, more puzzled than angry.

I said, "Why would you sell for *them*?"

Blizzard knew he'd made a mistake. "Don't worry about it, guys. Their stuff's not as good as yours." As if that were the issue.

"Spitfire . . ." Bobby stood rubbing the back of his neck, clearly bewildered. "Who's running it?"

Blizzard had his hand on the doorknob. "Nobody. Nobody you'd know."

Taking a couple of long strides across the room, Bobby blocked him at the door. "Look, Martin, I don't know who these Spitfire guys are, and if they've copied our standard kites, it probably doesn't matter any more. We're about through making them, anyway. But don't let them copy the Swallowtail."

I thought, *He's begging Blizzard*! Yet I still found myself echoing, "We've spent a lot of money developing that kite, and time too. It wouldn't be fair." *We're practically on our knees here, pleading for our lives.*

"Don't worry, you guys." Martin laughed. "I'd never let them do that." Imagining he'd reassured us, he left.

Bobby strode into the back, and I stood there with the conversation ringing in my head. Let them. Since when did Martin Blizzard let — or not let — some other company copy our designs? What was he anyway, the overseer of kite-copying? Why had he even brought it up? Nothing made sense, and I had the feeling Martin had, in some way, been toying with us.

Then I heard shouting, and going back to investigate, I found Chris nowhere in sight and Bobby yelling at Ram: ". . . and also what did you say those stupid things for, huh? You trying to make enemies, Price? Martin's selling a lot of kites!"

Ram said, "He was just too interested in everything. I'm suspicious."

Bobby hung right over Price's bench. "Sure he's interested, why wouldn't he be? He's gotta know what he's selling! Sometimes your mouth gets too big! Martin could get mad and quit, and we need all the dealers we can get. So next time he's here, shut up!"

"Oh pipe down," Ram said. "He won't get mad at you anyway, just me. If I'm wrong about him, so I'm wrong."

I felt obliged to speak up. "Remember, Bobby, Dad hated that guy from the beginning. Maybe we *shouldn't* tell him everything we know."

For the first time in years Bobby advanced on me, and for a fleeting instant his fists were up. "Why don't you stay out of it, huh?" he shouted with his big face next to mine. "Keep your opinions out of this, and Dad's too. Neither one of you knows what's going on. Sometimes I wish you weren't working here, you just get in the way!"

Furious, I said, "Watch it, Bobby! You can't afford to

alienate Dad and me, we — "

"Then don't be butting in!" He gave me a push.

I pushed him right back. "Don't *ever* do that! Don't even *touch* me! Now or any time!" I faced him down with my fists clenched. Nose-to-nose we stared at each other for seconds, both insanely angry. And then it all seemed futile and discouraging, so I gave up and went back into the office.

"WHY DON'T YOU GET OUT OF THIS BUSINESS?" Bobby bellowed after me. "WE DON'T NEED YOU HERE!" In the distance I heard the thumping of the back door.

All that time Ramsey Price went on working as though he'd heard nothing.

I was at my desk crying. And then Chris was there, standing in the doorway. "I was coming in from the alley as Bobby left. Don't take it too hard, Mom."

I picked up my purse and began rummaging inside. There had to be a Kleenex there somewhere. "Do the rest of you feel this way?"

Chris shook his head and stood close to my desk. "No, Mom. We need you. Just ignore Bobby. Right now he's out of control."

"I thought he'd changed."

"It's a lapse, that's all. He hasn't been like this in a while."

My things were gathered, ready to go home. But I paused a minute longer to soak up some of Chris's natural warmth. "When Bobby *wants* to be mean, he sure is an expert."

Chris nodded. "But it isn't often, Mom. Not any more."

For no reason that Chris could explain, Hollywood stopped calling, and we heard no more about the hang gliding movie. When I inquired, Chris said, "I don't *know* how long it's been. I haven't kept track." I suspected he *had* kept track but didn't want to talk about it. And he preferred not to discuss his medical school applications either. The replies had been coming to our house for some time, and every few days I'd hand him some, saying only, "Here's another batch, Chris."

With permission to open them, I'd know by the first few words what the answer would be.

"We're sorry to inform you. . ."

"Due to the large number of applicants . . ."

"Regrettably, our openings for this year . . ."

I read them and Chris read them and Betty-Jo read them, and the only comment among the lot of us was Betty-Jo saying, "Well, there are twenty-seven more still out."

July. Martin Blizzard had moved to Nevada, where his customers in the Reno area flew east off Slide Mountain. I happened to be alone in the front office the day a Dudley Piedmont called from nearby Carson City, asking about his new kite. He had a puny voice, which sounded ever punier as he said that his Swallowtail sail had been stitched twice and didn't look very good. "Could you send me a new one?"

"What do you mean, stitched twice?" I asked, having no idea what he was talking about.

Ram, who happened to walk in just then, glanced at me with a question mark.

"The sail has holes in it," the man said. "You can see where somebody stitched it and then ripped out the old threads and did it over. It looks very bad." For all that explanation, he didn't sound convinced himself.

"Just a minute," I said, putting my hand over the phone. "It's one of Blizzard's customers," I explained to Ram, "who says his sail has been double-stitched. Do you know what he's talking about?"

Ram frowned. "Get his number, Maralys. Tell him you'll call him back." So I did.

And then Ram was pacing the room. "I *know* that sail. We haven't sold so many these days. I cut it, in fact, and looked it over after it was sewn. Hell, I remember watching them put it on the frame . . ." He stopped, suddenly agitated. "I'll bet I know who did it! Call him back."

I did, and asked quickly before the man had a chance to think, "Mr. Piedmont, who *really* double-stitched that sail?"

He must have been caught off-guard because he mumbled "Well . . .," and I said, "Did Martin Blizzard do it?"

Unbelievably, he whispered, "Yes," and I said, "Why?"

"He needed a pattern."

"For what?"

"For his own Swallowtails." The man's voice was now so low he was barely audible.

I put my hand over the phone. "Blizzard's making Swallowtails." Ram just stared at me. Into the phone I said, "Then why are you asking us for another sail when it was your dealer who stitched it twice?"

"Martin Blizzard told me to."

Holding the phone away, I locked eyes with Ram and raised my eyebrows. I was speechless. It was the kind of statement you could hear but not believe you'd heard it. I said again, "Why?"

No answer, so I asked, "He wants another sail. Is that it?"

"I guess so." The customer was quite unhappy.

"What's he doing for *you*, Mr. Piedmont? Is he paying you?"

"Not exactly." The voice had faded again and was scarcely above a whisper. "He's just taking something off the kite—giving me a discount."

It was all so incredible, and the man was such a weakling—a dupe for whoever happened to push him at the moment—I felt he'd do anything I asked. So I said, "Would you be willing to sign a statement? I promise we'll make it worth your while."

He said he would, but when he gave me his address, I was certain he'd back out before putting anything on paper — because by then he'd have spoken to our dear friend, Martin Blizzard. Telling him we'd be in touch, I let him go. It was like throwing your biggest fish back in the river.

After I'd told Ram the parts he couldn't hear, Ram said, "You can be sure Blizzard'll scare him out of signing anything. Blizzard controls Slide Mountain, you know. Only his people can fly from it. I've heard the stories. He threatens people he doesn't like."

"Oh, come on, Ram. Your grapevine's got a disease."

"Don't laugh," he said. "It's true."

Suddenly I had an idea. "Let's see what Blizzard has to say."

And then Martin and I were talking. Our conversation was brief, me asking if he'd taken our Swallowtail sail apart, him saying he had because it needed fixing. "Did you trace our sail on your floor?" I felt him drawing up short. And suddenly I understood. *"You own Spitfire!* . . . You *are* Spitfire!"

His answer was innocent, as smooth as silk. "I have an interest in it, that's all. It belongs to someone else."

"Who?"

"It doesn't matter who."

"It matters to us," I said, trembling with anger. Pausing just long enough for a very large breath, I said, "You know what, Martin? Your customer just told us everything, everything we needed to know, and you're the biggest crook that ever set foot in hang gliding!" And I hung up on him.

"Asshole!" said Price.

Soon afterwards Chris and Bobby came in together, and Ram and I told them they'd better sit down because they weren't going to believe what we had to say.

As we talked, Bobby was resistant, not wanting to believe

our story. He tried to interrupt once or twice, but Ram and I wouldn't let him. We took turns pouring it out until he'd heard it all. As for Chris, he didn't seem surprised.

After we'd finished, Bobby said, "I taught him to fly. I never held back anything." He said it without spirit, without energy. Ram and Chris and I were outraged. But Bobby was depressed. "I was good to that guy."

I said, "I don't think I've ever hated anyone more than I hate Martin Blizzard."

"What about his partner?" Chris asked.

Ram said, "I'm going to find out who it is — if he has one."

It was Roy, the next day, who offered the final word on the subject. "Maybe we should put a contract out on Blizzard," he said gleefully, "I know someone who'd relish the job."

"Who?" I asked.

With a flick of his curly head, he said, "Mr. Wills, that's who."

33

MARALYS: Rob, predictably unpredictable, took the news of Martin Blizzard calmly.

"Bobby's really down," I said. "He feels betrayed."

Rob didn't gloat or say we all should have listened to him. Instead he said, "I can understand how it's tough for Bobby. But one of these days Blizzard will get what's coming to him." His expression turned ironic. "There's a saying that fits this situation perfectly: 'Time wounds all heels.' I like to think it's true."

I was ready for Time to start doing its job.

When things go sour, I thought, they go sour everywhere at once.

Ramsey Price kept bringing us bulletins: "Blizzard's Swallowtails look exactly like ours — except they're a hundred dollars cheaper and fly like crap." He sleuthed out a mysterious sponsor, supposedly with unlimited funds — whose existence we doubted until we learned Blizzard's copies were being produced in a building three times the size of ours, with all the latest machinery.

As Ram summed up with an ironic smile, "Once you have money, all it takes is stealing a good design."

Our sales dipped again. The first flood of orders for Swallowtails slowed to a trickle, and the Twentieth Century Fox movie, which we'd once hoped would bail us out, disappeared like a shadow. Nobody knew why.

When even Chris's normal ebullience waned, I said, "Don't take it too hard, Chris. This business won't be your life forever."

"How do I know that?"

"You'll get into *one* of those medical schools, I'm sure of it."

But I wasn't sure. Half his applications had already been rejected, and there was no reason to believe anything would be different with the second half. Under the shower I composed imaginary letters to unknown admissions boards: "As his mother I realize I'll be considered biased, but . . ." My letter would be a little different with each shower but always full of anecdotes that would prove Chris was singularly imaginative, intelligent, and dextrous and likely to be the best surgeon since DeBakey.

I never sent any of them, of course.

Yet we hadn't reached our lowest point. That came when we learned through a tendril on Ram's grapevine that the movie wasn't actually dead after all—someone else had it. With the way things were going, it seemed a wonder that Blizzard didn't get that too, but he didn't.

Bill Bennett did.

Bill Bennett and his Delta Wing Kites and some Hollywood stunt men were going to make our movie instead of us. Ironically, the stunt men had learned what flying they knew from Bobby and Chris. Fox had already bought a number of Delta Wings, perfectly legitimate for them to do, Chris said glumly. And then Ram found out the studios were also arranging a test film with the kites and the stunt men. But *we* weren't going to be there.

For the second time I wanted to let our company go and return home for good. *You'd have been discouraged, Eric,* I thought. *It isn't turning out well at all.*

Bobby didn't want any questions, so he didn't confide in us that his relationship with Jeremy Tanner was sagging. We just didn't see her very much. And then, on a flying date, Jeremy had an accident, and for several weeks Bobby was out of the office more than in.

He came back briefly to tell us what had happened. Looking haggard, he said, "Maybe I shouldn't have let her fly that day because there wasn't much lift. But she thought she could do it and she ran hard and finally got airborne and went up to about 150 feet. I thought she was doing okay, but then I saw she wasn't straight in her seat. She kept fooling with it, trying to get it adjusted — so busy with that danged seat, she forgot to fly the kite. All of a sudden the wind turned her around and she flew right back into the hill, with all of us yelling at her." He looked away. "You know the rest."

Jeremy suffered compound fractures of the major bones in one leg and lesser fractures throughout her body. She was taken out by helicopter. For the first few days, Bobby kept vigil at the hospital day and night.

Sadly, their already-failing relationship drifted to an end soon after Jeremy's second surgery, and with Jeremy walking again Bobby returned to the shop, grim and silent.

One day I became aware of a strange man hanging around the back of our shop. With a youthful, eager face, short round torso, and short legs, he reminded me of one of those dolls you push over and it comes bobbing right back. Every time I saw him, he was huddled with Bobby and oblivious to the rest of us. If anyone tried to break in, he waited impatiently, as if we were an intrusion.

Peter Donawitz was there to push Bobby into building the Rube Goldberg of the decade: a flying motorcycle. "I used to think about doing this," Bobby said, "about using the forward speed of a motorcycle to get airborne and the sail of a kite to fly. But I just never did it."

I paid little attention to what was happening in back until Rob stopped by and said to me, "I wish you'd get that man out of there."

"Oh . . . Donawitz. Why?"

"Because he's wasting Bobby's time, and no good's going to come of it. Furthermore, I don't trust the man."

"But you only met him once —" I began and stopped, remembering Martin Blizzard. By whatever radar Rob homed in on a man's character, it was worth taking note of. I said, "Bobby does what he wants, Rob. You know that."

For days Bobby worked with Donawitz, mostly out of my view, while Ram and Chris made periodic irritable comments about "oddball stuff that has no practical value." Ram muttered, "It's not as if we could ever sell 'em."

Eventually Bobby carted the pieces of a sail down to our sailmaker and the next day left for Wisconsin to fly in the Northwest Regional hang gliding championships.

Calls came while he was gone, mostly Donawitz demanding to know when he'd be back. After one such call, Ram swore and said, "Donawitz is a pain. He acts like Bobby's got nothing to do but work on that flying murder cycle."

When at last Bobby strolled through the front door carrying another towering trophy, he hardly slowed to take note of the general excitement over his first-place win. "It worked out okay," he said, and placed the trophy on a high shelf next to the others. Then he was at my desk. "Mom, has the seamstress finished my sail?"

When I left that evening, Donawitz's big black Honda motorcycle was out in the alley, fitted with a jaunty sail held rigid by aluminum supports — rather like Rambo wearing a pink bonnet.

The project dropped out of sight until Bobby loped into the house one night with a can of film. "I brought you a movie, Mom and Dad. I think you're going to be surprised."

With Chris running the projector, we had a 16mm view of Bobby on a dry lake bed in the desert, literally "flying" a motorcycle off a small ramp and out into space, leaning over the handlebars like a jockey over the neck of his horse. When he came down softly, a dozen spectators charged across the lake bed after him and others danced in ecstatic circles, shaking their fists over their heads.

As for Bobby, he sat on his cycle waiting calmly. He'd known all along it would work.

"Well," Rob asked, "is Donawitz satisfied now?"

Bobby grinned. "Not yet, Dad, he's building a bigger ramp. He thinks we can set a world record and jump farther than anyone's ever jumped a motorcycle before — beat Evel Knievel by a mile and get all the publicity and money."

Rob just looked at him, and then he stood up and abruptly left the room.

Bobby's expression changed. "What's Dad all mad about now?"

I said, "He thinks what you're doing's dangerous."

Bobby shrugged. "If I ever get hurt, it's not gonna be on this."

Over the next several months Bobby flew the cycle some three hundred feet off a tall ramp at the Riverside Raceway, and later, with only the park's owner watching, he flew the cycle off the thousand-foot hill at Escape Country, a motorcycle and hang gliding park. Donawitz was furious that Bobby did this without publicity or photographers, and they began arguing about who would decide when and where it flew.

Bobby's relationship with Peter Donawitz gradually took an odd turn. Donawitz became as possessive as a lover, rebuffed and angry when Bobby reverted to giving our business more time. Peter wanted Bobby to go on tour with their fly-cycle, promising the venture would earn them thousands of dollars.

Bobby didn't think so. "There's no future in jumping for the public. I just wanted to prove a motorcycle could get airborne — and now I know it can."

Not long afterward we learned Donawitz had found another rider and was about to put on a demonstration at Escape Country. And then the park's owner turned up in our shop. A friend of Bobby's, Jim Robinson had a farmer's leathery, hills-and-valleys face and a laconic grin. "I heard you've put a much larger sail on your own motorcycle, Bobby. Why don't you come out and fly off against Donawitz's man? His flights are a joke."

Bobby's mood had been dark for weeks. "I don't think so, Jim. I've got a backlog of kites to test."

"Come on, Bobby, it's only for one day."

"What's the point?"

"The point is, you could jump against him and prove you're still the best. Hey, where's your competitive spirit? Think of the publicity, two flying wizards in the world's first jump-off. Think what it will mean to me — and to you."

Bobby looked away. "It won't help me any."

When Bobby finally decided to do it — the "competitive spirit" bit must have gotten to him — Donawitz called him at home and said, *"You'd better not,"* and the next day his lawyer phoned the shop with vague, unspecified threats.

Bobby called his Dad. "What can he do to me?"

"Nothing," said Rob, "unless he gets an injunction. But this is Friday afternoon and the courts are closing soon. Don't worry, Bobby, if you want to do this fly-off, you should."

As five o'clock arrived with no sign of an injunction, Bobby glanced at the clock, smiling. "I guess he was bluffing. I'm going home." The truck gunned out of the alley.

Then it happened. A bearded, aggressive-looking man came in the door and barked, "Where's Robert Wills?"

I froze. So did Roy at the next desk.

Bobby wasn't there, I said, and the man asked nastily when he'd be back. When I said I didn't know, he held out a wad of papers, which I ignored. We glared at each other briefly, and he turned to go. I thought it was over.

Not so. Hand on the doorknob, the man swung back and tossed his papers into the room. "You're served!" he said. And he was gone.

The silence was stunning. Roy stared at the floor and so did I. Roy said, "Well . . . what do we do with them?"

"Nothing. We just leave them there."

As I stood to leave, detouring wide around the malevolent bundle, Roy smiled. "Too bad he threw 'em in the middle. They could burn a hole in the rug."

Saturday Rob and I headed for Escape Country.

"Do you think they'll let him jump, Rob? With that injunction sitting on our office floor?"

"Who knows about it, Babe, except Donawitz?"

After forty minutes of driving through undeveloped oak country, we reached the official entrance. The dream of its founder-owner, Jim Robinson, Escape Country was a ranch comprised of thousands of acres set among the brown hills of south Orange County. People came to camp, hike, ride motorcycles, fish, bicycle, and fly hang gliders. In its first year of offering hang gliding, Bobby had been given a free pass, a privilege later extended to Ram and Chris.

Inside, we found mobs of people and the symbolic rows of colored pennants flapping gaily in the breeze. It reminded me of the Nationals, and suddenly Rob began walking faster and shaking his fingers.

After a brief search we found Bobby sitting astride his motorcycle solemnly fielding questions from an eager crowd. The sail was over his head, a yellow thunderbolt zigzagging across a red field. In a blue mesh shirt, duck-billed helmet, and motorcycle boots, Bobby was like a rajah holding court under his canopy.

As we came closer, I caught a glimpse of the launching ramp, and my heart almost stopped. Midway down an almost-perpendicular hill, was a wooden ramp so large it looked capable of launching him into orbit. I couldn't believe its size or the way it reached out into space. It had to be six feet tall!

Rob saw it too and frowned. But he said casually, "Hello, Bobby."

Bobby acknowledged us with a small nod, and I edged in closer, wanting to discuss that ramp with him — had he known it would be so high . . . that the hill leading down to it would be so steep? I wanted to point out that only a madman would consider launching off *that*!

But we were obviously past such questions — and Bobby had always been a little mad. Instead I said something inane, like good luck, and he said something equally meaningless back and I thought, The bigger the moment, the more trivial the words.

Just as the loudspeaker crackled into life with welcomes and announcements, a man appeared from nowhere and stood in front of Bobby's cycle, legs spread à la John Wayne. "You Robert Wills?" he growled, and a hand shot out with papers that looked sickeningly familiar.

Bobby went blank. His face emptied of expression, and he turned his head away as though he'd heard and seen nothing.

Rob and I stood transfixed. Around us the crowd shrank back perceptibly.

"Here . . ." The man waved the papers at Bobby as one might wave a bone at a dog.

Face averted, Bobby gripped his handlebars tighter and said nothing.

"You're served!" the man said, and threw his bundle in the dirt at Bobby's feet. For a long moment Bobby sat there with his blank stare. Then he quietly pushed the motorcycle away.

"Bastard!" Rob said.

I half expected to see a policeman next, with billy club and handcuffs, but none materialized.

Partway up the savage hill, Dick Larkin, the other cyclist, prepared for flight. He tugged at his clothes and adjusted his helmet. Then he climbed aboard his motorcycle and, in a sudden hush from the crowd, gunned his motor and raced down the hill and onto the launching ramp. In seconds he was off, flying through the air on his motorcycle as quietly as any kite. For a short time he floated, held up by the sail, while the crowd remained silent as death. A brief journey through space and the gap closed and he settled back to earth—though it was more as if the earth rose to meet him.

He came down fast and he wasn't prepared.

As he hit, the front wheel of the motorcycle spun crosswise and the cycle tipped over. The crowd gasped. The pedal dug into the ground, the machine slewed, and the man flew off. On its side, the cycle skidded across the landing area, digging a furrow in the ground.

Men in the area leaped out of the cycle's path and others chased after it and ran it to ground. The cyclist got to his feet slowly, made a halfhearted attempt to brush himself off, and hobbled away.

Rob said, "This is insane!"

The loudspeaker came alive. "He's all right, folks, he's fine! We're measuring now. Ah! He jumped 262 feet. A very good jump. And now we have the challenger, Robert Wills!"

Beside me, Rob groaned. His jaw was hard, his lips a thin line. I didn't need to ask what he was thinking.

How typical, I thought, Rob's fear becomes anger, mine makes me weak. Trembling inside, I searched for Bobby and found him poised high on the face of the hill. For a split second he seemed frozen there, his body inclined over his motorcycle in that moment of concentration I'd come to recognize as intense focusing. One moment he was motionless. The next, a blur of action.

He came fast. Accelerated. Stretched out over his handlebars to reduce drag, reached for more and more speed, extended to the limit.

Lying low, he hit the ramp and leaned back. The wing began lifting and the wheels left the ground even before the ramp ended.

Like a great bird, the motorcycle sailed above the hill. Under the sail Bobby leaned forward again, reaching, urging the machine to greater distance.

The sail fluttered, the cycle floated and floated. I wanted to look away but couldn't. Inside, I was screaming silently. It was bizarre, a fantasy.

I felt his peril and my heart pounded with fear, but the fascination remained. Bobby was up so long it took on an unrealistic, dreamlike quality . . . he seemed more than human — impervious to natural law.

Then, as Bobby eased off, moving to the back of his seat and slowing pulling up the front, his machine settled to earth on its rear tire as gently, as smoothly as any of his foot-launched landings — one light tire-kiss and both tires were down. The cycle rushed ahead fast and straight.

A dozen more yards and Bobby stopped and put down the kick stand. He got off and stood next to his machine, waiting.

People ran to him, laughed and cheered, banged him on the back.

Bobby took it as matter-of-factly as he always took such things; calmness and solemnity were his trademarks.

I had a strange reaction: I began to cry.

The announcer told us he'd jumped 323 feet. A world record. Not even close to any other, better than Evel Kneival with all his Snake Rivers and rockets.

My mind took in the facts, and some part of me rejoiced. But it wasn't the facts that mattered. It was Bobby standing there by his cycle afterwards in one perfect, whole, undamaged piece.

Though Rob never said so, I sensed there came a time when he finally thought it was worth it . . . from the secure position of looking back, of knowing Bobby hadn't been killed.

But it was the last time Bobby would ever ride his motorcycle-kite in public. Sometime later, when Bobby had a chance to ride for millions of eyes, Donawitz pursued him with threats, court orders, and legal maneuvering. Rob fought back, tried to prove to the court the injustice of what Donawitz was doing. It was hopeless. Donawitz just kept coming with more papers, more injunctions, and, in the meantime, Bobby couldn't ride.

When it was finally decided by the court that Donawitz's claims had been unfair, that Bobby was equally entitled to the use of their joint invention, it no longer mattered.

34

MARALYS: Bobby's record motorcycle jump was an isolated triumph in a grim summer. I couldn't quite put away my grief over Eric. Just when I'd have a few days without missing him so much, I'd be called on to search through our old bills, and I'd find his familiar handwriting spread roundly across a page. The look of it brought him back: his patience, his dry, laconic personality. A tight feeling would start in my throat, and I'd wonder again what we were all doing there, carrying on without him.

Bobby had his grief too, burdens greater than mine. He'd lost Eric *and* Jeremy, and it told on him. His usually somber face seemed longer those days. He worked quietly in back, hardly bothering to argue with the other boys. It was as if he couldn't muster enough spirit to get involved.

One day I said to him, "I'm sorry about Jeremy. I know how you miss her."

"I'm not sure you do, Mom." It wasn't an argument, just a statement of fact.

Our problems had a certain fairness about them, in that everybody had his special source of disappointment. For Chris it was failing to get into medical school. The last of the forty-two rejection letters came in, flat no's all the way, in spite of a few interviews.

Like Bobby, Chris mostly kept his feelings to himself, reacting to each rejection with stony silence. It was only from Betty-Jo that I learned Chris planned to apply all over again the following year. "I was sure he wouldn't give up," she said, "but after he graduates, two quarters from now, you know where he'll be—working in the shop."

So he might spend his life running Wills Wing after all! Oh Lord.

Summer dragged into fall, with our sales on par with everything else. Since Martin Blizzard had, a few months after stealing our Swallowtail design, actually boasted about his deeds in a national publication, with the justification, "Bobby's all right, but I never did care for the rest of them," I often fantasized various fitting ends for him, such as murder by an irate lover. And then I thought, No, no, justice would be served much better if he killed *himself*—in the act of another theft. And I worked out a tidy plot, whereby Blizzard steals another of our kites and takes it to a mountain for testing, and Bobby, aware that the kite has problems, races up the mountain to stop him. Meanwhile Blizzard, seeing Bobby coming, rushes to get off the mountain, but in his hurry fails to hook his harness into the kite. In the end Bobby watches in horror as Blizzard flails his way down the mountain, desperately hanging on to the control bar until his arms give out. Then he falls to his death. As I finish the scene, I realize it is more "justice" than any of us want, so Ram says, "Why didn't he live—so we could beat him up?"

I always thought I'd use that scene some day. But when I had my chance, I realized getting even with Martin Blizzard wasn't worth telling a whopper of a lie.

For a while Ram reported regularly on what he could glean of Twentieth Century Fox's preparations for its test film, but he soon stopped mentioning it. None of us wanted to know.

Increasingly, Rob and I looked to the other children for

our encouraging moments. Kenny had been offered swimming scholarships at Stanford, UCLA, and Tennessee, and after much soul-searching chose UCLA, hoping ultimately to go to law school. Over the last few years Kenny had become less wasplike, more thoughtful. His non-swimming hours found him flopped on his bed reading books with unexciting titles like *The Essays of Ralph Waldo Emerson*.

Tracy was now working hard at her tennis, having learned to inject all of her five feet, eleven inches into a forehand return of serve that blistered over the net like a jai-alai ball. The ball didn't always land in the court, but you had to admire its speed. Never without a boyfriend, Tracy won brownie points from Rob and me when she told us after a school dance that she'd singled out one of the shorter, shyer boys and asked him to dance because "nobody else would do it."

Of the three younger children, only Kirk seemed to be losing his way. Though his tennis was better than ever, he'd lost his fight, sometimes dumping matches when he seemed to have them won. His schoolwork had slipped too. Ready to enter high school, he brought from junior high grades that were mediocre or worse. Rob and I kept assuming he'd soon do better. It would be years before we learned his brother's death had hit him harder than anyone knew.

On a Friday in late November, the photographer Greg MacGillivray called our shop asking for Bobby and, learning he was out testing kites, asked that I give him a message when he got back. It was urgent, Greg said.

Naturally my curiosity boiled right to the surface, and the minute Bobby ambled in the door with a kite on his shoulder, I was after him.

"Did Greg tell you what he wants?"

"No, but maybe it's something good."

"I doubt it," Bobby said, and picked up the phone.

Minutes later his face changed. His eyebrows went up and he said, "Yeah?" Then he smiled.

I watched him hopefully.

"Sure," he said, "I can be there. Sure, Greg. Sunday night. With all my stuff." He paused, a brief hesitation. "Hey, and thanks. I hope it works out too."

Bobby swung around laughing. "They're making the test film early Monday morning, Mom — Twentieth Century Fox — to decide if they really want to make a full-length movie. Greg told them he didn't want to do it without me, so they said okay, bring me along."

"Bobby! That's great!"

And then Chris was there and Bobby was telling him the good news.

"Yeah?" Chris said. But his tone was merely polite.

"I'm going to do it, Chris. We're going out to Palomar Sunday night." Bobby moved through the office restlessly. "He said I should lay low, not cause any waves, just let the producers see for themselves how I fly."

Chris shrugged. "It's better than nothing, I guess. At least they'll see you fly circles around the stunt men." He wasn't expecting any miracles. He'd been closer to the movie than this once before.

Bobby said, "That Greg is one loyal guy."

When Chris didn't respond, Bobby said, "What happened wasn't Greg's fault — or even Fox's fault. The Hollywood stunt men claimed they could do anything we could do and they're part of the union and we're not, so the studios were forced to use them for the flying scenes."

"What about all those Bennett kites?"

"You know how Bennett has been catering to them." Bobby grinned. "I guess they got 'em cheaper than ours."

Chris absently picked up one of our order sheets. "Go ahead out there, Bobby. Maybe your flying can do what my talking couldn't."

"Gee, Chris, I thought you'd be excited."

Chris made a face. "They screwed us before, and they'll probably try to screw us again." And he walked out of the room.

A little life experience thrown in here, I thought, tempering Chris's normal, irrepressible optimism. Most people would call it being realistic.

35

CHRIS: I should have told it to him straight, "Bobby, don't get your hopes up — except for Greg and Jim, you can't trust the people in Hollywood out of your sight."

But he knew. He could see what I was thinking.

One day out there, I thought, and that would be the end of it. He would out-fly the stunt men easy enough — they were rank beginners — but they'd somehow maneuver behind the scenes to get us excluded. We'd told the filmmakers from the start the stunt guys wouldn't be safe in the same airspace with helicopters. And they'd told *us* the job was ours. Yet they'd suddenly dumped us without a word. What happened before could happen again.

So I was surprised when Greg called me that night at home. "Since Bobby is coming, Chris, they've agreed to let you come too." He repeated what Bobby had already said — lay low, play it cool. The movie didn't belong to us. We were just there by the grace of God. "I can't promise you anything except the chance to fly and be physically present. The stunt guys are union and you're not, so as long as they can do the job, they'll get it." He paused. "Let your flying do the talking. It's your only chance." Then he gave me a number and told me to call the assistant producer and let him know I was coming.

It wasn't a call you could cheer about. The minute I said I'd be there with my kite I could feel hostility coming over the wire. "With your kite?" the man said. "What in hell for? We *have* kites!"

"Do you mind if we bring our own?"

"What's the matter, can't you fly Bennett kites?"

I took a slow breath. "Sure we can. We used to fly them all the time. But ours are better. They'll stay up longer for filming."

No comment.

"We figured nobody would care. It would save wear and tear on the movie kites."

He grunted. "Do what you want."

A great start. Greg had said, Don't cause waves, and already here was a tidal wave. His attitude ticked me off.

Then I figured, what the hell, we weren't any worse off than we'd been before.

Without much enthusiasm, Betty-Jo and I threw a few clothes into suitcases, drove past Bobby's apartment, and followed him to a motel in Rancho California. Our first look at the group milling around the lobby wasn't exactly warming. Three Hollywood stunt men and two flyers from Bennett's shop were already there, and when the three of us walked in, they barely acknowledged us.

One of the stunt men came up to me. "You can put your stuff—your helmet and harness—over there," pointing to a corner. "You won't be needing them for the next few days. And why'd you bring those kites? Most of us-fly whatever the studio provides." He laughed sarcastically. "Why wreck your stuff when you can wreck studio gear? It's a different game when you're flying for cameras. You'll learn."

Bobby and I exchanged looks and kept our mouths shut. I was glad Ram wasn't there. He'd have taken about one minute of that guff before he let someone have it.

The good news was steak for dinner, and the bad news was Bill Timpson, the head stunt man, dark and stocky with a mustache, giving us instructions. He held up a blue helmet. "These are what you'll be wearing tomorrow," tipping it to one side so we could see the interior. "We've got radios in here. We'll all be on the same frequency, and I'll be giving orders while you fly, so you'll have to listen carefully. I don't want you to talk back. Just do what I say." The cameras, he explained, would be at the launch site, at the bottom, and also in a helicopter filming from above. "As head flyer, I'll be directing the helicopter too. But the main thing for all of you to remember is, *Don't look at the cameras*. Just fly as if they weren't there."

He looked around. And then he fixed on me. "Some of you have flown for cameras before . . . but some of you haven't."

Wrong, I thought. Dead wrong. Various movies flicked through my mind: the Busch Gardens film, all the filming I'd done for Greg and Carl Boenish. *But you're not going to push me into anything.*

I felt Betty-Jo give my leg a pinch.

After dinner Greg took me aside. "Don't let Bill get to you, Chris. Stay cool. I have a feeling this may work out."

"I'll be all right. But I can't speak for Bobby."

"Bill won't lord it over Bobby. The stunt men know how much filming he's done. They've got a lot of respect for him. They just want to make sure everyone knows who's boss. Well, better get some sleep, shooting starts at dawn." Greg gave me a knowing smile and headed down the hall.

Four A.M. It was hard getting up. Betty-Jo yawned and said, "I could do without this dawn business."

It was twenty minutes from our motel to the base of the mountain. After that, a narrow, paved road led off the main highway and wound sharply up the side of a steep canyon. Curves, one after the other, took us through chaparral and scrub trees. We came to the Lookout Restaurant overlooking Elsinore Valley, and everyone piled out.

Bill Timpson gave us the once-over and warned us again about looking at the cameras. "And keep the helicopter in mind always." He gestured toward the truck. "Let's get started."

Nobody had said Bobby and I had to use the Bennett kites, so we quietly unloaded our Swallowtails. I glanced at the Bennett standards coming off the truck. Their performance would be no match for the Swallowtails.

Bobby touched my shoulder. "You think they'll let us use these, Chris?"

About then the director started running around yelling instructions and trying to be everywhere at once, and I said under my breath, "I don't think he'd notice if we were setting up water wings."

Bobby tried not to laugh.

Betty-Jo slid over next to me. "Remember, Chris, don't do anything to bug them."

I nodded, and we turned to watch Bill Timpson getting ready to launch.

Boy, I thought, the guy is nervous! We'd given him lessons only on small training hills, and it suddenly occurred to me he might never have flown off a mountain before. In fact, it was possible he'd had no training in cliff launches at all! If so, he had plenty of reason to be nervous.

We were standing on a paved parking lot that led to a near-vertical dropoff. Almost two thousand feet high, the mountain became less steep farther down the slope, and fanned out into a valley of orange groves and thick shrubs. Out ahead we could see Lake Elsinore and orchards to the left and right. Directly below, the landing area was rimmed with trees and brush.

Timpson lifted his kite, obviously not sure about it. Then he got off to a near-disastrous start, not running fast enough to get good flying speed and stalling over the edge. For a split second his harness swung perilously close to the mountain, and even after he'd cleared the site, he flew tentatively and straight down, with no turns or maneuvers. He barely cleared a fence near the landing area and crashed spectacularly in the field.

Bobby stared after him shaking his head, an unconscious gesture. But he kept his mouth closed.

I stood there mentally calculating my path of flight.

A walkie-talkie crackled, and someone announced Timpson's landing. We heard later he'd skidded, veered crazily, and rolled up in a ball. A cameraman had to grab his tripod and run.

It was my turn to fly. I ran a few steps and launched, secured my foot stirrups, and heard Jim Freeman's voice in my helmet directing me to hug the hill if I could. I did. Then Freeman asked if I could fly out a way and make two turns, first to the left, then to the right, which I did, hearing the thrumming of the helicopter to my side and keeping careful track of it out of the corner of my eye — but taking great care not to look. Since there was no more from Freeman, I set up for a gradual 360, completed it, then did a moderate stall followed by a dive, trying to show what hang gliders could do.

I put down a few feet from the cameras.

Standing behind the camera, Greg flashed me a quick smile.

And then Timpson came running up. He was obviously aware of the differences in our flying, which would have been apparent to anyone, but he was trying to make the best of a bad situation. "That was an excellent flight," he said. "You did just what I told you to," he lied. "I'm sure glad I went first in that bad air to check out conditions. Next time do a 360 each way so we can get the best camera angle."

It was hard to imagine, but Timpson was the best of the stunt men. The other two shouldn't have been flying off Elsinore at all. The next man down crashed dramatically, not a landing exactly but more a matter of staying with the kite until the machine decided to stop flying. His kite smashed against a rock and became rubble. If he hadn't been trained in falling, the man would have been hurt. After the dust settled, he untangled himself from the debris, stiffly refusing offers of help. He said the kite had run away with him.

The last of the stunt men wouldn't take off. Down on the ground, Timpson kept telling him through the walkie-talkie to start his flight, and we kept not seeing him. After about fifteen minutes he finally appeared, with the bar pulled in all the way. He landed hard but on his feet. The whole flight lasted about thirty seconds.

Three stunt men, I thought, and none really knew how to fly. How had those guys ever talked their way into the job? With what they'd shown everyone, the whole project could be scuttled. Yet it was all I could do to keep from grinning. If the stunt men had been regular hang glider pilots, I wouldn't have looked so impressive. As it was, those guys were so bad I'd looked unbelievably good.

The two Bennett men flew next, and they were okay pilots, except they had a big disadvantage — they didn't have high-performance kites.

It was Bobby who made that first round last forever. He'd launched before the Bennett men and he was still up, working some unexpected lift. He played around in it, doing 360s and graceful, bird-dance wingovers.

Bobby looked fantastic and followed Jim's directions exactly.

When he landed, he set down smoothly, shaking the kite in his unorthodox style and landing directly in front of Greg's camera.

The truck was already down with Betty-Jo and the launch director. I looked around. They'd seen it all. Bobby threw me a deadpan look, and I could feel a current of excitement running between him, me, and Betty-Jo. But none of us said anything.

Then the helicopter landed, and the pilot ran over to Greg. "This isn't going to work, not with some of those guys. I won't fly with them anymore. I'm afraid I'll kill one of them — or, worse, they'll kill me. I don't want to be picking 'em out of my rotors." And then Jim Freeman ran over to Bobby and me and raved about the great footage he'd gotten of the two of us.

Greg said to the helicopter pilot, "Just give it the rest of the day, John, okay?"

"Well . . ." the pilot cast a dubious look over the stunt guys, "I'll have to stay high, way the hell out of their way. The film isn't gonna show much."

Before lunch we flew a second round, but two of the stunt men refused, saying conditions didn't look good. Timpson took one more flight and said he was hanging it up for the day.

With the stunt men watching, Bobby and I and the two Bennett men huddled up top, planning a formation flight. I laid out the pattern, describing it with my hands, and Bobby went along. That was when Timpson walked over and said sheepishly, "A formation would look good if you can keep your group together."

"Your group," he'd said. I fought back excitement. Something could still go wrong.

Our formation had the beginnings of a pattern, with me flying last to direct the others and keep them organized. I concentrated hard, watching the other three and not thinking about my own flying. I'd never done anything like that before, and it was exhilarating, shouting directions over the mike and watching it take place in front of me.

By dusk I could hardly hold back my excitement.

That night at dinner Bobby and I cracked jokes with the other pilots. They weren't such bad guys when you got to know them.

After dinner Greg took me aside, smiling. "Don't worry, Chris, the difference is obvious."

At breakfast the next morning Bill Timpson walked over to my table. "It's yours," he said. "That mountain's more than we bargained for." He smiled ruefully. "We'll be taking off in a couple of hours." He stood there, hesitated, then stuck out his hand. "Good luck."

Back at Elsinore, we began the day the way we'd left off, and our formations were better, but not good enough. The standard Bennett kites weren't keeping up with the Swallowtails and kept dropping through, so the formations were ragged.

When the day's flying was finished, Greg asked, "Chris, can you round up some other flyers for tomorrow? I've made a suggestion to the producers — that we use only Swallowtail kites. We won't get our money's worth with the others."

Christmas, I thought, grinning. Fourth of July. "How many guys do you want?"

"Three more," said Greg.

And that was how Ram and Curt Kiefer and Dix Roper, a stockbroker friend, happened to land in the test film. It also marked the Bennett flyers leaving — a lot more graciously, I was thinking, than Bobby and I would have gone if the same thing happened to us.

For four days our gang of five flew together with me in the tailgunner's position directing traffic. "Bobby, fly left . . . Price, down the middle, Kiefer, to the right . . . Dix, drop back, drop back, okay, follow Bobby in. I'm right behind you, Price, speed up. Helicopter, high and to the left!" I shouted until I could hardly force my voice. Then I shouted some more.

I was high, there was no doubt about it, so damned high I wondered if I'd ever come down. I felt like Napoleon with an army, taking on the world. I'd never done anything remotely like this, making a movie with five men flying as a perfect, coordinated team. Five experts, and we were putting on a show you'd never believe. It was going to be a movie that would stop everyone, make people in Hollywood know that flying like this could take your breath away.

It was going to be fantastic!

On my last flight I set the kite down perfectly, exactly where I intended, and began walking around aimlessly, just pacing to burn off my excitement. And that's when I noticed something missing. I got on the mike again and talked to the helicopter, still circling. "Hey, John, I left my jacket up top. Can you bring it down when you come?"

"Sure, Chris," the voice came right back, the tone faintly quizzical, "and where shall I take it to have it dry-cleaned?"

36

MARALYS: Greg MacGillivray and his partner, Jim Freeman, edited the test film carefully, adding music. One night Twentieth Century Fox invited the flyers and special friends to go to Hollywood to see it. As we entered the building, I found myself walking beside Jeremy's mother, Lois, whom I hadn't seen in months, though Bobby was still good friends with the family.

Lois beamed, "Isn't this exciting? I'm so glad Bobby invited us!"

"What's Jeremy doing?" I asked, trying to sound casual.

"Oh, she's busy." Lois, tiny and sparkling, passed off the question, and I thought that would be all she'd say. But she surprised me a moment later, pulling me to one side and confiding, "She's working hard at getting over Bobby. It makes me so sad. Those two had something special. You know I've always felt Bobby was one of ours, a member of the family. I just wish things had worked out between them. This is the first time Bobby's called in a while."

"It's been a bad time for us."

"I know. I'm sorry, Maralys. About Eric. About everything. Perhaps this is the beginning of better times."

I nodded. Perhaps, I said.

Moments later Rob and I were squeezing each other's knees in the dark because Jim Freeman and Greg MacGillivray had produced a mini-masterpiece. When it was over, the important men at Twentieth-Century Fox rose as one and gave our film a standing ovation.

A few days later it became definite: Fox and Freeman-MacGillivray and the flyers at Wills Wing would soon be making the world's first full-length motion picture featuring hang gliding.

Lois Tanner had guessed right: winning the movie back breached our dam of dreariness. The boys had hardly finished the test film when, a few days after Christmas, the second U.S. Nationals were held at Escape Country.

Rob couldn't make it the first day so I went alone and arrived with Ramsey Price. Together we made our way across a stubbled field, trying to ignore away the light rain that blew in our faces. We walked fast, as if by hurrying we might somehow outdistance the wet. He said, "I feel like I've been on bennies or something for two weeks running!"

I nodded. It had all happened very fast. And there'd been the holidays, too, shoehorned in between. I asked, "How did you cram your whole Christmas into three days?"

He grinned. "That's about all the time I give it anyway. But it's hard getting up for the Nationals. I've been high about one week too long. And now *rain!*"

I looked ahead. How different this Nationals was from the first. A drizzly winter was not conducive to spectators, but, more than that, the purists in the sport had decided this year to spurn commercial sponsorship, which meant nobody was out there trying to interest the media. Few people outside the hang gliding community even knew the contest was being held. Though seventy flyers (double the first year) had come from all over the United States, they'd be playing to less than a packed house.

We'd almost reached the speaker's stand when we found Bobby coming the other way, his step buoyant. "Hey, Price, they may cancel if the rain gets any worse! Wanna go to Torrey Pines later?"

"Who's going?"

"Everybody! And with this storm . . .," Bobby held out his hand and looked reverently at the sky, "it's going to be great down at Torrey! You've gotta go!"

How like him! Everybody else wanting sun and Bobby wishing for rain.

Two hours later it went Bobby's way. The meet was canceled, and an exuberant Bobby went south, leading a caravan of flyers from all over the United States, the Pied Piper of hang gliding.

From all the flat and inland states they went, gawping at the way kites gathered energy at the top of the Torrey Pines cliff. Like greyhounds straining at the leash, the kites buffeted against the wind and, once released, billowed straight up into flight. Nearly everyone flew, a covey of kites wheeling through the air like ecstatic birds. The sky above Torrey could hardly contain the multi-colored flock. More kites flew that day than anyone had ever seen there before.

Most of the pilots said afterwards that that one day had made the trip to California worthwhile, whether the Nationals were ever held or not. And Bobby, who took so much happiness from everyone else's flying, had been a kind of transformer, absorbing feelings and sending them out multiplied.

Throughout the meet, they kept talking about the day at Torrey Pines as somehow mystical, with an aura that touched everyone who flew there.

Rob and I went to Escape Country for the last few days of the contest, though Rob was grumpy about the small crowds and no color, and kept complaining, "Where's the excitement of last year? Where's the media? Where's anything? Now '73 . . . *that* was a contest!" We looked around. Half the spectators perched on a distant hillside and seemed as remote as shrubbery.

I glanced at the five-hundred-foot hill, brown and bare without flags or cameras, and felt let down.

If Bobby noticed any of those things, he gave no sign.

At the end of the first day Ram said, "Nobody's going to beat him. Bobby is serious this time. He isn't making any mistakes. Look at his score on that speed run. Who's gonna top that?"

Chris said, "I am," and finished his speed run ahead of everyone. But it was his only first-place score. Bobby finished first on everything else: first on bull's-eye points, first on rounding the greatest number of pylons, first on style. By the third day of flying nobody could catch him. He could, if he wanted, coast to a win.

The family, making its headquarters on a log near the landing area, all stopped thinking about Bobby and concentrated instead on Chris and Ram, who battled for second place with four other pilots. Betty-Jo kept track of their scores on a pad of paper, noting how many pylons each pilot rounded, how close he was coming to the bull's-eye. But she wasn't always sure of the point designations, so all we had was an educated guess.

Ram's luck ran out toward the end. He'd just come down the speed run in the day's best time and was about to rack up an impressive score when nature threw him a curve. He suddenly ran out of lift at the far edge of the landing area. Still yards from the foul line — a white ribbon which separated points from no points — Ram seemed to have no option except to put down his feet and resign himself to a bad finish.

He didn't do it. He chose instead to float in his harness, inches above the ground, pushing his one-of-a-kind, self-designed kite to the limit.

Our group watched spellbound. Like Mike Larson the year before, Ram lay perfectly still in his canvas cocoon and stretched out the flight. Flying thus, he skimmed slowly, agonizingly, inches above the ground, letting the sail carry him a foot at a time, and finally yards, on what is called "ground effect." When at last the kite dropped him on his stomach, he'd made the outer ring of the bull's-eye!

As Ram stood up, wrapped in a smile that seemed to involve his whole body, everyone cheered and kept cheering. Ram was so genuinely, gratefully happy he appeared almost shy.

The last day the flying finished at dark to an empty arena. Only the pilots and their staunchest supporters were still there. In almost total darkness, Rob and I and a few others huddled on the field against a cold wind, waiting while the judges in their trailer tallied up points.

It was a long, chilly wait.

After what seemed hours, two cars pulled near the empty speaker's platform and turned on their headlights, alleviating the sensation that we were all lost on a dark, windy plain. Beside me, Rob muttered, "Ridiculous! Some National Championship. It looks more like a car rally! When this is over, who will even know?"

Bobby, standing nearby, said, "We will."

At last John Lake, the meet director—very thin with high cheekbones and sunken cheeks—climbed to the headlight-illumined platform to announce results. Because there was no suspense in first place, he smiled and said, "Will Bobby Wills please come up?"

The crowd pushed Bobby forward and then he was standing on the platform shaking John's hand, pausing solemnly with his trophy in his hands. Voices yelled, "Speech! Speech!"

Momentarily Bobby stood in the headlights, tall and uncertain. He began, "I think it's been a fair contest . . ." and that was all he could say because laughter erupted and someone shouted, "You would!"

Embarrassed at his blunder, Bobby retreated, stepping back into darkness.

Chris went next. Grinning so wide his eyes became mere

slits, Chris took the trophy for second place.

I thought, They did it, Coles Phinizy! The head is still on the ginger ale.

Then, to a sudden burst of cheering, John called Ramsey Price for third. As Ram moved to the platform, the flyers wore out his back, pounding and thumping him all the way.

Afterward, Rob took us all to a pie shop for dinner, not only our group but some out-of-town pilots as well. As the boys heaped their congratulations on Ram, I saw a new person emerge: saying almost nothing, for once, he couldn't stop smiling.

His happiness, so genuine and unaffected, was contagious. I couldn't get my eyes off him. That blond, curly hair. The strong, masculine planes of his face. But most of all his smile, which was radiant without his usual traces of sarcasm. I leaned closer to Rob. "Winning suits him," I whispered. "He's never looked handsomer."

Rob nodded. "He ought to win something every day."

Calmer days ensued, and Chris began sending out medical school applications again, this time with more doggedness than hope. It was January, and we'd long since stopped talking about his future beyond Wills Wing. Yet I could see the hope wasn't quite gone because he still spoke about his work there as if it were temporary. "When I'm not here, Mom, you're going to have to set up a long-range ordering program for A-N bolts."

I wondered that he could still think that way.

In February Bobby went to Canada again for the third Canadian championships, and four days later came back with the aging but still glamorous winged lady, whom he carefully placed back on her wine barrel. For yet another year she'd preside over our shop.

"Overall champ again, Bobby?" Rob asked warmly, and Bobby said, "Yup!"

We were taking his wins for granted now.

And they were doing Bobby good. Day by day he blossomed. I could see a largesse of spirit developing, that he was becoming kinder. More generous. It seemed the more the world cheered him on, the more cheerable he became.

A few mornings later Ram thumbed through our order book, and glancing at our trophies lined up on a shelf above my desk, he asked, "What does it take? I figured by now we'd be rolling in orders."

"It takes spring," I said. "Sunshine."

"So how come Blizzard doesn't need sunshine? He's selling kites like crazy."

"How do you know he is?" Roy spoke up, telephone in hand. "I'll bet he just hands out phony information to throw everybody off."

Bobby came in on the tail end of the conversation. "He's *giving* the kites away, Price. That's why they're selling. When you've got money you can do that. He's hoping the rest of us will go broke. But it's not going to work. Once the Swallowtail's obsolete, who will design for him?"

Ram laughed sourly. "If you're good enough at stealing, you don't need a designer."

Though our Swallowtail had more than lived up to the boys' hopes for it, Bobby felt he could create something still better, and in those flat midwinter days after Canada he squatted on the cement in back, designing a new sail and, soon, a whole new kite.

One day I overheard Chris and Bobby arguing in back. "It won't work, Bobby," Chris shouted angrily. "If you weren't so danged stubborn, you'd open your eyes and see it. What you're doing is crazy, it doesn't make sense."

"Sure it'll work," Bobby said. "I know what I'm doing, Chris. I've thought it all out. Every time I fly I imagine how this is going to be."

"Yeah, but thinking isn't enough. You have to follow

certain principles. What you're doing doesn't follow them, so it won't work."

"Chris," said Bobby, still patient, "am I usually right in the end?"

A pause. And then Chris said, "Well, you're going about this design wrong, Bobby. It's obvious — as obvious as knowing you can't take off downwind. Why are you always doing things the oddball way? Why are you always trying to fly downwind?"

Bobby laughed. "But I do it, Chris, don't I? I do it whenever I want. And I'm still here."

37

MARALYS: Sometime that year, Ram married bright, reserved Carol Boenish, sister of the photographer Carl Boenish, who'd first come into our lives at the fly-in at Coyote Hills.

Ram's wedding, marked by his unexpected, almost shy demeanor, his irrepressible grin, and his look of someone literally basking in happiness, was reminiscent of the day he'd won third place in the Nationals. I hardly remember Bobby's and Chris's even being there because it was Ram who outglowed them all.

And then Bobby met Suzette Lowry under circumstances which struck the family as somewhat mysterious. "Has anyone seen Bobby?" Chris asked one day in the winter of '75, and no one had. For three days we kept asking the question, and when nobody had answers, it was generally assumed that any disaster short of the Bermuda Triangle would produce tangible evidence and some sort of official notice. Therefore, Bobby must be on a mission of his own.

And so he was. Bobby was with his new friend, Suzi. The proof came after he reappeared, in a thank-you telegram from Suzi that cast an all-too-bright light on their tryst. The telegram made an unfortunate tour around the front office before it ever reached its intended recipient.

By then everyone's curiosity was, to say the least, aroused, and we couldn't wait to meet her.

As it turned out, Suzi was blonde, pretty, very religious, and game for any adventure. Bobby taught her to fly, and to our astonishment she was almost as fearless as he—not only willing to fly tandem, but bold enough for aerial acrobatics, such as hanging by her knees from the control bar and flying tandem under marginal conditions. Drawn to the adventurous, reckless side of his life, Suzi was thrown emotionally by Bobby's singleminded attention to hang gliding. His frequent neglect provoked her to extreme responses, and those two strong-willed people barely survived a stormy spring to get right with her church and marry—on two weeks' notice—in early June.

In late June the three boys and their wives left for Greece to make the Twentieth Century Fox movie, *Skyriders*. With them went Kurt Kiefer, two other friends, and Roy, who had signed on as equipment manager. For the first time since we'd started the company, I had the shop almost entirely to myself. A few production men remained, but I was the boss. Also the buyer, head salesman, production whip—everything. It was frightening in a way but gave me a certain grand sense of power too.

Letters from Greece came in bunches. Scrambled, squirrely letters from Ram, almost unreadable, with his cockeyed sense of humor darting in and out between the lines. One letter began, "So anyway . . ." and another ended, "And we'd almost come to this . . .!"

Focused on the dramatic, preferably the dramatic with a touch of calamity, Suzi wrote, "Everyone who has ever worked on movies agrees this one is jinxed. . . . Bobby rode the motorcycle without permission and did wheelies RIGHT INTO THE MOTEL LOBBY! The director has been tearing his hair out over Bobby. He's been sliding down the banister and shooting watermelon seeds, and he stole the motorcycle again and put a sail on it and flew it up and down the street, blocking traffic."

Later Suzi wrote, "The director was going to let Bobby fly his motorcycle for the circus scene. But Donawitz got an injunction, so now Bobby's riding for fun around the hotel parking lot — backwards."

Betty-Jo wrote about quaint Greek customs: about dinners by the sea in Athens and waiters tossing empty wine bottles into the ocean. She wrote about poor plumbing and emergency cords in their bathroom not connected to anything.

Chris printed his letters, which were breezy stories about the hotel clerk who shouted at him when he asked for a replacement for his week-old towel. The man blamed Chris for getting the towel dirty! He wrote about the jet-ranger helicopters that hovered over the hotel at four A.M., waiting to take pilots to the top of the mountain — a recurring event that so incensed one of the lady guests that she threw her shoe at the nearest member of the filming party, who happened to be Betty-Jo. He described hazardous flights between mammoth rock formations — "the gaps" — and playing backgammon, with scorpions lurking nearby, atop a narrow, thousand foot pinnacle, waiting for turbulence to subside. He spoke of Suzi's spectacular tandem flight when she undid her seat belt, climbed down a rope ladder, and hung by her knees — while Bobby put the kite through tight 360s.

Still another of Chris's letters mentioned the director who asked Chris to soar for hours of filming — except that Chris was to fly fifty feet over the director's head, dive down and do a touch and go, take off again, and fly three hundred feet to a spot where he was to land, left foot forward and right foot back, on two markers placed next to an umbrella in the sand! Chris tried not to laugh.

He told of the excitement of filming with James Coburn, Susannah York, and Robert Culp — and he talked about the crowds of Greeks who materialized, literally from the bushes, to watch the goings-on. In a parenthetical aside he mentioned the Fourth of July firecracker war between himself, Bobby, Ram, and a few other Americans positioned across the hotel grounds.

On one occasion, Chris said, the film crew threw a dummy off a pinnacle, rigged in a kite so the craft would fly momentarily, then go into a screaming dive. "A crowd of French tourists happened to be watching from the bottom, and I found myself, later, in discussion with one of the Frenchmen. When I asked him about the event, the Frenchman said it looked perfectly normal to him. He said all the hang glider pilots he'd seen in France landed like that every time!"

From Bobby we never got a letter. It didn't surprise me. I never thought of Bobby writing—only doing. Toward the end Suzi wrote, "Bobby is relieved the filming is almost over. He's not crazy to do any more flying with helicopters. He thinks they're dangerous. We're all getting restless now. I could die for a taco." She ended the letter by asking me to bring a supply of nebulizers for Bobby, whose asthma had gotten worse in the last few weeks.

He'd have them soon, I thought, folding her letter. In three days we'd all meet in England for the first British hang gliding championships.

The chain of command at the shop passed to Rob's father, Neal, who took over the front office with a perplexed smile. "I've done a lot of things in my life, Maralys, but never anything quite like this."

I handed him the order book. "I wish I could tell you we've got a big operation here, but we haven't. You'll do as well as any of us—probably better. At least you've been a commander in the Navy. What have I ever been?"

His eyebrows went up and he gave me a quizzical smile. You've been a mother of five boys."

I sighed. "I suppose that should have prepared me to be a

leader, but it didn't. I am, however, a very good follower."
And we both laughed.

Six days later, Tracy, Kirk, Rob, and I stood among a
hundred British flyers watching Bobby accept yet another
trophy. He had just become the first British hang gliding
champion, and Chris was runner-up. The scenario was
familiar: Bobby pleased but somber in his happiness, Chris
joking with the other pilots, Rob full of energy and
bonhomie, and me feeling effervescent joy. With a start, I
realized that Bobby was, at the moment, the British, American, and Canadian champion.

To the Brits, however, Bobby's exploits during their meet
were what they'd remember . . . when, on his last flight, for
instance, he nearly put himself out of contention by missing
one of the pylons. Watching from a cliff, we could see
Bobby must have realized his mistake, because, to our
horror, his kite slowly turned back to *re-circle the pylon*. With
his altitude almost gone and the kite far from the finishing
gate, I knew he'd lost everything. I stood holding my breath
as Bobby somehow eked out a few yards, and then a few
more, and, flying literally inch by inch, made it through the
gate and saved his win.

The crowd cheered him unreservedly, happy to root for
the Yank who'd already become something of a legend. It
had all started on the first day of flying, when the meet
director was explaining the rules and pointing out that
maximum points could be gotten only if both feet were
inside the smallest circle. It seems that Bobby looked at the
circle and looked at his own size-thirteen shoes and said,
"Both my feet won't *fit* inside the circle!"

A burst of laughter, and the matter was dismissed. The
size of Bobby's feet was his own problem.

After Bobby finished his first flight, Rob and I were
astonished at the stream of words, the shouts and laughter
that came over the loudspeaker, all in a British accent, of

course . . . cries of "Good job, Bob Wills! Fine show!" over what appeared to be a normal flight. We must have looked baffled because someone came over and explained to us. Bobby had just earned maximum points — by landing on one foot!

The meet director, Tony Fuell, wrote about the incident: *"A swooshing noise, and a hard SLAPP! Bob was standing in the centre of the circle. On one leg. The control frame was off the ground. He wobbled a bit, then got it under control. I ran in with the tape. One giant (and rather dirty) sneaker had obliterated the skewer at the dead centre of the circle. It was so central that the skewer holding the tape was under the ball of his foot. The other foot was waving violently in the air as he fought to keep it off the ground. Just for a moment, neither of us could believe it. We looked at each other. I felt a grin break out on my face. 'I did it right?' he said. 'Yes,' I said, 'you did.'"*

Tracy and Kirk were getting restless. They wanted to get on with our trip. I wanted to stay forever. It was a wonderful moment, and I willed it to last. The warm feelings communicated by the British stirred me to a rush of affection. As I'd felt on other occasions, coming to England was coming home. This time, though, we were basking in our children's accomplishments, and we'd been given a hero's welcome. Somehow, I knew it would have to last a lifetime.

Reluctantly, we left that perfect place — the little town of Mere.

Eric, I thought, *this was your kind of year!*

Skyriders. Greece. The British Nationals. Once again we were riding high at Wills Wing, and as though we deserved additional good fortune, our sales picked up and the business threatened to become profitable.

One afternoon I picked up the phone and heard the hollow, dead-air sound that told me the caller was thousands of miles away. It had been the fourth such call that week. "Allo, Wills Wing," a voice said after an echoing pause. I drew in a breath, readying my long-distance muscles. My friend, Pat — who now worked in the shop because Roy had had a flying accident in Greece and was still recovering — observed she could always tell when the call was overseas because I seemed to be trying to span the distance with my voice.

The man asked for Bobby, and when I said I'd get him, the speaker was clearly surprised. "I will talk to Bobby Wills — himself?"

Running into the back, I caught Bobby leaving with a kite on his shoulders. "It's from Italy," I said, "Genoa, Italy. Hurry."

Bobby laid his kite down. "That must be the guy who got his SST last month." Bobby's newest kite, the Super Swallowtail, had brought him bursts of appreciation from all over the world — from England, Australia, Norway, Canada, Japan. Now blue-jeaned legs carried him swiftly into the front office. Then he was poised on one leg, looking temporary. After some intent listening, he smiled and folded himself into one of our office chairs, and I knew the call would go on longer than it should. They always did.

The enthusiasm out there nurtured him. Today, as always, he expanded visibly as the call went on. He was soon laughing out loud.

When he finished I glanced at the clock. He'd been talking fifty minutes. "You've got to get those kites tested — " I began, but he was still too absorbed to listen. "The man said his SST is the greatest thing he's ever flown, and he wanted to talk about it. Today he soared above a cliff more than two hours. No one in his town's ever done that before. He was so excited, half his words were Italian." The news seemed to bring Bobby profound joy.

I smiled. "Two hours soaring and one hour telling you about it long distance."

He shrugged good-naturedly. "I can spare an hour."

38

MARALYS: Bobby was so engrossed designing new kites he didn't compete seriously again for almost a year, until the Nationals at Dog Mountain in Washington state. Riding up with a group of pilots in a motor home, Bobby became restless and pulled his big Samsonite suitcase out of the back. When he opened it, his friend, Ken deRussy, stared at the contents, amazed. "I expected to see clothes, but there weren't any, not a stitch. Inside he had nothing but games — chess games, three-dimensional tic-tac-toe, checkers, about thirty different games, and all the way up he kept challenging us to play with him — and of course sooner or later we all did."

Mid-trip, someone suggested that they stop at popular Fort Funston to practice, but Bobby voted no. "Everybody will want to talk to me and I won't get to fly." So they stopped instead at a lesser known mountain with a narrow, winding dirt road, and there Bobby borrowed a truck and drove everyone up in his usual terrifying style. At the top a flyer who didn't know him well jumped out of the back cursing and shouting, ready to fight because he'd feared for his life. Bobby just looked at him, surprised.

The pilot took one of his friends aside. "Let's give him a dose of his own medicine." Then, to Bobby, "On the next trip up *I'm driving!*"

"Sure," Bobby agreed affably. "Go ahead."

This time Bobby rode in back and the angry pilot drove, and, as someone said later, "He drove so damn fast and so dangerously he scared even himself."

Near the top of the mountain, a passenger looked back to see Bobby's reaction. He wasn't reacting at all. "I couldn't believe it," the man said. "He was leaning against the cab reading a magazine and eating peanut M&M's."

The contest was beset by variable weather and a new set of rules which specified, among other things, that no control bar was to touch the ground during landings. Sometime during the event Ram noticed that Bobby's aluminum control bar was seriously bent. "How did that happen? You never crashed."

Bobby looked puzzled. "I don't know. I don't remember tweaking it."

Some time later Ram found the answer in a photograph. Pointing to Bobby's legs, he shouted, "Hey, everyone, look at this!" Bobby was standing in the bull's-eye straining to keep his kite off the ground. His arm muscles bulged with effort and his bare feet were planted hard, toes clenched. And there was the control bar — bent down around his thighs.

Bobby didn't win at Dog Mountain. And he hadn't had enough flying, either, so he persuaded his party to stop at Mount Shasta on the way back. Ken deRussy reported, "He wanted to fly off that mountain, and he wanted us to go with him. None of us wanted to stop, but Bobby badgered and bullied until we did. We parked at the foot of the mountain and Bobby started up, literally running. Then he'd stop and look back at us, trying to entice us onto the slope. We just stood near the motor home with our arms folded. He thought if he went high enough we'd come, so he ran some more and turned around, and damn! he made me feel guilty.

"We managed to wimp out on him. But I wasn't happy about it. It was one of those things, later, I knew I should have done."

The next spring we were called back to the Twentieth Century Fox studios in Hollywood for a private showing of *Skyriders*.

Again the Tanners were there, and this time I saw Jeremy. She smiled at me almost shyly. "Bobby invited us all to come. Mom asked if he meant me and he said sure, if I wanted to. So here I am."

It was wonderful seeing her again and I said so.

Her blue eyes sparkled. "Isn't this exciting?"

I noticed she sat behind Bobby and Suzette, and that Suzette kept her hand on Bobby's arm.

It was a good movie. Not great, I decided, just diverting. As a lyrical song of hang gliding, the test film was better.

The following year, in October, Bobby and Suzi were expecting a baby. As the day approached, I asked them to call me, day or night, so I could be there — and naturally the baby chose two A.M. As I climbed out of bed, Rob mumbled groggily, "You're crazy, it's the middle of the night," and I said, "This is our *grandchild*, Rob . . . I'm going!"

The flight off Haleakala . . . my first grandchild . . . the lost sleep is now forgotten, but those moments will be in my memory forever. A few hours of waiting and I heard a scratchy cry from the delivery room. Unexpectedly, I had tears in my eyes. Bobby's little son, Robert Brandon Wills, had just reminded me that I am more emotional than I think.

Spring again. 1977. It was a Sunday, one of the long days in late May when twilight lingers like a guest at the door, reluctant to leave. Chris and Bobby had dropped by, and now sat with Rob and me at the patio table recalling other times. "Chris," Bobby asked, "do you remember the time we bombed Ensign Benson with oranges?"

"Sure," said Chris, throwing Bobby a quick conspiratorial grin. I could see it was going to be confession time in the old neighborhood. "I remember how you sat on the hill with your carbide cannon and I strolled down the street with a walkie-talkie directing your fire. And there was crabby old Benson out in his front yard with oranges dropping all around him, and he could never figure out where they were coming from."

The boys laughed and I glanced at Rob. Thank God we hadn't known at the time. Bobby leaned back in his chair and stretched out his long legs, smiling. "When Curt Kiefer came to visit me out at Granny's," he began, "we used to crash the drive-in movie by riding our bikes in the exit. We never got to see any movies though because the ushers always spotted us and started running. But we dodged between cars and they could never catch us. It was so entertaining we kept going back just for the chase. One day we came and *they* had bicycles too, but their bikes were too small, and they pedaled with their knees up around their chins, wearing their funny usher's caps. Kiefer and I almost couldn't pedal we were laughing so hard."

Bobby the raconteur, I thought . . . how long ago those bad-boy days seemed. And how well he told the stories, a man, now, sharing his dubious past for our entertainment. "I'm amazed you pulled that off," Rob said later, smiling at one of Bobby's tales, "but then you always were ingenious." And he was looking at Bobby with enjoyment—not as father to son, but as audience to entertainer.

We aren't Bobby's parents any longer, I thought, *we don't have to worry about him now*. He could come to our house and tell us stories, and we could relax and be amused.

We were finally just good friends.

One day soon afterwards Bobby found me alone in the shop after hours. He filled the doorway to the back. "Mom, there's something I've been wanting to talk to you about."

"Okay. But I was just going home."

"You can wait a couple of minutes." He moved into the room and loomed over my desk. "You know what I did last weekend, don't you . . . you heard?"

"No. What?"

"I was baptized. By total immersion. We went out to a lake, this minister and a group of Christians and me."

"With all your clothes on?" I asked stupidly, and thought back to an earlier baptism in a Presbyterian church—hardly total immersion, and he was a baby then, too, which somehow seemed more appropriate.

Bobby laughed. "Sure with all my clothes on. That's part of it, but not the important part."

I started to tell him we'd taken care of that once, but I thought, What would it mean to him? He'd had no choice in the matter. Now, for whatever reason—perhaps Suzi—he'd made the choice for himself.

He studied me earnestly. "I'm a Christian now. But I'm worried about you and Dad. When Jesus comes, are you going to be ready?"

The question was unexpected. I looked away, embarrassed. Was I really being called to task by my son? As always, I found such questions awkward, but I managed to fumble out an answer. "Well . . . I've always believed in God."

"But have you accepted Jesus?" He gave me a concerned look that seemed to reach right into my conscience, and I thought, Oh Bobby, what am I supposed to say?

He waited for an answer. "Well . . ." my teens came back to me. "I—I was saved long ago, when I was fourteen." But that had been another age, another person. Since those few years when I'd embraced fundamentalist religion so fervently that I refused to go to movies or dances because they were instruments of the devil, a great many things had changed. I believed in God, of course, and His Son, Jesus, but I'd never liked this kind of penetrating question. It always made me feel I hadn't measured up.

Bobby shook his head. "When the Rapture comes, I hope you're ready. And Dad, too. I've been worried about Dad."

Those eyes, those turned-down hazel eyes seemed weighted with worry. I had no answer to give. Rob had his own conscience, his own beliefs in fundamental decency, but they didn't mesh with orthodox religion. I couldn't persuade him of an afterlife or a God-ordered universe any more than he could convince me that religion was just a comforting answer to death.

"I'm afraid Dad won't go along with your ideas about the Rapture," I said.

"They aren't my ideas."

"Well, your church's ideas."

"It's going to happen, Mom. One of these days all the Christians will be swept up and the others will be left here. I want you and Dad ready. The alternatives aren't good."

How long was he going to keep me there discussing the disposition of our souls? "I'm glad you feel this way, Bobby. I'm glad you were baptized. It makes me happy for you." I meant it. I'd always thought if you had to take sides without proof, that was the side worth taking.

He smiled again, gently, and I had the feeling he was forty-seven and I twenty-six. "It isn't me we have to worry about anymore. It's you and Dad. Give it some thought, Mom. There may not be as much time as you think."

At last his eyes released me.

As I drove along the familiar eucalyptus-lined streets in Santa Ana, a reassuring thought came to me: when Rob and I were old, Bobby would take care of us very well.

Four days later Bobby went out to Escape Country to film a commercial. I knew very little about it except that he'd be gone several days, shooting from sunrise to dusk.

On the third day I was trying to run the office alone, the plum I always got when we were between office managers. After his flying accident in Greece, Roy had eventually healed but chose not to return to the shop. Chris and Ram were elsewhere. There is something to be said for not being quite so reliable, for not having it known that if no one else would open the doors, I would.

Our door swung wide and I glanced up. It was Jeremy. "Oh!" I said, "come in!"

She stood in the doorway in a blue sleeveless dress with a white belt hugging her waist and white piping forming a *V* above her breasts. Her hair fell in soft brown waves around her face. She was the prettiest thing I'd seen in our doorway for a long time.

Yet she didn't come in. She poised hesitantly. "Is Bobby here?" Her glance went past the front office into the back.

He wasn't, I said, he was out at Escape Country, but I expected him back soon. "Come sit down. You look wonderful!"

She pulled a chair toward my desk. "How long since we've chatted, Maralys . . . years?" Shyly, "Bobby and I talk once in a while. But Suzette doesn't like it." She smiled. "My husband, Don, doesn't mind. He trusts me. He knows Bobby and I are just friends."

I said, "Years ago I wanted to ask you something, Jeremy . . . I wondered what went wrong between you and Bobby. But I couldn't ask. The time was never right."

She said, "It wasn't anything special. Bobby could act very immature at times, trying to get my attention. I had another boyfriend, you know . . . I was pretty mixed up."

"I heard."

"It was mostly bad timing. I didn't know what I wanted." She hesitated. "It might have been different later. We had a lot of good times together, doing crazy things. Out at Borego, for instance, on the sand dunes, he'd drag a snow shovel behind his truck and I'd ride on it . . . and we went skiing once on the rim of the world, and he needed something out of the bed of his truck, so I crawled out the window into the bed while the truck was moving, and crawled back in again, and neither of us thought a thing of it. And once when we drove up Saddleback in the snow, he said, 'I'm losing traction, Jeremy. Go hang on the tailgate,' and I did because he was so sure, so competent . . . I knew it would come out all right."

And I rode with him tandem, I thought, off the cliffs of Hawaii — for all those same reasons.

"When I had my accident," she went on, "all the guys were crying, but Bobby was the rock. He was always there."

I nodded. "I remember he sent you flowers . . ."

"They were tea roses." She grew thoughtful. "He has a sensitive side to him. He gave me fragile, delicate things — a clear leaded-glass ball with a butterfly inside. And seashells, which he glued together into a delicate pyramid . . . even artichoke flowers that he cut and dyed because he knew I liked them." She fell quiet, and I wondered if she'd say more. When she spoke again, it was offhanded, and she was shifting in her chair, ready to leave. "It took me too long to figure out what he's really like. But I know now. He's a gentle giant."

39

MARALYS: The cleaning lady came later, a hunched and arthritic gnome of a woman with black, straw-like hair — an improbable person whom I'd hired both because she needed the job and seemed extraordinarily kind. Soon I realized she was vacuuming the metal filings off our disreputable carpets as if they were three-inch plush and giving our battered desks the kind of dusting usually reserved for the executive suite.

Now, as she carefully moved papers on the spare desk, I watched her idly. Thorough as usual. And then the phone rang. It was a young male voice. "Is Suzette there? Suzette Wills?"

I sat up, startled. Why would he think Suzette was in the office? "No, she isn't. May I ask who's calling?"

"I'm a friend of Bobby's. You may not remember me. I flew with him a year ago. I'm just . . . I'm just trying to get in touch with someone. I don't know who to call."

"I'm his mother," I offered.

This conversation had a ring to it. A horrible familiarity.

"I'm out at Escape Country," he said. "There's been an accident."

I gasped, "Who?" But I knew who.

"It's Bobby, Mrs. Wills. It happened about twenty minutes ago."

"God. Oh, God." The sound was more moan than

words, and the gnome looked up, startled. She started for my desk.

Quickly the boy said, "I think he's okay. He has internal injuries, but they said he's in stable condition."

The words burst out of me before I could stop them. "Oh my God! No!" I knew so much more than he did. I understood what those terms meant. They had nothing to do with small things like broken bones.

I must have given him Suzette's number, but I remember only that I began shaking uncontrollably. All of this had happened before. I'd already lived through it once. The pain of Eric's death multiplied what I felt a thousand times, for I wasn't over him. I'd never be over him, and he was all I could take.

The woman had her arm over my shoulder. She looked into my face, clearly frightened.

"Is he . . .," I began. But the boy went on, "They just took him away in a helicopter. He's going to Mission Viejo hospital."

"Thank you." He was gone and I sat for a moment, my head in my hands. "It's Bobby," I mumbled to the woman. "It's my son Bobby. He's been hurt."

She stood next to me silently, the smell of a hard day's work emanating from her raised arm, and I noted this fact blankly, and the fact that she was so kind, and at the same time a numbing barrier made her seem hardly there.

An inner voice fought back terror. You're being unreasonable, Bobby's alive, he's "stable." It isn't like Eric.

Clinging to hope, I called Rob at home. To my relief, he was calm, not upset at all.

He must know, I thought. Rob must know it's not bad. He said, "Meet me at my office, Babe. In the parking lot."

Together we drove south in Rob's car, talking about unimportant things. Part of me was thinking, Why is the sky so red? Why does it look so ominous? And another part thought, How foolish of me to get hysterical. Bobby's all right. We wouldn't be sitting here like this, rational and calm, if he wasn't going to be fine. Thank heavens Rob didn't see me earlier, the way I overreacted. By the time we arrived at the hospital thirty minutes later I was almost my normal self.

As Rob pulled up to the emergency entrance, I jumped out of the car, determined to see Bobby immediately. Swinging doors lay ahead, and I was about to go through when a nurse appeared and barred my way. "You have to go around by the front entrance."

"All right. But I'm Bobby Wills's mother. How is he?" It was a small hospital. She had to know.

It was as if she hadn't heard the question. With an expression that was all business, she said, "Around by the front entrance . . ." She pointed.

At a full run, I arrived at the reception desk, panting. The lobby was small and open, sparsely furnished with a few chairs. Across the counter the receptionist gave me an impersonal glance. I said, "I'm Bobby Wills's mother. He came in a little while ago. How is he?"

A blank look, as though she spoke a different language. "Just a minute," she said, and disappeared.

Fear started again.

When the woman came back, Rob was there, and now she held a pen and a hospital form. She had already filled in today's date: June 24, 1977. "I need some information. His name is Robert Wills?"

Rob nodded.

"Birthdate?"

"July 16, 1950."

"Place of birth?"

Before Rob could answer, I said rudely, "We don't *care* about this. *How is he?*" Incensed that Rob was standing there calmly answering her questions, I had the feeling we were all fiddling while Rome burned.

She didn't try to respond. Instead, to my surprise, she scurried away like a startled rabbit.

I turned on Rob. "They won't tell us a thing!" The trembling started again.

Then a uniformed man appeared from the back and came around the desk. He was wearing a holster, guns, and boots. His badge said "County Sheriff." "You his father?"

"Yes I am. What happened?"

In an instinctive gesture, the officer's hand went to his holster. "Your son hit a post—a marker of some kind. His kite broke up."

Rob and I stared at him in disbelief.

"A marker?" Rob asked. "How big a marker?"

The man didn't know.

"It would have to be something big to break up his kite."

"We haven't finished our investigation . . ." He shrugged and walked away.

A nurse returned to stand behind the desk in place of the receptionist, and, lo, she held the unfinished form. "Now—where was he born?"

Furious, I glared at her. "I want to know how he is!"

Her voice turned icy. "They're working on him. They're doing all they can."

Sickened, I turned away. This was another world, a world where people had their hearts excised, where they looked at you with empty heads and no feelings.

Rob was answering her questions. I couldn't understand how he was putting up with this because I was half crazy wanting to know. The scene had an unreal quality, and I felt like a boxer trying to punch out Jell-O. We'd been there twenty minutes and knew nothing. Somewhere behind that wall, Bobby was . . . what? Things were happening with our son, he needed us, but he might as well have been in Siberia, so completely were we cut off.

After a while, with the insane paperwork finished, Rob came and stood by me. "I'm scared," I said. "Rob, I'm scared."

His mind was on something else. "A marker—if that's

what it was — wouldn't have broken his kite."

Battered by fear and unable to stand in one place, I left him to pace the room.

From somewhere a priest appeared, wandering into the lobby on no particular mission, it seemed. Never had those vestments looked so comforting. "Sir," I began, "my son's been hurt. Would you . . . would you pray with me?"

The man looked down from a vast distance. "Of course. I'm sorry about your son. Let's sit down together." We chose two chairs next to a wall and prayed aloud in this public place. "Oh Father," I murmured, "help my son who's been hurt, help him, Lord, please . . ." In a deep voice he rumbled out the familiar assurance of God's enduring love.

Rob saw us and his eyes widened.

Then I was pacing again, with fear springing up anew. Had we been praying, perchance, for Bobby's soul? Oh dear God, I thought, the boy is still ours. It isn't time, yet, to pray for his soul. My pacing took me past the door to the emergency room just as a nurse came out. I rushed over and touched her shoulder. "Please . . . my son's in there. Tell me how he is!"

She looked at me compassionately, a human being at last. "He's critical," she said softly.

When I told Rob, everything changed. His strange passivity vanished and in its place was a man thundering at the nurse behind the desk. Did Bobby need a neurosurgeon? By god, a neurosurgeon damn well better be called. This kind of injury couldn't wait. Rob stood at the counter with his body thrust against the separating wall as if he were about to break into the room. Jaw hard, teeth clamped down, Rob had finally taken charge.

The nurse was frightened. "Sir, our doctors are very good."

Rob glared at her. "If he needs a neurosurgeon, you'd better call one!"

"Well," she said, flustered at such an unheard-of request,

"if they need one, I'm sure they'll find someone." For a moment longer Rob stood there, glaring. But she was all there was, her unresponsiveness a mushy barrier against which he could make no inroads. His thundering passed like a fading storm.

Presently the door of the emergency room opened and a man came out, then a nurse. The nurse said, "The doctor will see you now," pointing at the man's retreating figure, already headed down a long hall.

Rob went after him meekly, but I stood where I was. *If Bobby was still alive, the doctor would have spoken to us here.* When I remained rooted, she took my arm gently. "Come."

I shook my head. The others disappeared into a room. "No," I said, "I can't. I can't go down there. Please." I pulled away from her. I'm going to die from this, I thought. My heart is going to stop. Bobby's dead. If I go down the hall to that room, I'll hear him say it. He'll say Bobby's dead. And then I'll die too. I shook my head vigorously.

She tugged again, firmly but gently.

"No! No! Please! My husband can tell me." I was whispering. "Please. I have to go outside now. I have to run. Just let me go outside and run."

"Come." She pulled me along.

"No . . . no . . ."

She tugged and my feet walked by themselves. I couldn't feel myself walking.

Rob was sitting across the room when I arrived. Calm. Unruffled. I stared at him, horrifed. *He still doesn't know!* Oh Rob. You poor man. You poor, poor man.

The nurse stood close as I leaned against the wall. From the corner of my eye I could see her wary expression as she watched me. *You never know how they're going to react.*

The doctor began almost matter-of-factly. "If he'd lived," he said, "he would have been a vegetable."

That was how he said it. And it meant nothing. Not to

me. I already knew. I had already made the transition and started back.

But not Rob. His face dissolved like a sugar lump in coffee. Everything went out of it, all the muscles collapsing inward. In that second before he put his hands over his face I saw all the despair — the bleak, empty, terrifying despair of losing another child. I ran to him, as desperately sorry for him as for Bobby. "Oh, Rob. Oh Rob. I'm so sorry."

The tears wracked me and my thoughts wrestled with pain. Two of our sons were gone. How was I to live?

Eric — gentle, defenseless Eric.

Now Bobby, a giant, a man grown to a giant at the end. I thought, I can't live knowing you've died, Bobby, I can't, I can't.

Eventually Rob and I walked out of the death-room, supporting each other.

"Can I give you something?" the nurse asked. "A shot?"

Shaking my head negatively, I tried not to show my scorn. A shot? Did she have something magic, a shot that would bring him back? If not, I'd pass.

Like cripples, Rob and I passed slowly through the lobby where we'd waited so long. We were different people now. We'd come in as the parents of Bobby. We were leaving no longer connected to him.

The room had changed too, and dimly, as if through a waterfall, I noticed it was now filled with people. An assortment of young men hung around, some clustered along the walls. One of them came up to me. "You must be Bobby Wills's mother. How is he?"

Before I could answer, Rob spat out angrily, "He's dead!" I think he wanted to shock them, to make them suffer as we were.

The group exploded, literally flew apart, each man to a different place along the wall. Voices cried, "Oh, no!" Men groaned.

We drifted along between them, unaffected. How could

their sorrow touch us, we who could no longer feel?

Outside the hospital another man waited.

I stared at him, for he was openly crying. He said hoarsely, "I loved that man. I only knew him for a week, but I loved him!"

It was only as we started home—Rob driving, God knows how—that I remembered Suzette and Brandon.

Oh, Suzette, what will happen to you, how will you manage with your baby? And I thought of Jeremy too . . . because she'd loved him as well.

The bleakness of it, Bobby's leaving everyone to cope as best we could . . .

I cried again for us all.

Tracy, white-faced, greeted us at the back door. She'd already called the hospital, she already knew. She fell into my arms.

Kirk huddled unhappily alone. Why didn't we see?

And Kenny. He was more philosophical, more kindly. Changed. Deepened.

Rob had changed too. He was bitter.

Chris—I had to call Chris.

Six of us left now. All changed.

Flowers again.

Friends.

Chris, home from New York, found out what happened, knowing as surely as he knew Bobby that Bobby would never have died by his own hand . . . that his hitting a tiny marker at the top of the hill was insignificant. Then he discovered the presence of a filming helicopter, which none of us knew had been there.

Instantly Chris knew what had happened. The helicopter blew him down. In the trial that followed later, nobody disputed that fact.

It was all so bitterly ironical: that Bobby had survived all the wild, reckless, foolhardy acts he'd committed in his lifetime, only to have *somebody else* kill him . . . like an alien force, unknown and unexpected, creeping up from behind. But it wasn't even a malevolent force. It was just some jerk who got careless.

Another funeral.

And now we knew coffins meant nothing, that which one you chose was unimportant. Rob let Suzi and me do it without him.

I wrote my memories of Bobby for the funeral.

Chris organized the rest of it. Ramsey Price tried to help but couldn't. He was too devastated. Ram had lost a brother.

And Chris had lost a best friend.

The moments after the funeral. The crowd fills the social hall of the church and waits quietly while Chris works at the projector. He makes a last adjustment and says, "Lights."

The place grows dim and I see the image flickering, jumping, and settling down.

Bobby.

Beside me I hear Suzi draw in her breath, then she is quiet, we're both quiet, watching.

He flies across the screen in front of us, turning abruptly to face us head on and wave, the butterfly kite with its red leading edges and large yellow circles on a blue field— beautiful, lyrical, and I feel better, suddenly. He is back where he should be, it is natural and right, the world is ordered again.

Bobby does a 360, turning easily, his pushing out thus on the control bar, his leaning against the turn bringing the kite full circle. He does it as though he were born knowing how.

My pain eases further.

Every scene is about him, as if he were summarizing his life for us in the way he might have done it best. Flying.

Suzi whispers, "It's so beautiful!"

In the dark I nod.

I think, what does the number of a man's days matter if he's lived a lifetime?

I remember his standing near the garage yelling at his father, "I don't want to do what everyone else has done! I want to be different!"

Well, he'd been different. Wonderfully different. And he'd made the rest of us different too. And richer.

I watch him floating away serenely, the sail rippling in a whisper of sound, the sun splashing across the fabric. One hand rests easily on the control bar, the other in his lap. Up here, I think, he is perfect. Flawless. This is Bobby, and this is the way he'll always be.

EPILOGUE

Bobby's death sent shock waves through the hang gliding community. "We decided long ago," a pilot said, "if anything happened to Bobby, the sport wasn't safe for anyone." A young man wrote, "He will always be one of my heroes of flight."

Letters came from all over the world:

". . . we heard in Norway about the accident . . . even no pilote in Norway knew him personally, we all knew what great pilote he was . . ."

From Guatemala, ". . . we have great respect for the figure in the sport whom we admired the most . . ."

From England, ". . . he was a legend."

Another from England quoted Johnathan Livingston Seagull: "'. . . he was not bone and feather but a perfect idea of freedom and flight limited by nothing at all.' For a great number of us Bobby *is* our 'JLS,' *is* our inspiration, and each day as we turn our eyes to the sky he will be ever in our thoughts."

And Ramsey Price in *Hang Gliding Magazine*: "He was an Eagle among men."

The world had reached out to us, drawing us into a universal hug.

I went back to the shop after a while and looked around. It seemed empty. Oh, there were people there, but none of them had faces, none of them were Bobby. And it all seemed so pointless because it was *Bobby's* company, and without him what were we working for—who were we keeping it alive for anyway? One morning I spent hours picking metal filings out of the carpet—not because I cared about the carpet any longer, only because it was a mindless, deadening kind of thing to do.

It was Price who told me to go talk to Curt Kiefer. "Something happened, Maralys, you oughta know."

So I found Kiefer and he didn't want to talk. But then I pressed and he finally did. "Right after Bobby died," he said in a matter-of-fact voice, "I was riding my motorcycle pretty fast, and suddenly I couldn't turn the handlebars and I knew—don't ask me how, I just knew—that Bobby had a hold of them and he wanted me to listen."

I stared at him. Kiefer wasn't religious and he wasn't psychic. And he didn't want to say any of this either. That was plain enough.

He went on reluctantly. "Bobby said something. I couldn't hear it. I just knew what he was saying inside my mind. He said, 'It's okay, Kiefer, it's beautiful. There's music and colors. It's like doing 360s forever.'"

He stopped talking and turned his bland blue eyes away and shrugged. I could believe it or not, he didn't care.

I didn't know what I believed—only that the words sounded like Bobby and they didn't sound like Kiefer. And something else . . . if Bobby wanted to tell us something, he'd figure out a way.

Of the three friends who began their hang gliding together, only Ramsey Price still flies unpowered gliders. He's a veteran now, at thirty-seven philosophical, oft-consulted. No longer tapping into the grapevine, Ram is a giver of information. Ram is "where it's at." Even the newcomers know.

With his second round of applications, Chris was accepted into New York University medical school. His interview on the way home from London was a turning of the last stone. Robert Morris, the doctor who interviewed him, was impressed with Chris's rich and varied life outside of academia. "The admissions board listens to me," he said. "Everyone I've recommended has done well."

Chris *did* do well, securing a choice residency in orthopedics. He is now an orthopedic surgeon in Santa Ana, in partnership with a man like himself — warm, optimistic, and adventuresome. Chris and Betty-Jo have four children.

Though Chris no longer flies unpowered hang gliders, he has his own ultralight craft, and flying still is — and probably always will be — an important part of his life.

Suzi remarried. Her new husband is a fine man who is stable and a good father to fourteen-year-old Brandon. And Brandon himself? He is spunky and well-adjusted and loves *both* his fathers!

Rob defends doctors in his own law firm now, a mile from home. Though he claims a lifelong bitterness over his sons' deaths, I rarely see it. Instead I see a once angry man replaced by a gentler one, a man on whom the family all leans. Without meaning to, Bobby changed Rob most of all.

As for me, I stayed with the company a year, trying to keep it alive. "Why?" people asked me. "Why are you hanging on?"

I answered them fiercely. "Eric died and Bobby died. And I can't let the company die too." It became symbolic, a fight to stave off the last disaster, as though the company were somehow *them*. In the end I won, breathing life into the place until other young people came along to buy it and make it prosper.

At last I went home to write books — some with Betty-Jo, some alone. In a quieter sort of family I would have done that years earlier.

Occasionally, now, I wonder if I might have changed destiny so it all ended some other way. I ask myself when, at what point, I might have intervened to alter events. Should we have quit our business after Eric died? Would that have made any difference?

I think not. By then it was too late. Bobby loved flying too much. A pilot is what he *was*. Without us, he would simply have flown for someone else.

Before Eric died, we might have saved them both by stopping Chris — but does anyone think that was possible?

So a part of me rejoices that Bobby, at least, had so much. In a way he still lives. I see him flying majestically in the Smithsonian's Imax film *To Fly*; twice he's been on the cover of calendars; and sometimes we catch glimpses of him on television, soaring through ads.

In unexpected places, at odd times, I continue to find out more about him. It was on Kauai, where the family went on vacation years later, that a tennis pro looked up when he heard the name Wills. "I remember a Wills, once," he said, smiling. And then he told us a story. "There was this kid on the island, years ago, making a movie. I wouldn't have paid much attention, except for what he did in his off-hours. He found this bicycle, you know, and he rigged up a bed sheet into a sail, and he *sailed* the bicycle down the island, using the wind. It was so ingenious we all stood around and watched. He went surprisingly fast going with the wind. But coming back," and here the man laughed, "he had quite a bit of trouble trying to hold the sheet and ride the bike and tack into the wind. But, by golly, somehow he did it!"

And so, years later, I remember the sympathy letter that touched me most. It was from Mrs. Underwood, the boys' first fan from the old days of bamboo and plastic. She wrote, "Bobby didn't just live — he devoured life!"